Laozi: Quest for the Ultimate Reality

An appreciation of the *Dao De Jing*

Jingwei (景维)

jjingwei11@gmail.com

Singapore
October 2013

This monograph is also presented in the Google site:
https://sites.google.com/site/laoziappreciation/

Disclaimer:
Every precaution has been taken in the preparation of this book.
The publisher and author apologize for any errors and omissions that may remain.
The publisher and author assume no liability, whatsoever, for damages resulting from the use of this book.

Copyright © 2011
This work is registered with the UK Copyright Service.
All rights reserved.
Copying is allowed for individual private use.
Copying is not allowed for commercial trade.

Self-published by Jingwei (景维)

Address: Jingwei,
           My Mail Box 882907,
           Singapore 919191.
Email: jjingwei11@gmail.com

Title availability
Singapore:
   Geo Arts N Crafts Ent.,
   Blk 183 Toa Payoh Central,
   #01-262, Singapore 310183
Worldwide (order online):
   Print-on-demand (POD) by Lightning Source Inc.
   Distribution through Ingram International
   The Book Depository.co.uk (with free delivery worldwide)
   Espresso Book Machine
   Amazon.com
List price: SGD $20.00

National Library Board, Singapore Cataloguing-in-Publication Data

Jingwei.
   Laozi : quest for the ultimate reality : an appreciation of the Dao De Jing / Jingwei. - Singapore : Jingwei, 2012

p. cm.

ISBN :   978-981-07-3758-0

1. Laozi. Dao De Jing.   2. Taoism.   3. Philosophy, Chinese.   I. Title.

BL1920

299.51482 – dc23   OCN811096051

The cover artwork is by Fiolita, Singapore.

First print in Singapore: 200 copies, October 2012

Print on demand: Lightning Source Inc., December 2012
Book type: B&W 6.14x9.21 in or 234x156 mm (Royal 8vo) Perfect Bound on White w/Gross Lam
Page Count: 204

Dedicated to the well-being
of all fellow travelers (~7 billions)
riding together
on the surface of the blue planet
in the space and time of a universe
computed to be 93 billion light-years across
14 billion years since the last "Big Bang"
on a journey to nowhere
with
The Ultimate Reality
being finite or infinite
and we know not

--//--

An ancient Chinese Bronze Tripod
(c.150BCE, Nanyue King Museum, Guangzhou)

The bronze age in China span over 3 dynasties, Xia, Shang and Zhou (c.2100-221 BCE).
Bronze metallurgy development reached its zenith in the Eastern Zhou Dynasty.
The largest known ceremonial tripod vessel weighs up to 875 kg.
The fire-power of the Chinese Bellows for such metal works must have impressed Laozi.

SYNOPSIS

The ancient text, known as *Laozi* or *Dao De Jing* (*The Primal and Virtue Classic*) has legion of commentaries.
It is a well known Chinese book in the West, and has been much translated like the *Bible*.
However unlike the *Bible*, the *Dao De Jing* (*DDJ*) is hardly read by, or known to, the public.
The reason is because the *DDJ* is not easy to read and understand; its ideas seem to border on mysticism.
Commentaries and translations are often even less comprehensible and do not make for good reading.
This monograph evaluates the *DDJ* on its own merits with evidence taken directly from its own text.

Laozi, an archivist in the imperial court of the Zhou Dynasty, ponders the existence of the universe.
He is impressed by power of the Chinese bellows that helped to produce huge bronze artifacts.
He postulates Dao, a primal entity in the bellows, formed before Heaven and Earth, the mother of all things.
Formless, Dao silently creates and nurtures, yet is master of none, and demands no worship of its creations.
Laozi urges us to emulate Dao, which is perceived to benefit others, does no harm, selfless in all its actions.
He suggests reconciliation in respond to grievance suffered, and to embrace the gentle, feminine way in life.
Weak and invisible in the bellows, Dao inspires him to believe in the triumph of the weak over the strong.

A keen observer of human behavior, he advises against self-promotion and frivolity.
He warns us not to indulge in the senses, to resist temptation and desires for glory and wealth.
He promotes simplicity, honesty, and the 3 treasures of love, thrift and dare-not-be-world's-first.
He encourages meditation and the cultivation of a serene, stress-free way of life by not contesting.

A thinker, he accuses rulers for causing poverty and rebellion with high taxes and oppression.
He insists that wars are only for defense as a last resort, not for the expansionism and glorification of rulers.

In the *Dao De Jing* of about 5000 words, the legendary Laozi leaves us with 2 great legacies.
Firstly, the spirit of inquiry in his quest for the Ultimate Reality (Dao).
Secondly, pacific Daoism, a way of life with humility, unselfish actions, benefiting, and doing no harm (De).

P.S.
Development of concepts and ideas are not presented sequentially in the Dao De Jing.
Hence, one has to read the whole book at least once in order to appreciate it fully.

PREFACE

Philosophers are thoughtful people who have acquired wisdom and useful experience.
Personally among all the philosophers, I have found Laozi to be the most helpful.
His *Dao De Jing* (*The Primal and Virtue Classic*) has about 5000 Chinese characters in total.
Inside is a wealth of inspirational sayings which alleviate stress and suggest proper actions to take.
In times of difficulties and dilemmas, I search through this book for guidance.
Whenever I am faced with conflict of interests from colleagues or friends, I find encouragement in, quote:
"Success achieves, do not claim credit
For credit not claim, will not go away" (ch.2)
Whenever I am confronted with a rebellious family, I find liberation in, quote:
"Create, but do not possess" (ch.2)
Truly, Laozi will not do your work for you, like in a miracle.
However, accepting his way of thinking calms the nerves and balances the mind.
Then one is better able to resolve a situation amicably and move on.

The *Dao De Jing* (*DDJ*) covers a remarkable wide range of topics with so few words.
From the creation of the universe, to principles governing nations, to survival advice for individuals.
It has been listed among the 100 most influencial books ever written (Seyour-Smith, 1998).
And the *DDJ* has been translated more times than any book other than the *Bible*. (Harrington, 1998)
Yet compare to the *Bible*, the *DDJ* is hardly read by the public, despite such academic interest.

The reason may not be hard to find.
To explain existence of the Universe, Laozi postulates that the primal entity, Dao, creates all things.
Hence, most Chinese commentaries are spiritually inclined with their treatment of Dao in the *DDJ*.
Whereas most Western interpretations and translations tend to develop the mystical aspects of Dao.
These biases have often resulted in the *DDJ* becoming incomprehensibly presented, at best.
And at worst, the *DDJ* becomes an unbelievable fantasy which will obviously put off the casual reader.

These past 4 years after my retirement, I have studied the *DDJ* very closely.
I am a research scientist in biological science by profession.
Naturally, I am highly critical of anything I read.
And nothing is sacred in, or out of bounds to, my investigative questioning.
For the ancient meaning of the Chinese text, I have also consulted the dictionary of Xu Shen (c.58-147CE).
Transmitted down through the millenniums, there are omissions from, and additions to the text by scholars.
Hence, areas of controversy and sections that have become incomprehensible are to be expected.
But by and large, I have found the *DDJ* consistently sensible and highly inspirational.
Reading the Dao as a hypothetical concept only, the *DDJ* is far from being spiritual or mystical.
It is the writing of a philosopher scientist seeking the Ultimate Reality of the universe.
The scientific format of discourse is consistent in each chapter.
Laozi first makes one or more observations of nature or society.
Next, he draws his deduction or conclusion.
He does not go beyond reasonable inference with wild speculation or fantasy.
And when he does not know something or is in doubt, he is not afraid to declare his ignorance.
At places where he borrows a quote, he stated it and hence, the *DDJ* is unlikely to be an anthology.
Along the way, in his search for the Ultimate Reality, Laozi's thoughts spawn pacific Daoism.
But most importantly, he inspires us with his questing spirit for the Ultimate Reality.

In this study, I attempt a direct, primary interpretation of the *DDJ*.
I find his pacific Daoism conducive to life with minimal stress for the individuals.
I find his quest for the Ultimate Reality, an inquiring spirit that might unite all individuals.

CONTENTS

2	**PUBLICATION DATA**	
3	**DEDICATION**	
4	*Illustration 1*	An ancient Chinese Bronze Tripod
5	**SYNOPSIS**	
6	**PREFACE**	
7	**CONTENTS**	
11	*Illustration 2*	*Laozi, text on silk*
12	**INTRODUCTION**	
17	**DAO DE JING (81Chapters)**	
18	*Illustration 3*	無　Wu (Have-not);　有　You (Have)
19	Chapter 01*	Laozi: Quest for the Ultimate Reality (道可道, 非恒道)
20	Chapter 02*	All correlatives respected (天下皆知美之为美)
21	Chapter 03*	Rulers unselfish, find all citizens governable (不尚贤)
22	Chapter 04	Dao formless, precedes the existence of all forms (道冲)
23	*Illustration 4*	*The Chinese Bellows*
24	Chapter 05*	Dao in the emptiness of the bellows (天地不仁)
25	Chapter 06*	Dao in procreation, female (谷神不死)
26	Chapter 07	Dao, selfless like Heaven and Earth (天长地久)
27	*Illustration 5*	上善若水　*High goodness like water*
28	Chapter 08*	Benefiting and not-contesting like water (上善若水)
29	Chapter 09	Be no-hoarder, halls full gold cannot be guarded (持而盈之)
30	Chapter 10	Self, a meditation on primal virtues (载营魄抱一)
31	Chapter 11	Paradox: Emptiness, utility of the Hub (三十辐共一毂)
32	Chapter 12	Beware, indulgence of the senses (五色令人目盲)
33	Chapter 13	Life-death: Cultivate selflessness and have no fear (宠辱若惊)
34	Chapter 14*	Dao, not detectable with our senses (视之不见)
35	Chapter 15	Daoist behavior (古之善为道者)
36	Chapter 16*	Life-death: Cycle of life-death mellows (至虚极)
37	Chapter 17	Rulers, types and ranking (太上，下不知有之)
38	Chapter 18	Virtue, conventional (大道废，有仁义)
39	Chapter 19*	Virtue, primal (绝圣弃智)
40	Chapter 20	Daoist conduct (唯之与阿，相去几何？)
41	Chapter 21*	Dao in procreation, male (孔德之容, 惟道是从)
42	*Illustration 6*	曲则全　*Bend and be whole (preserved)*
43	Chapter 22	Salvation, bend and be whole (曲则全)
44	Chapter 23	Heaven and Earth, power limited (希言自然)

Contents

45	Chapter 24	Self-promotion, counter-roductive (企者不立)
46	Illustration 7	有物浑成　　Matters mixed and formed
47	Chapter 25*	Dao formation, before Heaven and Earth (有物浑成)
48	Chapter 26	Beware of Frivolity (重为轻根)
49	Chapter 27	Salvation, nothing is abandoned (善行无辙迹)
50	Chapter 28	Daoist Leadership is Humility, Responsibility (知其雄)
51	Chapter 29	Freedom, the world belongs to everybody (将欲取天下而为之)
52	Chapter 30	War, is mass destruction (以道佐人主者)
53	Illustration 8	杀人之众　　Killed people in large number
54	Chapter 31	War, is mass killings (夫兵者，不祥之器)
55	Chapter 32	Daoism for rulers (道恒无名)
56	Chapter 33	Self-knowledge is difficult; longevity is remembrance (知人者智)
57	Chapter 34*	Freedom, as Dao is master of none (大道氾兮)
58	Chapter 35	Dao is not detectable (执大象)
59	Illustration 9	将欲取之　　Wishing to take it
60	Chapter 36	Paradox: Strategies for triumph of the weak (将欲歙之)
61	Chapter 37	Be unselfish in all actions (道恒无为而无不为)
62	Chapter 38*	Virtues Ranking (上德不德)
63	Chapter 39	Daoism is Anonymity (昔之得一者)
64	Chapter 40	Dao is cyclical in action and gentle in use (反者道之动)
65	Chapter 41	Daoism is laughable ! (上士闻道)
66	Chapter 42	Daoism is harmony, humility and non-violence (道生一)
67	Chapter 43	Daoism is unselfish and teaches by example (天下之至柔)
68	Chapter 44	Life-survival versus fame-wealth (名与身孰亲？)
69	Chapter 45	Paradox: Greatness not apparent (大成若缺)
70	Chapter 46	Be Contented (天下有道)
71	Illustration 10	不出戶　　Without stepping-out the door
72	Chapter 47*	Paradox: Travel more, know less; the written archives (不出戶)
73	Chapter 48	Daoism is unselfish (为学日益)
74	Chapter 49	Salvation is Universal (圣人恒无心)
75	Chapter 50	Life-Death: Do not go into harm's way (出生入死)
76	Chapter 51*	Freedom, a primal right (道生之)
77	Chapter 52	Salvation in Self-discipline (天下有始)
78	Chapter 53	Beware of Temptation (使我介然有知)
79	Chapter 54	Self first in cultivating virtues (善建者不拔)
80	Chapter 55	Daoism is Harmony (含德之厚)
81	Chapter 56	Daoist cannot be influenced (知者不言)
82	Chapter 57	Daoist in Government (以正治国)
83	Chapter 58	Paradox: Cycles of good-fortune and misfortune (其政闷闷)
84	Chapter 59	Rulers: Thrift for nation building (治人、事天)

8

85	Chapter 60	Daoism: Governing is as easy as cooking a small fish (治大国, 若烹小鲜)
86	Chapter 61	Rulers: Humility for diplomacy (大国者下流)
87	Chapter 62	Daoism is Refuge for all things (道者, 万物之奥)
88	Chapter 63	Repay grievance with kindness; Be prepared for difficulties (为无为)
89	Illustration 11	千里之行　Journey of thousand miles
90	Chapter 64	Paradox: Journey of a thousand miles starts beneath the feet (其安易持)
91	Chapter 65	Rulers: Govern not with cleverness (古之善为道者)
92	Chapter 66*	Rulers: To rule is to serve (江海所以能为百谷王者)
93	Chapter 67*	Three treasures: Love, Thrift and Not-dare-be-world's-first (天下皆谓我道大)
94	Chapter 68*	Be Respectful to Talents (善为士者)
95	Chapter 69	Wars only for defense (用兵有言)
96	Chapter 70	Laozi's sayings are easy to know, easy to practice (吾言甚易知)
97	Chapter 71	Beware, not knowing acts knowing is sick (知不知)
98	Chapter 72	Ruler: Rebellion arises from oppression (民不畏威)
99	Chapter 73*	Retribution: Net of Heaven does not leak (勇于敢, 则杀)
100	Chapter 74	Retribution: From society risks miscarriage of justice (民不畏死)
101	Chapter 75	Rulers: Hunger arises from high taxes (民之饥)
102	Chapter 76	Paradox: Gentle path to life, rigid path to death (人之生也柔弱)
103	Chapter 77	Heaven: Reduce the have-excess, supplement the have-not (天之道)
104	Chapter 78	Paradox: Triumphs of the Weak and Gentle (天下莫柔弱于水)
105	Chapter 79	Salvation: Sow no grievances (和大怨)
106	Chapter 80*	Paradox: Small nation, few citizens, back to basics (小国寡民)
107	Chapter 81*	Heaven: Benefit, and do no harm (信言不美)

108 **DISCUSSION**
109 Dating the *Dao De Jing* (Dao and Virtue Classic)
110 Authorship

111 Is Laozi writing for the rulers?
112 Is Laozi a mystic?
113 Is Laozi religious?
114 Is Laozi a philosopher?
115 Is Laozi a scientist?
116 Is Laozi a pessimist?
117 Is Laozi laughable?

118 The Chinese Bellows
119 Concept of Dao (道, the Primal Entity)
120 Concept of De (德, the Primal Virtue)
121 Concepts of Wu (无, Have-ot) and You (有, Have)
122 Concept of Naming
123 Concept of Correlatives

124	On Benevolence, Righteousness and Etiquette
125	On Contentment
126	On Fame and Wealth
127	On Fears and Crises
128	On Femininity appreciated
129	On Freedom
130	On Greatness
131	On Happiness of the Daoist
132	On Honesty
133	On Human Desires and Failings
134	On Humility
135	On Life-Death, Survival
136	On Meditation
137	On Not-Contesting
138	On Paradoxes
139	On Problems and Difficulties
140	On Purpose of Life
141	On Retribution
142	On Salvation
143	On Self-Understanding and Cultivation
144	On Success and Failure
145	On Triumph of the Weak
146	On Trust
147	On Uncertainties of Life
148	On Wars
149	On WuWei (无为)
150	On WuWei, WuBuWei (无为,无不为)
151	**SUMMARY**
157	**CONCLUSION**
158	Laozi's legacy 1: Quest for the Ultimate Reality (Dao)
160	Laozi's legacy 2: Pacific Daoism (dos and don't s) (De)
166	Benefits from reading the *Dao De Jing* (de-stressing and liberating)
169	Going forward
170	**BIBLIOGRAPHY**
171	Publications in English
172	Publications in Chinese
173	**APPENDICES**
174	Acknowledgments
175	After thoughts
176	List of important dates
177	Glossary
178	The Chinese Language
180	*Illustration 12 Evolution of Chinese Characters*
181	Concordance Analysis
183	Copyright & Disclaimer
184	Alphabetical Index

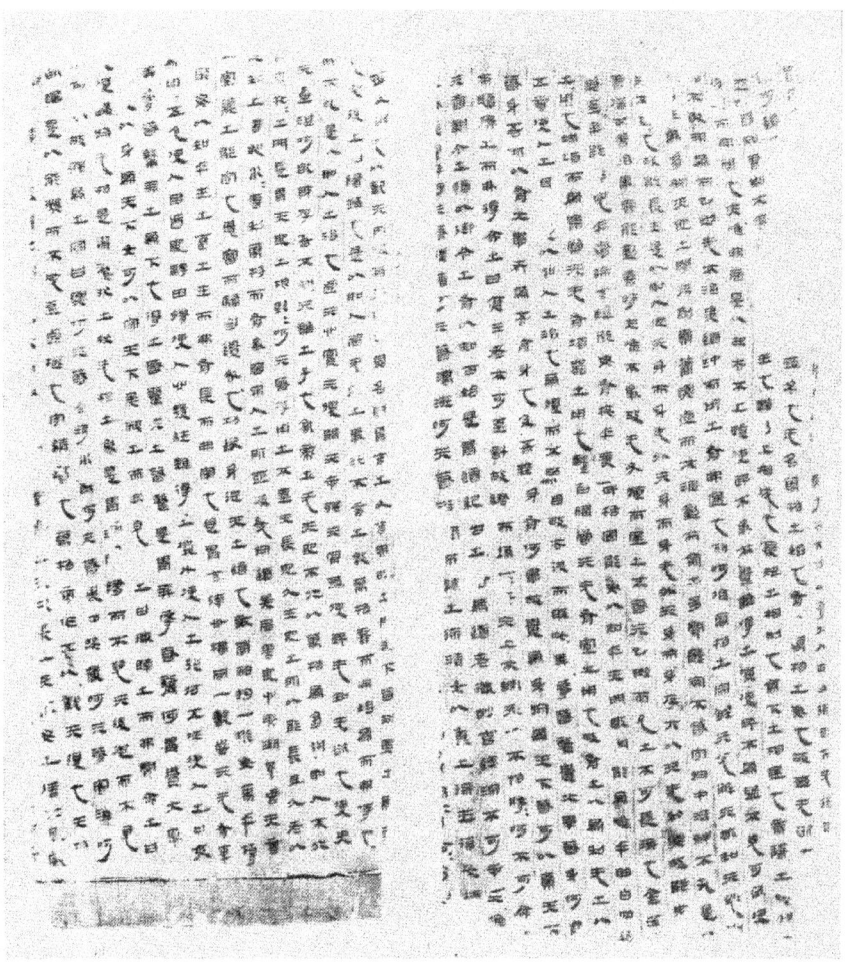

Laozi, text on silk

The second oldest version of *Laozi*, brushed on silk, recovered in 1973.
The Han tomb is from the excavation site, at Mawangdui, Changsha, Hunan.
It dates back to about 200 BCE.

INTRODUCTION

Introduction

Laozi

Our blue planet Earth is seen floating in dark space on a journey to nowhere (see book cover).
Where did we came from and where are we going?
Humankind has been pondering such questions since the dawn of written history.
Surprisingly Kongzi (Confucius, 551-479 BCE) has precious little to say on how the universe has came to be.
In contrast Laozi (c.500 BCE) is most concerned about how all things have come into existence.
Today in the Internet age of the 21st Century, we are blessed with much knowledge.
We have cracked the genetic code of life and we have sequenced the whole human genome.
The age of the universe is computed to be 13.7 billion years, the time that has lapsed since the 'last' Big Bang.
The diameter of the observable universe is computed to be 93 billion light-years across
However, it is still not known if the size of the universe is finite or infinite. (Wolframalpha.com)
And yet, we may still ask about what happened before the Big Bang?
Hence, regarding the Ultimate Reality of the universe, we are none the wiser than Laozi was in c.500 BCE.

The name, Laozi was first mentioned by Zhuangzi (c.369-286 BCE) in his writing.
The first biographical account of Laozi is in the *Historical Records* by Sima Qian (c.145-87 BCE).
The entry here says Laozi is a native of the State of Chu, with family name Li and given name Er.
He is in charge of the royal archives in the court of the Zhou Dynasty (Eastern, 770 – 221 BCE).
Laozi cultivates Dao and Virtue, his philosophy is to remain unknown and nameless.
After a long period of living in Zhou and observing the decline of the dynasty, he decided to leave.
At the frontier pass, the guard recognized him and knew that he was a learned man.
The guard said, "Since Teacher is going to retire, please make the effort to write me a book."
Laozi obliged and wrote the *Laozi* of about 5000 Chinese characters in 2 parts.
Then Laozi left and no one knows where he went thereafter.

The *Laozi*, later known the *Dao De Jing* (*DDJ*) is very "dense", its philosophy difficult to comprehend.
Down through the centuries, more than 2000 commentaries in Chinese have been written to interpret it.
There have been more than 200 translations into English and many other Western languages.
It has been listed among the 100 most important books ever written. (Seyour-Smith, 1998)
The *DDJ* has been translated more times than any book other than the *Bible*. (Harrington, 1998)
However comparing it to the *Bible*, few have read the *Dao De Jing*!
The reasons are not hard to find.
The Chinese commentaries usually develop the spiritual aspects of the *DDJ*.
Whereas the English translations are inclined to over-interpret the mystical aspects.
Extra efforts are often made by scholars to discover the inner-most layers of Laozi's thoughts!
The net results are often more confusing than clear!
Accept for academics and a few dedicated individuals, most casual readers are put off by the complexity.

Originally known as *Laozi*, the *DDJ* is a small book of only 5000 Chinese characters.
With sentences comprising of 10 characters or less, verses are formed and arranged into 81 chapters.
It analyzes formation of the hypothetical Dao, the primal entity that created the universe.
It analyzes the conduct of government, poverty, warfare and other such sufferings of human society.
It offers profound advice for good government practices and good conduct for individual survival.
It is remarkable that almost every alternate line is a quotable quote.
Ideas are often presented in one-liners, succinctly and with illuminating imagery.

Introduction

Sample quotations from the *Dao De Jing (The Primal and Virtue Classic)*

上善若水　　　　　　　　Top goodness like water (ch.8)
水善, 利万物而不争　　　Water good, benefits all things yet not contesting
Laozi philosophizes that we emulate water and act likewise, benefiting and not contesting.

金玉滿堂　　　　　　　　Gold and jade filling the halls (ch.9)
莫之能守　　　　　　　　None who can guard
Laozi warns of the futility of excessive accumulation of wealth that cannot be guarded.

企者, 不立　　　　　　　Whoever tip-toe, cannot stand (unstable) (ch.24)
跨者, 不行　　　　　　　Whoever standing astride, cannot move (forward)
With a measure of humor, Laozi illustrates that self-promotion can be counter-productive.

知其雄　　　　　　　　　Knowing the male (dominant role) (ch.28)
守其雌　　　　　　　　　Hold the female (support role)
为天下谿　　　　　　　　Be the world's creek (small stream)
Like the stream flowing low, Laozi chooses the female role in support rather than to dominate.

师之所居　　　　　　　　Where an army has occupied (ch.30)
荆棘生焉　　　　　　　　Thistles / thorns grow indeed
大军, 之后　　　　　　　Big army, after its (deployment)
必有凶年　　　　　　　　Certain to have bad years
Laozi laments the aftermaths of wars, supporting the idea that, not to contest is the sensible way of life.

知人者智　　　　　　　　Whoever knows people is knowledgeable (ch.33)
自知者明　　　　　　　　Whoever knows self is enlightened
Laozi's observation of human nature is penetrating enough to note that one's greatest enemy is often oneself.

祸兮, 福之所倚　　　　　Misfortune indeed, where good-fortune depends (ch.58)
福兮, 祸之所伏　　　　　Good-fortune indeed, where misfortune lurks
Laozi gives hope when misfortune strikes and cautions against the reverse when good-fortune is enjoyed.

报怨以德　　　　　　　　Repay injustice with virtue (kindness) (ch.63)
 Laozi is wise to suggests reconciliation, breaking the vicious cycles of demanding retaliation and justice

民之饥　　　　　　　　　The people's hunger (ch.75)
以其上食税之多　　　　　Because their rulers eat (take) taxes in excess
Laozi has no doubt as to the cause of people's hunger.
Today, in our 21st Century, corrupt governments still cause millions to live below the poverty line!

Introduction

Dao and Daoism

As an archivist at the court of Zhou, Laozi had access to all recorded knowledge up to his time. Written accounts of ancient mythology, history of preceding dynasties and current politics of states. Written theses in astronomy, medicine, laws, government, agriculture, commerce, you name it. Hence, without him having to step out the door, the archives give him knowledge in all departments.

不出戶, 知天下	Without stepping-out the door, knows the world
不窺牖, 見天道	Not looking out the window, sees Heaven's way (ch.47)

A quiet and studious person, Laozi did not involve himself in court politics.
Laozi has much time to ponder on the existence of the universe, the states and societies.
From the first writings on shells and bones, Laozi can trace history back to the Shang Dynasty.
Pushing back in time, there is no writing, probably only oral transmission of ancient mythology.
Pushing further back to the beginning of Heaven and Earth, there must have been nothing!

无, 名天地之始	Nothing, to name the beginning of Heaven and Earth (ch.1)

In the smith-shop, Laozi observed the bellows that never fails to work up the fire.
He probably believes Dao is in there, not visible itself but providing the inexhaustible energy visibly.
And by extension, he sees the space between Heaven and Earth as a huge bellows.

天地之间	Heaven and earth, the space in-between
其犹橐龠乎?	Is it not like the bellows?
虚而不屈	Empty but not yielding
动, 而愈出	Move (plunger), yet more come out (air, feeding the fire) (ch.5)

Laozi therefore bravely postulates the existence of a primal entity that exists before the beginning:

有物浑成	There are matters that mixed and formed
先天地生	Created before Heaven and Earth
吾不知其名, 字之曰道	I do not know its name, addressing it call it Dao (ch.25)

Laozi's hypothesis of Dao, the primal entity that creates the universe, does not stand today.
However, his perception of Dao's many gentle attributes has spawned the philosophy of pacific Daoism.
The invisible Dao quietly creates, claims no ownership, benefits, and does no harm.

大道氾兮	The great Dao over-flows
其可左右	To the left and to the right (pervasive)
万物恃之而生, 而不辞	All things depend on Dao to exist, but Dao speaks not (of dependency)
功成, 不名有	Success achieved, but (Dao) is not named (or credited).
衣养万物, 而不为主	Clothes and nourishes all things, but Dao will not be their master (ch.34)

Laozi aptly sums up pacific Daoism in the last four lines of the *Dao De Jing*.

天之道	Way of Heaven
利而不害	Benefit and not harming
圣人之道	Way of the Sage
为而不争	Action but not in contention (ch.81)

Introduction

Structure and writing style of this book
In the next section, the 81 chapters of the *Dao De Jing (DDJ)* are presented in 4 parts.
All 4 parts of each chapter are put together on the same page for easy reference.
The parts are: Chinese character text, English translation, Laozi's thinking and Comments.
Throughout this book, sentences are structured and confined to single line for easy reading.

The original Chinese character text
Liu Xiaogan's (2006) compilation of 5 versions of Laozi is consulted.
The Guodian version, on bamboo slips (dated c.300 BCE) is incomplete with only 1800-odd characters.
The Mawangdui version written on silk (dated c.195 BCE), has lost many characters due to deterioration.
The versions of Heshangkong (c.179 BCE) and Wang Bi (226-249 CE) are more complete.
Where there are text at corresponding positions of the *DDJ*, all 5 versions give contents of similar meaning.
The popular Wang Bi version has been adopted mainly, with corrections from other versions where needed.
Example, Wang Bi uses 常 to replace 恒, the name of a Han emperor; the earlier Guodian version uses 恒.
For the beauty and poetry of Laozi's eloquence, the original Chinese character text should be read.

The English Translation
English words implying gender are avoided as the Chinese characters are devoid of gender connotation.
Short and simple English words are preferred wherever there are choices.
The Chinese sentence structure is also adopted wherever possible with the English words.
These efforts are made so as to capture the brevity, the beauty and poetry of the original Chinese text.
Different words of similar meaning have been used in different sections, translated at different time.
They are not corrected for consistency and are left in place, as together they may give a broader perspective.
能无为乎?   Possible <u>without self-agenda</u>? (ch.10)
以至于无为   To reach till <u>no motive</u> (<u>not selfish</u>) (ch.48)

Laozi's thinking
This part is added to provide some background information on what is known then.
This is necessary as the text in the *DDJ* is so brief and condensed that comprehension is often difficult.
Such information is useful to show how Laozi may think and arrive at his ideas and philosophy.
Knowing Laozi's thinking will help readers appreciate what he wrote in the *DDJ*.
Laozi evidently admired the legendary rulers (Yao, Shun, Yu), whose successions are based on merits.
He is also appreciative of the righteous leaderships of founder kings of the Xia, Shang and Zhou Dynasties.
Virtues of these rulers are lauded in the ancient *Book of Change*, the *Book of Poems* and the *Book of History*.
"To govern is to serve" and such noble examples in the *Book of History* find much resonance in the *DDJ*.

Comments
This summaries the author's appreciation of what Laozi presents in each chapter.
There are substantial departure from the interpretations of other scholars.
Laozi's Dao is interpreted as his concept only, not the Ultimate Reality that he intended it to be.

Laozi has been wondering how the universe has come to exist.
He postulates Dao, the Ultimate Reality that creates all things, accounts for the existence of the universe.
Dao is perceived to be formless, silently creating, benefiting, do no harm, and is master of none.
Dao displays no supernatural power, needs no worshiping, and hence all things have complete freedom.
Laozi suggests we emulate Dao and do likewise, thus spawning pacific Daoism.

Laozi is great for giving us a philosophy of humility and respect for all things, for peaceful co-existence.
But he is greater for giving us the spirit of seeking for the Ultimate Reality of our universe.
Commitment to seeking it by all individuals will unite us all in one common universal understanding.
Focusing on this final possibility, the title chosen for this book is: *"Laozi: Quest for the Ultimate Reality"*

A word of caution
Development of concepts and ideas are not presented sequentially in the Dao De Jing.
For example, the concept of Dao is described in several chapters that include 5, 6, 14, 25, 42 and others.
Hence, one has to read the whole book at least once in order to appreciate any part of it fully.

DAO DE JING

81 Chapters

Note:
In the translation, extra English words (bracketed) are put in for implied meaning, so as to facilitate comprehension and easy reading.

無　　　　　　　Wu (Have-not)
名天地之始　　　To name the beginning of Heaven and Earth

(*Dao De Jing*, chapter 1)

有　　　　　　　You (Have)
名万物之母　　　To name the mother of all things

(*Dao De Jing*, chapter 1)

Dao De Jing

| 一章 | **Chapter 1** |

01 道可道, 非恒道	If Dao can be described, it is not the primal Dao
02 名可名, 非恒名	If Name can be named, it is not the primal name
03 无, 名天地之始	Wu (Have-not), to name the beginning of Heaven and Earth
04 有, 名万物之母	You (Have), to name the mother of all things
05 故:	Therefore:
06 恒无, 欲以观其妙	In the primal Wu (Have-not), if one wishes to observe wonders of Dao
07 恒有, 欲以观其徼	In the primal You (Have), if one wishes to observe manifestations of Dao
08 此兩者, 同出而异名	These 2 entities, are from the same source but differently named
09 同谓之玄	Both are said to be mysterious
10 玄之又玄	Mystery upon mystery
11 众妙之门	They are the door-ways to all wonders

Laozi's thinking
The daily cycle of the sun and moon and the yearly cycle of spring, summer, autumn and winter.
The life-cycle of human, animals and plants, that is, the never ending cycles of energy and of life.
The space between Heaven and Earth is like a huge bellows. (ch.5)
The bellows seems empty, yet the more you push, the more air it issues and it is inexhaustible.
To feed the fire that forges the tools that help to create the myriad of things.
There must be an primal principle in there to provide all of the energy and it shall be named Dao. (ch.25)
This primal Dao cannot be seen, heard, touched or tasted (ch.14).
Hence, we may describe Dao but we shall not be able to describe the primal Dao completely. L1

With the same object, people from the different kingdom states call it by different names.
Hence, an object may be named, but the Name is not its primal (or absolute) name. L2

There are written records of the Zhou (1066-771 BCE) and Shang (1,600-1,066 BCE) dynasties.
There are no written records of the Xia Dynasty (2,100 – 1,600 BCE), probably only oral history.
Pushing further back in time to the beginning of Heaven and Earth, there is nothing
Hence, we shall use Wu (Have-not) to name the beginning of Heaven and Earth. L3
And we shall use You (Have) to name the Mother that subsequently created all things. L4

Wishing to observe the wonders of Dao, we have to examine the primal Wu (Have-not). L6
Wishing to observe the manifestations of Dao, we have to examine the primal You (Have). L7
Although these two entities are named differently, Wu and You are from the same source, Dao. L8,9
Both are said to be mysterious, and mystery upon mystery, they are the doors to all wonders. L10,11

Comments:
Laozi: Quest for the Ultimate Reality (ch.1)

In the *Dao De Jing* (*DDJ*), concepts and ideas are not developed sequentially.
Hence, I understand this first chapter fully only at the end of my study of all the 81 chapters.
In Chapter 25, Laozi explores several names for the various perceived characteristics of primal Dao.
Hence, L1,2 really mean to state the hypothetical nature of his concept of Dao, and Naming names.
Likewise L3,4 are for defining his hypothetical concepts of Wu (Have-not), and You (Have).
Next, Laozi invites us to discover the mystery of the universe through examining these concepts.
Like the 'Big Bang' theory of the beginning of the Universe, these concepts have remained, theories only.
Laozi has not succeeded in explaining the Universe 2500 years ago, but neither can we, today.

In this first chapter, Laozi has already revealed himself as a seeker of the Ultimate Reality.

Dao De Jing

二章　　　　　　　　　　Chapter 2

01 天下皆知美之为美, 斯恶已	All the world know beauty as beautiful, then non-beauty is known
02 皆知善之为善, 斯不善已	All know goodness as good, then no-good is known.
03 故, 有无相生	Hence, You (Have) /Wu (Have-not) are correlatives in creations
04 难易相成	Difficulty/easiness are correlatives in manifestations
05 长短相形; 高下相倾	Long/short are correlatives in forms; high /low in inclinations
06 音声相和; 前后相随	Tone/sound are correlatives in harmony; front /back in sequence
07 是以: 圣人处无为之事	Therefore: the Sage manages unselfish tasks
08 行不言之教	Does non-verbal teaching (by setting good examples)
09 万物作焉, 而不辞	All-things in action, but makes no comment;
10 生, 而不有; 为, 而不恃	Creates, but does not possess; acts, but not presumptuous
11 功成, 而不居	Success achieves, but not dwell (takes credit)
12 夫惟不居, 是以不去	Indeed, only not dwell, hence (credit) not go-away

Laozi's thinking
When the whole world knows beauty as beautiful, then non-beauty, the correlative, is known. L1
When the whole world knows goodness as good, then no-good, the correlative, is known. L2

Hence Have and Have-not are correlatives in creations. L3
Difficulty and easiness are correlatives in tasks. L4
Long and short are correlatives in forms; high and low are correlatives in inclinations. L5
Tone and sound are correlatives in harmony; front and back are correlatives in sequence. L6
Correlatives are natural in occurring; when you have one, you have the other.
Nobody can say which member of a correlative pair is bad and which is good.
For example, born with beauty seems good, and is preferred and a blessing.
But when selected for sacrifice to appease the river spirit, then beauty is not a blessing.
Therefore, all members of correlatives should be treated without bias.

Hence, the Sage manages affair not for self but for the common good. L7
The Sage teaches without speaking but by setting good examples. L8
Observing all things in action, but makes no comments for good or for bad, being not judgmental. L9
Creates, but claims no ownership; contributes and does not become presumptuous. L10
And when success is achieved, takes no credit. L11
It is because credit has not been claimed that the deserved credit will not be lost. L12

Comments:
All correlatives are respected (ch.2)
Defines beauty (A), then ugly (not A) is already defined as a correlative.
Say, someone is in front, and then there are others behind correlatively.
Correlatives are naturally occurring phenomena.
Therefore, there should be no bias against any member of pairs of correlatives.

The Sage (Laozi) is inspired to be unselfish in action, not-possessive in creation, not critical of all things.
The frog has beautiful, strong legs and can jump far and high graciously.
The snake seems ugly with no legs, but can move fast to catch the frog for supper.
All things may not be created equal, but have equal rights of respect and protection.

Correlatives have inspired Laozi to describe a great philosophy of respect for all things.

Dao De Jing

三章　　　　　　　　　　Chapter 3

01	不尚贤, 使民不争	Not exalting the virtuous-talented, causes citizens not to contest
02	不贵难得之货	Not valuing hard-to-obtain commodities
03	使民不为盗	Causes citizens not be robbers
04	不见可欲	Not being seen with desirables
05	使民心不乱	Causes citizens' heart (feelings) not be confused
06	是以:	Therefore:
07	圣人之治	The Sage's administration
08	虚其心	Humble their heart
09	实其腹	Fill their stomach
10	弱其志	Weaken their ambition
11	强其骨	Strengthen their bones
12	恒使民无知, 无欲	Constantly causes citizens not to know, not to desire
13	使夫智者, 不敢为也	Causes the unscrupulous, not dare to act (manipulate citizens)
14	为无为	Act not selfish
15	则无不治	Then none not governable

Laozi's thinking

A truly virtuous and talented person needs no exaltation to come out and serve the citizens.
Not exalting the virtuous-talented will help discourage unhealthy rivalry among citizens. L1
Not valuing rare goods discourage robberies as these goods will have no value on the black market. L2,3
Not seen amassing great wealth will not cause confusion in citizens, hence inciting no disturbances. L4,5

Therefore, the Sage's principles for government are: L6,7
To humble the citizens' heart so that they may be kind, honest and helpful to each other. L8
To fill their stomach so that they do not go hungry and feel restless. L9
To weaken their ambitions so that they do not have excessive expectations. L10
To strengthen their bones so that they have good health and are strong to defend the nation. L11
Constantly causing citizens not to know extravagance and indulgence, hence not to desire. L12
Then unscrupulous people will not find it easy to manipulate the citizens for their own selfish gain. L13

Act with no selfish motives, but for the common good of the people. L14
Then none that is not governable as the people are well taken care of and living as well as the Sage. L15

Comments:
Unselfish leaders find all citizens governable (ch.3)

It seems highly controversial to suggest, "Not exalting the virtuous and talented …..".
However with these suggestions, Laozi seems to target the leaders themselves more than the citizens.
He warns leaders not to glorify themselves so that citizens aspire not and contest not for leadership.
He warns leaders not to hoard rare commodities so that citizens aspire not for possession and be robbers.
He warns leaders not to flaunt their wealth, thus confusing the citizens as to why they are so poor.
In good government, leaders are healthy, humble, honest and undemanding - like the citizens.
Leaders do not live extravagantly, hence, citizens know no indulgences and have no desires.

Laozi concludes, " When leaders are not selfish, no nation not governable".

Dao De Jing

四章 Chapter 4

01 道沖	Dao charges out (such as from the bellows)
02 而用之，或不盈	Yet use it, may not be depleted
03 淵兮	Deep indeed
04 似万物之宗	It seems to be the ancestor of all things
05 挫其銳	Blunt its sharp edges (Dao keeps low-profile)
06 解其紛	Resolve its conflicts (Dao is peaceful)
07 和其光	Harmonize with lights (Dao does not dazzle)
08 同其塵	Blend in with dusts (Dao is inconspicuous)
09 湛兮	Submerged indeed (Dao is unseen)
10 似或存	Seems like existing (not existing)
11 吾不知誰之子	I don't know whose child (Dao is)
12 象帝之先	Preceding Emperor of Forms (Dao is formless)

Laozi's thinking
Dao charges out (such as from the bellows) and seems inexhaustible in use. L1,2
Dao is deep like the ocean and seems like it is the origin of all things. L3,4

Dao is everywhere, creating and contributing, yet not to be seen or felt.
It is unobtrusive, peaceful, blending in with the lights and the dusts of the universe. L5-8

Dao submerges in the universe, like it exists and does not exist at the same time. L9,10
I don't know who has created Dao. L11
Dao must have existed before the existence of all forms and that is to say, Dao has no form. L12

Comments:
Dao is formless as it precedes the existence of all forms (ch.4)

Here Laozi elaborates on his concept of Dao.
Ch.5 says the space between Heaven and Earth is like a bellows.
Laozi speculates that Dao is in the air that is issued out to feed the fire.
The fire creates the tools that make all things, and Dao's use is inexhaustible.
Today, modern science tells us it is the oxygen in the air that makes the fire roar.
Hence, Dao per se as an Ultimate Entity envisaged by Laozi cannot be substantiated.

Here Laozi can only describe his perception of Dao in these poetic words of uncertainty
He cannot do a scientific investigation on Dao.
Suspecting Dao is in the air, Laozi is at a loss to find it
In ch.14, Laozi directly states that Dao cannot be seen, be heard or be hold.

Laozi honestly admits his ignorance not knowing who created Dao.
Hence, his famous first line in chapter 1, "Dao that can be described, is not the primal Dao".
He speculates that Dao precedes the existence of all forms, that Dao is formless.

Admitting ignorance, Laozi reveals himself, an honest thinker in quest for the Ultimate Reality.

Laozi: Quest for the Ultimate Reality

The Chinese Bellows

天地之间	Heaven and Earth, the space in-between
其犹橐籥乎？	Is it not like the bellows (barrel and plunger) ?
虚, 而不屈	Empty, but not yielding
动, 而愈出	Move (plunger), yet more come out (air, feeding the fire)

(*Dao De Jing,* chapter 5)

23

Dao De Jing

五章   Chapter 5

01 天地不仁	Heaven and Earth not benevolent
02 以万物为刍狗	All things treated like straw dogs
03 圣人不仁	The Sage not benevolent
04 以百姓为刍狗	All citizens treated like straw dogs
05 天地之间	Heaven and Earth, the space in-between
06 其犹橐籥乎？	Is it not like the bellows (barrel and plunger) ?
07 虚, 而不屈	Empty, but not yielding
08 动, 而愈出	Move (plunger), yet more come out (air, feeding the fire)
09 多言, 数穷	More said, numbers lacking
10 不如守中	Better then hold the center (position)

Laozi's thinking
When Heaven and Earth are not humane, such as during earthquakes, floods and droughts. L1
All matters suffer without bias, like the straw dogs discarded after ritual ceremonies. L2
When the Sage is not humane, for example during an unintentional miscarriage of state's affairs. L3
All citizens suffer equally, like the straw dogs discarded after ritual ceremonies. L4
Thus Heaven and Earth together with the Sage always act impartially.

The space between Heaven and Earth, is it not like a big bellows? L5,6
Inside, it looks empty, yet it strongly resists plunger movements. L7
Pushing hard against it, the more you work the plunger, the more air comes out to feed the fire. L8
And all manner of tools may be fashioned to create all the things in the world.
Furthermore, this energy or principle (Dao) comes forth without ever being depleted.

At this stage it is not good to say more when the facts and figures are lacking. L9
It is better then to hold the present position and not speculate beyond. L10

Comments:
Dao in the emptiness of the bellows (ch.5)

This is the only chapter where Laozi says Heaven and Earth and the Sage can be evil.
Treating all things like straws dogs implies impartiality
Indeed, when natural disaster strikes, all will be destroyed indiscriminately.
All that are present at the wrong place and at the wrong time.

The space between Heaven and Earth is like the big bellows that we can see in the smith shop.
This is one critical observation that must have fascinated Laozi.
One that made him conceived the primal entity of Dao as invisible, yet possessing inexhaustible energy.
That continuously enables creation and contribution to the universe through the tools that are forged.
Simple science today, but Laozi cannot know that it is the oxygen in the air that makes the fire burn.

Without more facts and figures on this 'bellows' phenomenon, Laozi wishes to say no more.
With great integrity, he would rather hold on to the current position than to fantasize about the unknown.
The concept of Dao may not be substantiated, but Laozi's philosophy still stands in the 21st century.

Laozi honestly resisted temptation to build his concept of Dao on fantasy and unbridled imagination.

Dao De Jing

六章	Chapter 6

01 谷神不死　　　　　Valley-spirit (of fertility) never die
02 是谓玄牝　　　　　Is said to be the primal female
03 玄牝之门　　　　　The primal female's doorway
04 是谓天地根　　　　Is said to be foundation of Heaven and Earth
05 绵绵, 若存　　　　Softly, continuously, like existing (not-existing)
06 用之不勤　　　　　Is used without being depleted

Laozi's thinking
Through the ages, union of the two sexes constantly works to produce succeeding generations.
This is so with the human species, and is also true with the animals and some plant species.

The valley spirit of fertility that never dies. L1
It is said to be the primal female. L2
The doorway of the primal female (sex organ) through which all procreation emerge. L3
This is said to be the foundation of Heaven and Earth, producing all the living things. L4
Acting softly and continuously for procreation, the spirit of fertility is like existing, not-existing. L5
Nevertheless, it is used without being depleted. L6

Comments:
The Female in procreation (ch.6)

The phenomenon of procreation also fascinates Laozi.
He sees it as another manifestation of the existence of Dao. (see also The Male in procreation, ch.21)
The valley is large, well irrigated, rich in plants and animals, where civilizations first started.
The valley-spirit therefore is an appropriate symbol of fertility that never dies.

The Valley-spirit or Dao in procreation is unseen, and unheard, thus seems to both exist and not exist.
It is conceived to be the eternal energy that softly continuously enables procreation but is never depleted.
Laozi does not have the benefits of scientific knowledge of our time to understand the procreation process.
His description of the procreation process is shrouded in the mystery of the Valley-spirit of fertility.

Laozi's use of mystical words and descriptions is clearly not meant to deceive us with his superior knowledge.
But on the contrary, it expresses his fascination and puzzlement in the phenomenon of the creation of life.
He admits his ignorance of the procreation process with his choice of words "like existing, not existing".

Laozi is clearly an honest and sincere observer, a seeker to understand the procreation of Life.

Dao De Jing

七章	Chapter 7

01 天长地久 — Heaven is long (in years) Earth is lasting
02 天地, 所以能长且久者 — Heaven and Earth, the reason for being long and lasting
03 以其不自生 — Is that they do not exist for themselves
04 故能长生 — Hence can be long and lasting

05 是以: — Therefore:
06 圣人后其身, 而身先 — The Sage takes back-role, and finds a front-role
07 外其身, 而身存 — Disregards personal danger, and finds personal survival
08 非以其无私耶？— Is it not because there is no private-agenda (for self)？
09 故, 能成其私 — Hence, can achieve a private-agenda (for all)

Laozi's thinking
Heaven and Earth exist long before the ancients who sheltered in caves and lived in the wild. L1
Then civilization started with people staying in clean houses and living on cultivated land.
Kings and dynasties may come and go in succession, but Heaven and Earth stay on.
The reason that Heaven and Earth can be so long lasting! L2
It is because they do not exist for themselves, hence, can last forever. L3,4

Therefore, taking the cue from Heaven and Earth, the Sage does not live for the self. L5
Not wishing to contest and by taking a back seat role, the Sage is given a front seat role by the people. L06
Disregard personal danger in service, the Sage finds safety and protection from the people. L7
Is it not that the Sage has no private agenda for the self？L8
Hence he can achieve his private agenda which is for the common good of all. L9

Comments:
Selfless like Heaven and Earth (ch.7)

Laozi observes that Heaven and Earth are long lasting.
And infers that this is due to Heaven and Earth not existing for themselves.
Hence, he advises that the Sage should act likewise and be unselfish in the service of the people.

This chapter cannot be interpreted otherwise.
We certainly cannot accuse the Sage of being deceitful, taking a back seat with an eye on the front seat！
Otherwise it is like using the yard stick of evil to measure the actions of the good.
As a good leader, is it not possible that the private agenda of the Sage is for the common good of all？
In fact, chapter 49 states clearly that the wishes of of the Sage are actually the wishes of the people.
Hence, in fulfilling the agenda of the people, the unselfish private agenda of the Sage is also fulfilled.

"Be unselfish" is a basic principle of pacific Daoism.

Laozi: Quest for the Ultimate Reality

上善若水
水善,利萬物,而不爭

High goodness like water
Water good, benefits all things, yet not contending

(*Dao De Jing,* chapter 8)

Dao De Jing

八章　　　　　　　　　　Chapter 8

01 上善若水	High goodness like water
02 水善, 利万物, 而不争	Water good, benefits all things, yet not contending
03 处众人之所恶	Resides where all people will hate (bottom)
04 故几于道	Hence is founded in Dao
05 居善, 地; 心善, 渊	Residence good, has place (humble); Heart (feeling) good, has depth
06 与善, 仁; 言善, 信	Relation good, has kindness; Communication good, has trust
07 政善, 治; 事善, 能	Government good, has management; Service good, has capability
08 动善, 时	Action good, has timing.
09 夫, 唯不争	Indeed, only not-contesting
10 故, 无尤(说文解字:異也)	Hence, no differences (or rivalry with others)

Laozi's thinking
Water is high in goodness, benefiting all things in many ways. L1
Water irrigates the land for growing food, provides drinking liquid which is essential for all living things.
It provides liquid for washing, for pottery and other production activities.
It fills the rivers and ocean for the fishes and also supports an alternative means of transportation by boats.
It flows around any obstacle in its path, always yielding and not-contesting. L2
It always flows downwards, to occupy lowly positions where all people hate. L3
Therefore, the goodness of water is akin to Dao itself. L4

In life, we can emulate water, benefiting all things and not-contesting.
Good positioning has humility; good feeling has depth. L5
Good relation has kindness; good speech has trust. L6
Good government has governance; good service has capability. L7
Good action has timing. L8

Indeed, only by not-contesting, one has no differences with others. L9,10
Hence, no rivalry, and no worries.

Comments:
Not-contesting like water (ch.8)

Except for the occasional floods and drowning, water is essential for life in the sea and on land.
At the same time water is also soft and gentle, taking the shape of its container.
Water is therefore illustrative of benefiting and not-contesting.

Laozi further defines goodness in other spheres of human activities.
There is humility in status position, depth in good feeling, kindness in good relationship.
There is trust in good communication and efficiency in good government.
There are capabilities in good service and timing in good action.

Not-contesting is the quality that Laozi wished to highlight.
If practiced, there would be no division among individuals and a harmonious society would be ensured.

In water, Laozi observes one of the pillar principles of pacific Daoism, not-contesting.

Dao De Jing

九章	Chapter 9
01 持而盈之	Holds and fills it (will spill)
02 不如其已	Not better than let it be (not pushing to the limits)
03 揣而锐之	Strikes to sharpen it
04 不可长保	Cannot for long maintain (sharpness)
05 金玉满堂	Gold and jade filling the halls
06 莫之能守	None who can guard it
07 富贵而骄	Rich and noble but arrogant
08 自遗其咎	Self bequeath own destruction
09 功遂, 身退	Success achieved, bodily retire
10 天之道	Way of heaven

Laozi's thinking
Try filling a vessel to the brim and there will be messy spillage, so better let it be less full. L1,2
Try striking hard to sharpen an object, the sharpness may not be maintain for long. L3,4
When the halls are filled with gold and jade, none can guard them from thieves and robbers. L5,6

The wealthy and the privileged should not be arrogant, else they are sowing the seed of self-destruction. L7,8
Staying to claim the fruits of success often lead to conflict of interests and can endanger one's life.
Therefore, when success is achieved, one should physically retire. L9
This is the way of Heaven. L10

Comments:
Halls full of gold and such extremes, not defensible (ch.9)

Filling a container to the brim causes spillage.
Sharpness is not easy to sustain.
Halls full of jade and gold cannot be guarded
In life, Laozi makes observations which show that, going to extremes is not a good idea.

Wealth and status corrupt, giving rise to arrogance and sowing seeds of danger.
And Heaven's way is perceived to have created all things and not ask for anything in return (ch.51).
It may be easier to share misery than to share success.
The philosopher in Laozi therefore warns: it's better to retire after success than stay to claim credit.

Counter-intuitively, Laozi warns of the danger of maximizing, and staying back to claim credit for success.

Dao De Jing

十章　　　　　　　　　　Chapter 10

01	载营魄抱一	Carry and nourish the body-spirit to embrace One (Dao)
02	能无离乎？	Possible not to stray away (from Dao)?
03	专气至柔	Focus on the breath till gentleness (achieve)
04	能如婴儿乎？	Possible to be like the baby?
05	涤除玄览	Wash and remove mysterious visions (supernatural thoughts)
06	能无疵乎？	Possible without blemishes?
07	爱民治国	Love the citizen and manage the state
08	能无为乎？	Possible without self-agenda?
09	天门开阖	Heaven's door open and close (affairs of the world)
10	能为雌乎？	Possible to assume the female (support role)?
11	明白四达	Clear understanding in 4 reaches (all knowledgeable)
12	能无知乎？	Possible not aware of knowledge (its power for self gain)?
13	生之，畜之	Create it, nourish it
14	生，而不有	Create, and not possessing
15	为，而不恃	Contribute, but not presumptuous
16	长，而不宰	Have seniority, but not controlling (life and death)
17	是谓玄德	These are called primal virtues

Laozi's thinking
In carrying and nourishing the body-spirit to embrace Dao, is it possible not to stray away? L1,2
In focusing on the breathing, is it possible to be as gentle as the baby? L3,4
In cleaning out mysterious thoughts from the mind, is it possible not to have any blemishes? L5,6
In loving the people and managing the nation, is it possible not to have a personal agenda? L7,8
In affairs of the world, is it possible to assume the female role, supportive and not-contesting? L9,10
Having a clear understanding in all spheres, is it possible to not be aware of the power for self-gain? L11,12

The following are manifestations of having successfully embraced Dao:
Creating and nourishing all things; creating and not possessing; contributing and not presumptuous. L13-15
Having seniority but do not exercise controlling power for life and death. L16
These are called the primal Virtues. L17

Comments:
Meditation on primal virtues (ch.10)

Laozi advocates meditation to clean our mind of fantasy thoughts (L5,6 above).
With a breathing exercise to release all stress, so as to achieve total innocence like that of a baby.
Then to go on and better realize and appreciate Dao and its many virtues such as:
Having no personal agenda in the administration of the state;
Assuming the supportive female role in the affairs of the world;
Not using the power of knowledge for personal gain.

Laozi advocates meditation to cultivate primal virtues, not to acquire supernatural power for self-gain.

Dao De Jing

十一章	Chapter 11

01 三十辐共一毂	Thirty spokes share 1 hub
02 当其无	When it is empty
03 有车之用	Has cart to use
04 埏埴以为器	Mix water with clay to make container
05 当其无	When it is empty
06 有器之用	Has device for use
07 凿戶牖以为室	Open door and window to make room
08 当其无	When it is empty
09 有室之用	Has room for use
10 故:	Hence:
11 有之, 以为利	Has it, is of benefit
12 无之, 以为用	Empty it, to be of use

Laozi's thinking
The principle of the usefulness of emptiness can be seen everywhere.
The 30 spokes share a hub which is empty, so that the axle-rod can be inserted and the cart built. L1-3
Clay are made into earthenware, and only when empty can they be of use for holding and storage. L4-6
Chisel doors and windows to build a room and only when empty can the room be of use. L7-9

Hence, having these things can be of benefits. L10,11
But only when there is nothing or when they are empty can they be of use. L12

Comments:
The Hub, emptiness and utility (ch.11)

Laozi observes that the space between Heaven and Earth is like a bellows which never depletes. (ch.5)
Laozi believes Dao is there in the 'emptiness' of the bellows, unseen, formless, yet useful and inexhaustible.
Above are 3 more examples from daily life where Laozi can appreciate the utility of emptiness.

We are puzzled at such talks of the utility of emptiness.
When we first encounter them, these sayings do sound rather odd and counter-intuitive!
The world often looks at the positive sides of things and seldom consider their negative aspects.
However, Dao has inspires Laozi to question conventional wisdom, to examine the negative side of things.
The world favors 'contesting and going for it' kind of positive attitude.
Learning from Dao and water, Laozi sees the use of 'not-contesting' which may be a better way forward.
Like defense can be the best form of 'attack' by wearing down the enemy with a drawn-out war.

The 'emptiness' of Dao has inspired counter-intuitive thinking in pacific Daoism.

Dao De Jing

十二章	Chapter 12
01 五色, 令人目盲	Five colors, cause people's eyes blindness
02 五音, 令人耳聋	Five tones, cause people's ears deafness
03 五味, 令人口爽	Five flavors, cause people's mouths tasteless
04 驰骋田猎	Galloping fast on the flats hunting
05 令人心发狂	Cause people's heart to race madly
06 难得之货	Hard to obtain commodities
07 令人行妨	Cause people to take prevention
08 是以:	Therefore:
09 圣人为腹不为目	The Sage cares for the stomach not for the eyes
10 故, 去彼取此	Hence, discard that and choose this

Laozi's thinking
Excessive visual stimulation and colors can tire and damage the eyes of the people. L1
Excessive music and sound can deafen and injure ears of the people. L2
Excessive flavors can overwhelm and desensitize the taste buds of the people. L3
Indulgence in fast-pace hunting cause riots in people's hearts and minds. L4,5
Indulgence in hoarding rare commodities cause people to take preventive measures. L6,7

These indulgences can destroy the people and their nations.
Therefore, the Sage care for health through the stomach and not indulgence of the senses. L8,9
Hence, the Sage discards pleasure and opts for the healthy lifestyle. L10

Comments:
Indulgence of the senses, warning (ch.12)

Here Laozi warns of the dangers in over indulgence of the senses.
Hence the Sage chooses to care for the health of the people.
Rather than pandering to them through the excitement and pleasure of the senses.

These warnings are especially relevant in the 21st century today with ever increasing possibilities.
Excessive viewing of movies through internet download that are available 24/7.
Excessive video gaming among children which can impair vision.
Constant mobile music with head phones that can cause premature hearing impairment.
Indulgence in fast food can cause obesity and health problems even in rich, and developed countries.

Laozi is right, for over-indulgence of the senses can destroy individuals, and even nations.

Dao De Jing

十三章	Chapter 13
01 宠, 辱, 若惊	Favors, Insults, are like frightening
02 贵大患若身	Value (taking seriously) big trouble because of body (self)
03 何谓, 宠辱, 若惊？	Why says, Favors and Insults, are like, frightening ?
04 宠为上	Favors are highly (regarded)
05 辱为下	Insults are lowly (regarded)
06 得之若惊	Receiving them, likely be frightened
07 失之若惊	Losing them, likely be frightened
08 是谓, 宠辱若惊	This is to say, Favors and Insults, likely to frighten
09 何谓, 贵大患若身？	Why says, take seriously big trouble because of self ?
10 吾所以有大患者	The reason that I have big trouble
11 为吾有身	Is because I have a body (self)
12 及吾无身	When I have no body (ready to die)
13 吾有何患？	What trouble do I have ?
14 故, 贵以身为天下	Hence, value sacrificing self for the world
15 若可寄天下	Possibly can be keeper of the world
16 爱以身为天下	Love to sacrifice self for the world
17 若可托天下	Possibly can be entrusted with the world

Laozi's thinking
Receiving Favors or Insults are both likely to frighten. L1
We take big trouble seriously, because we have a body and fear for personal safety. L2
Why are Favors or Insults likely to frighten? L3
Favors are highly regarded and Insults are lowly regarded. L4,5
This is to say, receiving them are likely to frighten and losing them are also likely to frighten. L6-8
For we fear there may be sinister reasons behind these Favors and Insults.

What does it mean to say, taking big trouble seriously is because of having a body? L9
The reason I have big trouble is, because I have a body or a self. L10,11
When I have no body (prepared to sacrifice self), then what trouble do I have? L12,13

Hence if one will sacrifice oneself for the world, one can be keeper of the world. L14,15
If one loves to sacrifice oneself for the world, one can be entrusted with the world. L16,17

Comments:
Cultivate selflessness and have no fear (ch.13)
Normally we will say Insults are frightening but not Favors!
But Laozi is right to say Favors and Insults are both frightening
For we may not know the true reasons, sinister or otherwise for receiving or losing them.
Laozi is quite right too for saying, we fear great danger, because we have our physical body.
When we have no body, that is to be selfless and is ready to die, then what danger is there?

Without fear, balanced in body and mind, we can respond better to any crisis.
Hence, to confront fear of disaster, Laozi has prescribed self-cultivation of selflessness.
It is significant he has not advised us to seek outside help, from Dao or other supernaturals.

It is clear, Laozi is not a mystic philosopher, and teaches no mystical powers.

Dao De Jing

十四章	Chapter 14

01 视之不见, 名曰夷　　Look at it (Dao) and see not, name it Unseen
　　(说文解字:东方之人)
02 听之不闻, 名曰希　　Listen to it and hear not, name it Rarefy
03 搏之不得, 名曰微　　Grasp it and hold not, name it Micro
04 此三者不可至诘　　　These 3 entities cannot be investigated
05 故: 浑而为一　　　　Hence: Mixed and be One

06 其上不皦, 其下不昧　　Its top not bright, its bottom not dark
07 绳绳不可名; 复归于无物　Rope to anything yet cannot be named; again return to no-matter
08 是谓无状之状　　　　This is called the formless form
09 无物之象, 是谓惚恍　　The image of nothing, this is said to be indistinct, undefined

10 迎之, 不见其首　　　Go up to it, and not see its head
11 随之, 不见其后　　　Follow it, and not see its back
12 执古之道, 以御今之有　Hold to Dao of the ancient, is transport to the present Have (reality)
13 能知古始, 是谓道纪　　Able to know the ancient beginning, is called history of Dao

Laozi's thinking
Look at Dao and see not, so name it Unseen *(like barbarians of the east)*. L1
Listen to Dao and hear not, so name it Rarefy (as the air is thin). L2
Grasp it and hold not, so name it Micro (as the dust is micro). L3
As these 3 entities cannot be investigated; hence, mixed them together as One. L4,5

Combined, its top is not bright, its bottom is not dark. L6
Try connecting to something, Dao cannot be named and again return to no-matter. L7
Dao is said to be the formless form, the image of no matter, indistinct and undefined. L8,9

Welcoming it, the head cannot be seen; following it, the back cannot be seen. L10,11
Hold on to this ancient Dao so as to connect with today's matters. L12
To know the origin of the ancients is to know the order and discipline of Dao. L13

Comments:
The formless Dao is not detectable with our senses (ch.14)

With names like Unseen, Rarefy and Micro, Laozi tries to define Dao.
However with the senses of sight, hearing and touch, he cannot find Dao.
Hence he said these 3 entities cannot be investigated and be combined as One.

This chapter describes Dao in more detail, mainly negatively for what Laozi cannot observe.
Dao has the formless form, the image of no-things, indistinct and undefined.

Looking high and low Laozi fails again to define and name Dao in positive terms.
Going up to confront or following behind, Laozi is still not able to see the head or tail of Dao.
Finally, Laozi suggests we may look into the past, into the beginnings to understand the present.

Laozi conceptualizes Dao for the need of a primal energy for the creation of all things.
However, Laozi has not fallen for superstition and fantasy spinning on Dao, to worshiping Dao.
What Laozi does not know he states he does not know, and advises investigation into the past.

Again Laozi shows he is no mystic, but just a honest thinker seeking the Truth of Dao.

Dao De Jing

十五章	Chapter 15

01 古之, 善为道者	In ancient time, persons good at practicing Dao
02 微, 妙, 玄, 通	Subtle, wonderful, in-depth, knowledgeable
03 深不可识	The depth (of character) cannot be known
04 夫唯不可识; 故, 强为之容:	Indeed as (character) cannot be known; hence, perforce to describe it:
05 豫兮, 若冬涉川	Prepared indeed, it's like crossing a river in winter
06 犹兮, 若畏四邻	Hesitant indeed, it's like fearful of neighbors
07 俨兮, 其若客	Dignify indeed, it's like the guest
08 涣兮, 其若冰之将释	Gentle indeed, it's like ice on the verge of melting
09 敦兮, 其若朴	Sincere indeed, it's like the simpleton
10 旷兮, 其若谷	Open-minded indeed, it's like the valley
11 浑兮, 其若浊	Flow-together indeed, it's like muddy
12 孰能浊, 以静之徐清?	Whoever can be muddy, then by stillness be progressively cleared ?
13 孰能安, 以动之徐生?	Whoever can be inactive, then act to progressively enlivened ?
14 保此道者, 不欲盈	Whoever keeps this Dao, does not wish being-full
15 夫, 唯不盈	Indeed, only being not full (of oneself)
16 故, 能蔽而新成	Hence, can be the tiny-grass and be renewed
(说文解字:小艹也)	

Laozi's thinking
In ancient time, people good at practicing Dao is subtle, wonderful, in-depth, knowledgeable. L1,2
The depth of character cannot be known as it is so profound. L3

Hence, we can only arbitrarily describe the characteristics as follow: L4
Prepared indeed like crossing a river in winter; hesitant indeed like fearful of the neighbors; L5,6
Dignify indeed like the guest; cool and gentle indeed like ice on the verge of melting; L7,8
Sincere indeed like the simpleton; open indeed like the valley; L09,10
Mix-together (sociable) indeed with any company like a commoner. L11

Whoever can be muddy-headed, then by quietude be progressively clarified? L12
Whoever can be inactive, then by action be progressively enlivened? L13
Whoever keeps this Dao does not wish being so full of oneself. L14
Indeed, not so full of oneself, then one can be inconspicuous like tiny grass and be renewed. L15,16

Comments:
Daoist behavior (ch.15)

Laozi reveres the ancient Daoists, people who practice the principles of Dao.
As Laozi describes, the Daoists are:
Ever-prepared, careful, mindful and considerate of others, dignify in appearance.
Cool and gentle in manner, sincere and honest, broad-minded, common and sociable.

In muddy and tumultuous condition, Daoists are capable of quietude and be clear-minded.
In resting and inactive mode, Daoists are capable of action and be enlivened.
Daoists are not full of themselves in their knowledge and perfection.
Daoists are low-profiled and are capable of renewing themselves like the tiny grass.
Daoists are not powerful and overbearing people whom others fear and try to avoid.

As pacifist, Daoists are gentle, peaceful people who are welcome in the neighborhood, in the world.

Dao De Jing

十六章	Chapter 16

01 至虚极	Reach emptiness at its limit (clear the mind)
02 守静笃	Hold stillness seriously (maintain the clear mind)
03 万物并作	The myriad things simultaneously in action
04 吾以观复	This I have observed repeatedly

05 夫物芸芸	Indeed all things like evergreen grass
(说文解字:艸也,可以死而复生)	
06 各复归其根	Each again return to its root (in cycles of life and death)
07 归根, 曰静	Returned to root, is called Stillness
08 是谓, 复命	This is called, fulfilling Destiny
09 复命, 曰常	Fulfilled Destiny, is called the Constant (Death, unavoidable)
10 知常, 曰明	Knowing Constant (Death), is called Enlightenment
11 不知常	Not knowing Constant (Death)
12 妄作, 凶	Unscrupulously acting, ominous

13 知常, 容	Knowing Constant (Death), will be accommodating
14 容, 乃公	Being accommodating, will be fair
15 公, 乃王	Being fair, will be king
16 王, 乃天	Being king, will be Heavenly-attuned
17 天, 乃道	Being Heavenly-attuned, will be in accordance with Dao
18 道, 乃久	Being in accord with Dao, will be long-lasting
19 没身, 不殆	Till submerged body (death), not endangered

Laozi's thinking
To think and understand the world better, first reach emptiness at its limit so as to clear the mind. L1
Hold fast to this state with quietude, then we will realize that all things are constantly in action. L2,3
And I have made such observation over and over again. L4

All things are like evergreen grass, each will again return to its root, to die in cycles of life and death.. L5,6
At end stage, it is called Stillness, and it may be said that each has fulfilled its Destiny. L7,8
Fulfilled Destiny is called the Constant (Death), knowing Death is inevitable, is called Enlightenment. L9,10
To not know Constant (Death), and act unscrupulously is ominous. L11,12

Knowing that Death is inevitable, we will be accommodating, and fair. L13,14
We will be kingly, and be heavenly-attuned. L15,16
We will be in accord with Dao, long-lasting, and till death will not be endangered. L17-19

Comments:
The cycle of Life-death (ch.16)

Through meditation we may be more aware of the cycle of life-death of all things.
Life is limited, this is a certainty, an inevitability.
Not knowing this certainty, and act unscrupulously is dangerous.
Knowing this fact, we mellow, we become accommodating, fair, and kingly.
Be in accord with Heaven and with Dao, and experience no danger going through life.

Realization of the inevitability of the life-death cycle has mellowing impact on our psyche.

Dao De Jing

十七章	Chapter 17
01 太上, 下知有之	Great ruler, people know it exist
02 其次, 亲而誉之	The next best, love and praise it
03 其次, 畏之	The next, fear it
04 其次, 侮之	The next, insult it
05 信不足焉	Trust when not enough (from the top)
06 有不信焉	There is no trust then (from the bottom)
07 犹兮, 其贵言	At ease indeed, it (great ruler) rarely talk
08 功成, 事遂	Success achieved, and task performed
09 百姓皆谓: "我自然"	The citizens all said: "We are natural (in accomplishment)"

Laozi's thinking
The nation is at peace and there are no short supply of any commodities.
The justice and other departments run smoothly and there are no extra taxes to disturb the people.
The government is known to exist but not heard giving new orders or issuing new decrees.
This is the highest level of government when the citizens are just aware of its presence. L1
Next level of leadership is one that citizens love and praise. L2
Next level is one that the citizens fear. L3
Next level is one the citizens despise. L4
When there are not enough of trust from the top, in response, there will be no trust from the bottom. L5,6

Relaxed, and in control, the great leadership rarely needs to make an announcement or issue a decree. L7
When the fields are planted and the crops are in, the citizens said " We are naturally accomplished". L8,9

Comments:
Rulers: types and rankings (ch.17)

Clearly, the best leadership works for the best interest of all citizens and not just for the leaders.
Prosperity happens so naturally, the citizens feel they have done it all by themselves.

Directly and simply, Laozi has all rulers typed and ranked with uncanny accuracy.
Many scholars have interpreted Laozi as a philosopher for the lords and kings.
But clearly we can see here that Laozi is speaking up for the citizens.

Laozi is certainly a philosopher of the common people.

Dao De Jing

十八章　　　　　　　　　Chapter 18

01 大道废, 有仁义	Great Dao lost, there is benevolence and righteousness
02 智惠出, 有大伪	Knowledge and intelligence appear, there is great falsehood
03 六亲不和, 有孝慈	The 6 family-relationships not in harmony, there is filial piety
04 国家昏乱, 有忠臣	The nation in muddle upheaval, there are loyal ministers

Laozi's thinking
When Dao reigns, everyone is good, and no one is bullied, hence, no need for benevolence and righteousness.
When Dao is lost, there is a need for benevolence and righteousness to protect the weaker citizens. L1

When Dao reigns, the people are simple, and honest, and do not scheme, so there are no falsehoods.
When Dao is lost, some people are tempted to gain more, by using their knowledge to scheme falsehoods. L2

When Dao reigns, there is harmony, all family members are alike, as every member has filial piety.
When Dao is lost, and familial harmony is lost, then filial piety is appreciated in certain members. L3

When the nation is in order and prosperous, all ministers are alike.
When the nation is in disarray, then we can tell the loyal ministers from the disloyal ministers. L4

Comments:
Conventional virtues (ch.18)

When everybody embraces and practices the principles of Dao, Daoism reigns.
Everybody is good and nobody is bad in taking advantage of others.
Everybody is self-sufficient, and hence, no one needs benevolence from another.
Everybody is good and fair to each other; therefore, righteousness is not needed either.
Every member does its duty and there is harmony in the family; hence, no filial piety is needed.
Ruler manages the nation unselfishly and there is prosperity; hence, has no loyal or disloyal officials.

Primal virtues such as not-contesting, fairness, and unselfishness reign in the ideal land of Dao.
There is no need for conventional virtues such as benevolence, righteousness, filial piety, and loyalty.
Cultivation of primal virtues in each individuals prevents the occurrence of injustice, violence, and suffering.
Conventional virtues are open to abuses as the unscrupulous often steal in the name of charity.
Hence, teaching conventional virtues is like treating the symptoms of social ills.
Whereas teaching primal virtues is like curing social ills.

Laozi exposes the faults of conventional virtues, that appear when Daoism is lost.

Dao De Jing

十九章   Chapter 19

01 绝圣, 弃智	End Sage-hood, abandon intelligence
02 民利百倍	Citizens benefit 100-fold
03 绝仁, 弃义	End benevolence, abandon righteousness
04 民复孝慈	Citizens return to filial love
05 绝巧, 弃利	End ingenuity, abandon gains
60 盗, 贼, 无有	Robbers, thieves, none exist
07 此三者以为文不足	These 3 entities as written is not enough
08 故:	Hence:
09 令有所属	Additional instructions are given
10 见素, 抱朴	Show plainness, embrace original-self
11 少私, 寡欲	Lessen selfishness, reduce desire
12 绝学, 无憂	End learning, no worries

Laozi's thinking
Exalting sage-hood and virtues will cause unhealthy rivalry among citizens. (ch 3)
The appearance of intelligence will give rise to falsehood and deception. (ch18)
Hence, end Sage-hood and abandon intelligence will benefit the citizens 100-fold. L1,2
End benevolence and righteousness that are redundant, then citizens return to filial love. L3,4
End ingenuity and abandon gain, then there is no accumulation of wealth. L5
Citizens have no temptation and therefore no reason to be thieves and robbers. L6
These 3 written guidelines may not be enough to guide people. L7

Hence: L8
In addition, people should be encourage to take positive actions. L9
Such as, display simplicity and be honest and humble – one's original self. L10
Lessen selfishness and reduce desires for fame and fortune. L11
End learning to chase after more glory and wealth; reduce wants, and therefore have no worries. L12

Comments:
Primal virtues (ch.19)

In the ideal world of Laozi, everyone has embraced the principles of Dao.
Everyone contributing and not contending.
Everybody's rights are respected; nobody takes more than anyone else; nobody needs to take less.
There are no conflicts, there are no sufferings, no hoarding of wealth.
Hence, no charity is needed, no righteousness is needed.

This chapter is an extension that elaborates upon the preceding chapter 18.
Laozi warns of the negative aspects of benevolence, righteousness, ingenuity, amassing of wealth.
The antidotes are teaching primal virtues such as simplicity, honesty, and humility.
Be less selfish, reduce desires, and stop pursuing learning for more wealth and glory.

Laozi suggests abandoning conventional virtues, and replacing them with teaching primal virtues.

Dao De Jing

二十章   Chapter 20

01	唯之与阿, 相去几何?	"Wei" (soft response) versus "Ah" (loud response), how apart are they?
02	美之与恶, 相去若何?	Beauty versus non-beauty, how different are they?
03	人之所畏, 不可不畏	What people are afraid of, cannot be not afraid
04	荒兮, 其未央哉!	Wilderness era (prehistoric), such ethics have not stopped!
05	众人熙熙	All the people talking happily
06	如享太牢	Like enjoying a sacrificial feast (of cattle, goat and pig)
07	如春登台	Like ascending the tower in spring (in festivity)
08	我独泊兮, 其未兆	I alone anchor (in quietude) indeed, with no sign (of celebration)
09	沌沌兮, 如婴儿之未孩	Blank innocence indeed, like the baby yet able to smile
10	儡儡兮, 若无所归	Looking tired indeed, like having nowhere to return
11	众人皆有余, 而我独若遗	The people all have surplus, but I alone like on the run
12	我愚人之心也哉!	I am a fool at heart indeed!
13	俗人昭昭, 我独昏昏	Common people are most clear-minded, I alone am most dim-witted
14	俗人察察, 我独闷闷	Common people are most discerning, I alone am most boring
15	澹兮其若海; 漂兮若无止	Floating indeed like on open sea; riding on wind indeed like no limit
16	众人皆有以, 而我独顽似鄙	The people all have occupation, but I alone am stubborn and lowly
17	我独异于人, 而贵食母	I alone am different from others, only value nourishing-mother (Dao)

Laozi's thinking
In life, people are pleased with praise and angry with insults, perceived or otherwise.
"Wei" a soft answer versus "Ah" a loud response, how far apart are they? L1
Good versus no-good; how different are they? L2
What people are afraid of, we should also be afraid of. L3
Since prehistoric time, such ethical precautions have not stopped. L4

In the present world of reality, the people are happily talking. L5
Like enjoying a big sacrificial feast of cattle, goat and pig. L6
Like ascending the tower in spring, in festivity and celebration. L7
In my ideal world of Dao, I alone am anchored at the water-edge in quietude, with no sign of feeling. L8
Blank and innocence indeed, like the baby not yet able to smile. L9
Looking tired indeed, like having nowhere to return to. L10
The people have surplus, while I alone seemed lost; a fool at heart indeed as not wishing to contest. L11,12
The common people are most clear-minded, while I alone am most dim-witted, as not wishing to dazzle. L13
The common people are most discerning, whereas I alone am most boring, wishing to keep a low profile. L14
I feel relaxed, floating on the open sea; I feel free, riding on the wind, like no limit to where I may go. L15
The people all have preoccupation, whereas I alone appear stubborn and lowly. L16
As I do not wish to join the common crowd, contending for fame and fortune.
I alone am different from others as I treasure and embrace Dao. L17

Comments
Daoist conduct (ch.20)
Laozi first teaches us to be socially courteous, to be afraid and guarded as the general wisdom dictates.
He then colorfully depicts the different conducts of the common people and the Daoist in daily life.
It is clear that practicing the principles of Dao does not give the Daoist power or advantages over others.
The Daoist seems more restrictive and disadvantaged having to be gentle, not contending, and so on.
However, the Daoist with minimal desires is carefree, floating, relaxed at sea or riding free on the wind.

The Daoist, not-contesting in conduct, is relaxed and care-free.

Dao De Jing

二十一章　　　　　　　　　Chapter 21

```
01 孔德之容, 惟道是从        Contents of great Virtue, only with Dao do accord
02 道之为物, 惟恍惟惚        Dao itself as substance, all vague all elusive
03 惚兮恍兮, 其中有象        Elusive indeed  vague indeed, within there is image
04 恍兮惚兮, 其中有物        Vague indeed elusive indeed, within there is substance
05 窈兮冥兮, 其中有精        Far-away indeed dim indeed, within there is essence (semen)
06 其精甚真, 其中有信        The essence is very real, within there is trust

07 自古及今                  Since ancient time till now
08 其名不去                  Its Name (Dao) has not gone away
09 以阅众甫                  As to oversees all humankind (creation)
10 吾何以知众甫之状哉？      How do I know the condition of humankind's creation then?
11 以此                      By these (above observations)
```

Laozi's thinking
The contents of great Virtue only comply with Dao. L1
Dao itself as substance, all vague and elusive. L2
Elusive and vague, within there is image; there is substance. L3,4
There is essence, life-substance, or semen. L5
The essence is real; this reality can be trusted. L6
For without fail, a new life is formed and given birth to, in due course.

Since ancient times till now, Dao has not gone away. L7,8
Dao is always present to oversee the procreation of all humankind. L9
How do I know the condition of procreation of all humankind ? L10
By these observations of life-substance, or semen. L11

Comments:
Male in procreation (ch.21)

Modern science tells us procreation starts with the union of a sperm and an egg.
Modern science has even revealed the DNA code of life.
Today we know that there is no Dao as describes by Laozi; hence, there is no Dao lurking in procreation.

Of course, Laozi may not know the processes involved in procreation.
So he can only vaguely express the participation of Dao in procreation as above.
The union of man and woman, presence of semen transferred and subsequent formation of a child and birth.
These are daily phenomenon in procreation known to all individuals since the beginning of time.
To explain procreation, Laozi vaguely describes that Dao is present to make it all possible somehow.
Laozi seems vaguely suspicious that the semen is the physical form of Dao.
With vague words, Laozi actually admits not knowing how Dao participates in the procreation process.
To his credit Laozi has not fantasized on the role of Dao in the procreation process.

Indeed, so vague is this chapter that few scholars read it to mean discussing Dao in procreation!

曲则全　　　　　Bend and be whole (preserved)

(*Dao De Jing,* chapter 22)

Dao De Jing

二十二章	Chapter 22

01 曲则全	Bend and be whole (preserved)
02 枉则直	Incriminated and be straightened (vindicated)
03 洼则盈	Low-lying and be filled
04 敝则新	Worn and be renewed
05 少则得	Less and be gained
06 多则惑	More and be confused
07 是以，圣人抱一为天下式	Therefore, the Sage embraces One (Dao) and be the world's example
08 不自见，故明	Not self-focus, hence enlightened
09 不自是，故彰	Not self-righteous, hence illustrious
10 不自伐，故有功	Not self-praising, hence have credit
11 不自矜，故长	Not self-important, hence have authority
12 夫唯不争	Indeed because not contending
13 故, 天下, 莫能与之争	Hence, in the world, none can engage in contention with
14 古之所谓「曲则全」者	The ancient saying, "Bend and be preserved whole"
15 岂虚言哉！	Surely no empty talk indeed !
16 誠全而归之	Truth in total returns to this saying

Laozi's thinking
Resisting an armed robbery and being hurt or killed is not a good option.
Hence, sometimes, one needs to bow in order to survive the presence, and be preserved whole. L1
Similarly, to suffer incrimination, so that facts may be straightened out, and be vindicated later. L2
Take courage when down and low like in a pit, for when the rain (fortune) comes, you will be filled. L3
Things worn may not be unfortunate, as then they can be renewed, and with improvement. L4
When less is available, we may better appreciate the little we have, and therefore gain in enjoyment. L5
On the contrary, when there are more to be had, we may not know which to chose, and be confused. L6
Hence, the Sage embrace One (Dao) and lives as an example to the world. L7

Do not be self-focus, then we can appreciate other view-points and be enlightened. L8
Do not insist that we are always right, then we shall be illustrious. L9
Do not praise ourselves for success, then we shall have credit in the eyes of others. L10
Do not consider ourselves to be important, then others are willing to accept our authority. L11
Indeed, only when not contending, then none in the world can engage us in contention. L12-13

The ancient saying, " Bend and be preserved whole" is surely not empty talk. L14,15
In fact, much survival and many successes are owed to understanding and practicing it.
Hence, truth is in total support of this saying. L16

Comments:
Bend for salvation (ch.22)
Laozi acknowledges, when he borrows from the ancient saying,"Bend and be preserved whole".
Hence, the *DDJ* is no anthology, not just a collection of ancient sayings and wisdom.
Facing adversities, Laozi councils bending, suffering, lying-low to survive, to fight another day.
In life, Laozi advises not to self-promote, not to contest, for humility bears the best result.

Laozi's teachings actually encourage hope, not despair, especially for the weak !

Dao De Jing

二十三章	Chapter 23

01 希言自然	Less talk is natural
02 故, 漂風不終朝	Hence, whirl-wind cannot last whole morning
03 驟雨不終日	Stormy-rain cannot last whole day
04 孰为此者？	Who do all these ?
05 天地	Heaven and Earth
06 天地, 尚不能久	Heaven and Earth, even cannot last
07 而況于人乎？	So how can human then ?
08 故:	Hence:
09 从事于道者，同于道	Follower of Dao, conduct life in accordance with Dao
10 德者, 同于德	Follower of Virtue, conduct life in accordance with Virtue
11 失者, 同于失	Follower of Loss, conduct life in accordance with Loss (not Dao)
12 同于道者, 道亦乐得之	Follower who accords with Dao, Dao is happy to have follower
13 同于德者, 德亦乐得之	Follower who accords with Virtue, Virtue is happy to have follower
14 同于失者, 失亦乐得之	Follower who accord with Loss, Loss is happy to have follower
15 信不足焉, 有不信焉	Where trust is not enough, there is no trust then (in response)

Laozi's thinking
Nature rarely speaks or manifest. L1
Hence, a whirl-wind cannot last a whole morning; stormy-rain cannot last a whole day. L2,3
Who can do all these? Heaven and Earth. L4,5
Even Heaven and Earth cannot make whirl-winds and stormy-rain last. L6
So, it is only natural that empires of humankind come and go! L7

Hence: L8
The follower of Dao, conducts life in accordance with Dao. L9
The follower of Virtue, conducts life in accordance with Virtue. L10
The follower of Loss, conducts life in accordance with Loss (not Dao) L11
Follow Dao and Dao will love to have the follower. L12
Follow Virtue and Virtue will love to have the follower. L13
Follow Loss and Loss will love to have the follower. L14
When there is not enough of trust, then in response, there is no trust. L15

Comments:
Heaven and Earth, power limited (ch.23)

Even forces from Heaven and Earth are not sustainable.
How can the empires of oppression, build by Lords and Kings, carry on for long ?
The lesson is that using force is not sustainable.

Practice virtue, receive virtue; practice evil receive evil.
Show no trust, receive no trust.
The warning is that you reap what you sow.

Laozi recognizes the limitation of power; hence we are not protected from reaping what we sow.

Dao De Jing

二十四章   Chapter 24

01 企者, 不立	Whoever is on tip-toe, cannot stand (firm)
02 跨者, 不行	Whoever is standing astride, cannot move (fast)
03 自见者, 不明	Whoever is self-centered, not enlightened
04 自是者, 不彰	Whoever is self-righteous, not illustrious
05 自伐者, 无功	Whoever is self-praising, no credit
06 自矜者, 不长	Whoever is self-important, no authority
07 其在道也	These (defects) from Dao's (point of view)
08 曰余食, 赘行(形)	Call excess food, superfluous clothes
09 物或恶之	All things (and people) likely detest them
10 故, 有道者不居	Hence, follower of Dao will not dwell

Laozi's thinking
Whoever wants to be elevated by standing on tip-toe cannot stand firm. L1
Whoever proudly stands astride cannot advance fast. L2
Whoever is self-centered cannot see others' point of view, hence, not understanding. L3
Whoever is self-righteous is not liked by others and will not be spoken well of. L4
Whoever is self-praising will not be credited by others. L5
Whoever assumes self-importance will not be looked upon as an authority by others. L6

Such defects from Dao's point of view are like excess food, superfluous clothing. L7,8
All things will detest such excesses in their leaders. L19
Hence, followers of Dao will not dwell in such situations. L10

Comments:
Warning, self-promotion is counter-productive (ch.24)

Standing on tip-toes and standing astride are interesting images of instability.
Illustrating the negative effects of self-promotion and self-advancement.
The various self-promotion conducts have been first mentioned in Chapter 22.
They are reiterated here in the reverse form of expression.

Lesson: Self-promotion and self-advancement are self-defeating tactics that a Daoist will not practice.

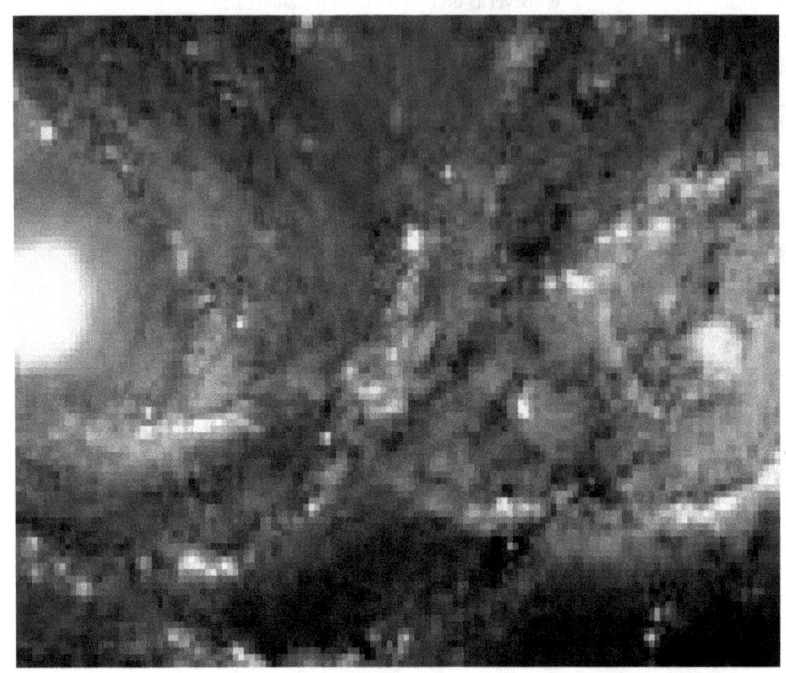

有物浑成	Matters mixed and formed
先天地生	Created before Heaven and Earth
吾不知其名	I do not know its name
字之曰道	Addressing it, call it Dao

(*Dao De Jing,* chapter 25)

Dao De Jing

二十五章　　　　　　　　Chapter 25

01 有物浑成, 先天地生	Have matters that mixed and formed, created before Heaven and Earth
02 寂兮, 寥兮, 独立而不改	Silent indeed, rarefied (formless) indeed, alone stand and not change
03 周行而不殆	Moving in cycles and not in danger (of stopping)
04 可以为天下母	Can be the mother of the World
05 吾不知其名, 字之曰道	I do not know its name, addressing it call Dao
06 强为之, 名曰大	Force to name it, call it Great
07 大, 曰逝	Great, is called Going-forth
08 逝, 曰远	Going-forth, is called Faraway
09 远, 曰反	Faraway, is called Returning
10 故:	Hence:
11 道大, 天大	Dao is great, Heaven is great
12 地大, 王亦大	Earth is great, King is also great
13 域中有四大	In the Universe there are 4 Greats
14 而王居其一焉	And King occupies one of them indeed
15 人法地, 地法天	Human models after Earth, Earth models after Heaven
16 天法道, 道法自然	Heaven models after Dao, Dao models after Nature

Laozi's thinking
Above Heaven and Earth in the dark reaches of the universe, stars are moving in never-ending cycles.
Therefore, created before Heaven and Earth there are matters that mixed and gel. L1
Silent and formless, it stands alone, never changing. L2
Moving in cycles with no danger of stopping. L3
It can be the mother of the universe. L4
I do not know its name; addressing it, we may call it Dao. L5
Including all the stars beyond Heaven and Earth, Dao must be very big, so maybe termed it Great. L6
We can see stars going forth to far-away places, then returning after many years, in never-ending cycles.
So, Going-forth, Far-away, Returning may all be terms to name and describe Dao. L7-9

Hence: L10
Dao is great, Heaven is great, Earth is great, King is also great. L11,12
In this universe, there are 4 Greats and King occupies one of them indeed. L13,14
Humanity models after Earth, Earth after Heaven, Heaven after Dao, and Dao after nature. L15,16

Comments:
Dao, birth of (ch.25)

Laozi is hypothetical in calling Dao with terms such as Great, Going-forth, Faraway and Returning.
Describing Dao as silent, formless, stand alone, never-changing, cycling in action, Mother of all things.
Laozi is probing the mystery of the universe by observing and examining the perceived attributes of Dao.

In our scientific understanding of the world today, we can safely say there is no such entity as Dao.
Equally unsubstantiated is our "Big Bang theory' as we shall still ask what happen before that?
So in comparison, Laozi has not done too bad, in seeking the universal truth some 2,600 years ago.

This chapter clearly shows Laozi to be a philosopher scientist on a quest for the Ultimate Reality.

Dao De Jing

二十六章   Chapter 26

01 重为轻根	Heavyness is the root of lightness (seriousness anchors frivolity)
02 静为躁君	Quietude is the master of impatience
03 是以：	Therefore:
04 圣人终日行，不离辎重	The Sage whole day on the move, strays not from the baggage wagon
05 虽有荣观	Though have grand palace
06 燕处超然	Prefers the swallow's common place, comfortable in Nature
07 奈何万乘之主	It is inexplicable why the master of ten thousand chariots
08 而以身轻天下？	Will in person slight the world (with frivolity)?
09 轻则失根	Frivolity causes loss of roots (base support)
10 躁则失君	Impatience causes loss of kingship

Laozi's thinking
What is heavy may be used as the base to stabilize what is light. L1
Quietude may be used to control and master impatience. L2

Hence: L3
The Sage, while on the move for the whole day, strays not from the heavy baggage wagon. L4
Though there are palaces with grand views, the Sage transcends nature. L5
And prefers to dwell simply like the mystical swallows under the commoner's roof. L6

The last king of the Shang Dynasty, King Zhou was frivolous to the extremes.
He was given to rash and irresponsible acts.
The last straw was when he lit up the Smoking-towers, signaling an emergency.
All his lords and their armies rode to him in a great hurry, creating a great sight.
All this was done to make Daji, his concubine, happy and laughed!
It is inexplicable why the master of ten thousand chariots would personally slight the world. L7,8
Such frivolity caused him to lose his base support from his people. L9
And in the end, he lost his kingdom and dynasty. L10

Comments:
Warning frivolity (ch.26)

The last king of the previous Shang dynasty, King Zhou, was famously frivolous and cruel.
Laozi must have had him in mind when he wrote this chapter.
However, throughout the *DDJ*, Laozi never used a single proper name.
And this fact has not helped in the accurate dating of the *DDJ* and identification of Laozi, the man.
Maybe Laozi was too cautious to name names and write in general terms for his own safety.

Writing against frivolity, Laozi is warning all individuals as much as he is warning the rulers.

Dao De Jing

二十七章 — Chapter 27

01	善行, 无辙迹	Good at movement, leaves no trails
02	善言, 无瑕谪	Good at speech, leaves no incriminating mistakes
03	善数, 不用筹策	Good at numbers, needs no counting aids
04	善闭, 无关楗而不可开	Good at lock-up, no lock that cannot be opened
05	善结, 无绳约而不可解	Good at knotting, no rope restrain that cannot be undone
60	是以:	Therefore:
07	圣人恒善救人, 故无弃人	Sage with absolute Goodness saves people, hence no abandoned people
08	恒善救物, 故无弃物	With absolute Goodness saves things, hence no abandoned things
09	是谓袭明	This is said to be total enlightenment
10	故:	Hence:
11	善人者, 不善人之师	A good person, is teacher of a no-good person
12	不善人者, 善人之资	A no-good person, is the material of a good person
13	不贵其师	Not valuing the teacher
14	不爱其资	Not loving the material
15	虽智, 大迷	Though knowledgeable, is greatly confuse
16	是谓要妙	This is called the important secret

Laozi's thinking

A person good at traveling leaves no trail behind that others can follow. L1
A person good at speech leaves no incriminating remarks. L2
A person good at numbers needs no counting aids. L3
A person good at locks and keys will be able to open any lock. L4
A person good at knotting will be able to undo any rope-knots. L5
Therefore, the Sage, with absolute Goodness saves people; hence, there are no abandoned people. L6,7
Similarly, with absolute Goodness, the Sage saves things; hence, there are no abandoned things. L8
This can be termed as total enlightenment. L9

Hence, a good person is a teacher of a no-good person. L10,11
A no-good person is the work-material for a good person to teach. L12
Not valuing the teacher, or not loving the material. L13,14
A person, though knowledgeable, is greatly confused. L15
This is an important secret that everyone should know. L16

Comments:
Salvation, no abandonment (ch.27)

There are scholars who take the first 5 lines to mean supernatural powers of people who have acquired Dao. But Laozi is merely describing 5 persons with special skills, each making no mistake in their own specialty. Similarly the Sage, good at saving, also makes no mistake in saving all people and all things.

Laozi supports absolute compassion, arguing here that we need not have abandoned people or things.

Dao De Jing

二十八章   Chapter 28

01 知其雄, 守其雌	Knowing the male (role), hold the female (role)
02 为天下谿	Be the world's creek (small stream)
03 为天下谿, 恒德不离	Being the world's creek, absolute Virtue not go-away
04 复归于婴儿	Again return to baby child (innocence)
05 知其白, 守其黑	Knowing the white (right), hold the black (wrong)
06 为天下式	Be the world's example
07 为天下式, 恒德不忒	Being the world's example, absolute Virtue not changed
08 复归于无极	Again return to infinity
09 知其荣, 守其辱	Knowing the honor, hold the disgrace
10 为天下谷	Be the world's valley
11 为天下谷, 恒德乃足	Being the world's valley, absolute Virtue is enough
12 复归于朴	Again return to uncarved-wood (Dao)
13 朴散则为器	Uncarved-wood (Dao) disperse to be instruments
14 圣人用之, 则为官长	The Sage uses them, then be official leader
15 故, 大制无割	Hence, Big Order (Dao) not cutting (harming)

Laozi's thinking
The Daoist has and is aware of the male dominant role. L1
But not wishing to contest, the Daoist holds the female role, serving the world like the lowly stream. L2
Thus, showing that absolute virtue has not gone away, and we can be returned to child-like innocence. L3,4

Similarly, the Daoist has and is aware of the positive or the white side of things. L5
But the Daoist wishes to take responsibility for the dark side of things and set the world an example. L6
Thus, showing that absolute virtue has not changed and we can be returned to infinity. L7,8

Again, the Daoist has and is appreciative of what is honorable. L9
But the Daoist is willing to bear the consequences of disgrace and be the world's valley. L10
Thus, showing that absolute virtue is enough and be returned to Dao. L11,12

Dao, formless, disperses and takes all forms of matter. L13
The Sage uses them and becomes the leader. L14
Hence, Dao does not harm. L15

Comments:
Humility, responsibility, Daoist leadership (ch.28)

The follower of Dao (Daoist) does not contest but set good examples to the world.
The Daoist does not dominate in a male role but takes the female (mother) role to support and serve.
By taking on affairs of the dark side such as tasks that are difficult, dirty and dangerous.
And by being responsible, bearing the consequence and disgrace when mistakes are committed.

"Benefits and does no harm" - the pillar principle of a Daoist leadership.

Dao De Jing

二十九章   Chapter 29

01 将欲取天下而为之	Wishing to take the world and govern it
02 吾见其不得已	I see that cannot be done
03 天下神器	The world a sacred instrument
04 不可为也	Cannot be manage indeed
05 为者败之	Whoever tries will fail it
06 执者失之	Whoever holds on will lose it
07 故:	Hence:
08 物或行, 或随	Matter may progress, may follow
09 或歔, 或吹	May blow-hot, may blow-cold
10 或强, 或羸	May be strong, may be weak
11 或载, 或隳	May carry, may destroy
12 是以:	Therefore:
13 圣人去甚	The Sage discards excesses
14 去奢, 去泰	Discards extravagance, discards extremes

Laozi's thinking
Whoever wishes to take the world and manages it for self-gain, I see that will not succeed. L1,2
The world is a sacred instrument, and cannot be taken for possession. L3,4
Whoever tries will fail and whoever holds on to it will lose it. L5,6

Hence: matters may move in advance, may follow, may blow-hot, may blow-cold. L7-9
May be strong, may be weak, may nurture, may destroy. L10,11
In the world, matters are highly unpredictable.

Therefore: L12
The Sage when governing the world, discards excessess, discards extravagance and extremes. L13,14
That is to say, the Sage is not governing for self but for the people, for the world.

Comments:
Freedom, the world belongs to everybody(ch.29)

The world is large and all matters in it are highly variable.
The world is therefore not manageable for personal ownership.
The Sage is wise to discard excesses, extravagance, extremes in government..

No individual can possess the world; hence, leaders must discard excesses, extravagance and extremes.

51

Dao De Jing

三十章 Chapter 30

01	以道佐人主者	Whoever uses Dao to assist the master of people
02	不以兵強天下	Do not use army to dominate the world
03	其事好还	Such affairs lead to retaliation
04	师之所居	After the army has occupied
05	荆棘生焉	Thistles and thorns grow indeed
06	大军之后	Big army (deployment) afterward
07	必有凶年	Certain to have bad years
08	善有果而已	Good to have fruits (victories) only
09	不敢以取強	Not daring to take dominance
10	果, 而勿矜	Victorious, but do not boast
11	果, 而勿伐	Victorious, but do not chop-down (like wood)
12	果, 而勿骄	Victorious, but do not be arrogant
13	果, 而不得已	Victories, that cannot be avoided (in defense)
14	果, 而勿強	Victorious, but do not dominate
15	物壮, 则老	Matters prime, will age
16	是谓不道	Is said not Dao (incompatible with Dao)
17	不道早已	Not Dao early demise

Laozi's thinking
Whoever uses Dao to assist master of the people. L1
Do not use the army to dominate the world. L2
Such strategy will only invite retaliation in kind. L3
Where the army has occupied, thistles and thorns proliferate. L4,5
Whenever the army has been deployed, years of hardships are certain to follow. L6,7

It is good enough to be victorious. L8
In victory, the Daoist does not dominate, does not boast. L9,10
Does not pursue and destroy, does not become arrogant. L11,12
In defense, victory cannot be avoided. L13
But in victory, never seek to dominate and oppress the enemy afterward. L14

When matters prime, aging starts; when dominance peaks, decline follows. L15
This is not in keeping with the principles of Dao. L16
Things not in accord with Dao will end prematurely. L17

Comments:
War is mass destruction (ch.30)

War is always evil with great loss of lives and destruction of properties and livelihoods.
One of the basic principles of Dao is not to contest; hence, war is never the first option.
When war is inevitable in defense, then victory is enough; never dominate afterward.

The Daoist denounces wars, appalled by the widespread destruction.

Laozi: Quest for the Ultimate Reality

杀人之众　　　　　　　Killed people in large number
战胜, 以丧礼, 处之　　　Victory in battle, with funeral rites, administer it

(*Dao De Jing,* chapter 31)

Dao De Jing

三十一章   Chapter 31

01	夫兵者, 不祥之器	The Army, instrument of misfortune
02	物或恶之	All matters likely hate them
03	故: 有道者不居	Hence: whoever has Dao do not dwell (embrace)
04	君子居, 则贵左	The Gentleman in residence, then favors the left (where scholars stand)
05	用兵, 则贵右	The Army in deployment, then favors the right. (where generals stand)
06	故, 兵者, 不祥之器	Hence, this Army entity, instrument of misfortune
07	非君子之器	Not instrument of the Gentleman
08	不得已而用之, 恬淡为上	Unavoidable then use it, best done peacefully and minimally
09	胜而不美	Have victories but do not glorify
10	而美之者, 是乐杀人	And whoever glorifies it, is happy to kill people
11	夫乐杀人者	Whoever happy to kill people
12	则不可得志于天下已	Then cannot achieve ambition in the world indeed
13	吉事尚左; 凶事尚右	Matter of fortune favors the left; matter of misfortune favors the right
14	偏将军居左, 上将军居右	Deputy general stands to the left, top general stands to the right
15	言, 以丧礼处之	This is to say, use funeral rites to handle it
16	杀人之众, 以悲哀泣之	Killed people in large number, with sadness and sorrow to grieve it
17	战胜, 以丧礼, 处之	Victory in battle, with funeral rites, administer it

Laozi's thinking
The army is an instrument of misfortune and all matters are likely to hate it. L1,2
Hence, whoever has Dao do not embrace and use it. L3

The Gentleman king in peacetime favors the left where the scholar officials stand. L4
In war time, when the army is deployed, generals on the right are favored. L5
Hence, the army is an instrument of misfortune, not an instrument of the Gentleman. L6,7
When it is unavoidable, then use it in defense when attacked, and only minimally too. L8
When victorious, do not glorify, as whoever glorifies victory is said to be happy killing people. L9,10
Whoever is happy to kill people will not achieve their ambition in the world. L11,12

Matters of fortune favor the left (which stands for Heaven, the sun, male, etc.). L13
Matters of misfortune favor the right (which stands for Earth, the moon, female, etc.). L13
Hence, deputy generals stand to the left and senior top generals stand to the right. L14
That is to say funeral rites are used for administrative procedures in war. L15
People killed in large numbers should be grieved with sorrow and sadness. L16
Victories are to be administered with funeral rites. L17

Comments:
War is mass killings (ch.31)

Laozi is right; there is really no victory in walking over many dead bodies.
Even in victories, funeral rites are practiced to take care of the aftermath.

The Daoist sanctions war, horrified by the mass killings.

Dao De Jing

| 三十二章 | Chapter 32 |

01 道恒无名　　　　　Dao primal have no name (unknown)
02 朴虽小　　　　　　Uncarved-wood (Dao) though small
03 天下, 莫能臣也　　　In the world, none can subject it
04 侯王若能守之　　　Lords and kings if can keep it
05 万物将自宾　　　　All matters will be self-willing guests (subjects)

06 天地相合　　　　　Heaven and earth mutually united
07 以降甘露　　　　　To rain-down honey dew
08 民莫之令, 而自均　　Citizens have not commanded, yet are naturally shared

09 始制有名　　　　　Starting systems (kingdoms) have names
10 名亦既有　　　　　As names already have
11 夫亦将知止　　　　Whoever (lords and kings) also will know the limits
12 知止, 可以不殆　　　Knowing the limits, then can have no danger

13 譬道之在天下　　　Proclaiming Dao is to the world
14 犹川谷之于江海　　As streams and valleys are to the rivers and seas

Laozi's thinking
Dao primal has no name. L1
Dao also called original-self; though small, none in the world can subject it. L2,3
If lords and kings can practice Dao, all matters will self-submit to them as their subjects. L4,5

People are willing subjects because rulers with Dao are benevolent and impartial.
Like Heaven and Earth uniting to rain honey dew. L6,7
Which distributes evenly among the people who have not demanded it to be so. L8

Lords and Kings first established their kingdoms and have their names or titles. L9,10
They should embrace Dao, know the limits, and rule in peace with no danger. L11,12
Else ever expanding their territories with fightings and wars, disasters are at hand.

Daoism will benefit the world like streams irrigating the valleys, like rivers filling the seas. L13,14

Comments:
Daoism for rulers (ch.32)

Heaven and earth are observed to rain impartially, the rivers to irrigate beneficially for all citizens.
Laozi urges lords and kings to do likewise, be contented, know their limits, and not indulge in expansionism.
Daoism for government means equality, contentment, no expansionism, only peace and prosperity.

Laozi advocates that rulers embrace pacific Daoism for government.

| 三十三章 | Chapter 33 |

01 知人者, 智　　　　Whoever knows people, is knowledgeable
02 自知者, 明　　　　Whoever knows self, is enlightened
03 胜人者, 有力　　　Whoever victorious over another, has strength
04 自胜者, 强　　　　Whoever victorious over self, is strong (in character)

05 知足者, 富　　　　Whoever knows contentment, has abundance
06 強行者, 有志　　　Whoever forces action, has ambition
07 不失其所者, 久　　Whoever has not lost life-direction, last long
08 死而不亡者, 寿　　Whoever is dead but not lost, is long-lived

Laozi's thinking
Paradoxically, it is easy to find faults in others than to admit to faults we have in ourselves.
So in self-denial, we would rather try to change others than change ourselves.
Hence, whoever knows people is knowledgeable, whereas whoever knows self is enlightened. L1,2
Whoever is victorious over another has strength, whoever defeats self is strong in character. L3,4

Whoever knows contentment, and knows that enough is enough has abundance. L5
Whoever is forceful in action has ambition, purpose and perseverance only. L6
Whoever acts without losing life-principles and direction will stand the test of time. L7
Whoever is dead but not lost to memory and whose inspiring legacy lives on, is long-lived. L8

Comments:
Self-knowledge is difficult; Longevity is remembrance (ch.33)

Laozi rightly argues, self-knowledge is more difficult and more enlightened if achieved.
Often unaware of self-denial at work, we are our own greatest enemy.

Ambition knows no bounds; hence, Laozi argues that in contentment, we have abundance.

It is interesting that Laozi equates Longevity with a life of integrity not lost to memory after death.
Laozi does not equate Longevity with the time one lingers on earth regardless of the quality of life.
Hence there is dignity in death and likely Laozi would find euthanasia to be an acceptable proposition.

These observations show the depth of Laozi's wisdom in analyzing human nature and behavior.

Dao De Jing

三十四章   Chapter 34

01 大道泛兮	The great Dao over-flows
02 其可左右	To the left and to the right (pervasive)
03 万物恃之以生, 而不辞	All things depend on Dao to exist, but (Dao) will not mention
04 功成不名有	Success achieves but (Dao) is not named (credited)
05 衣养万物, 而不为主	Clothes and nourishes all things, but (Dao) not be master
06 恒无欲	Dao has no desires
07 可名于小	Can be named Small
08 万物归焉, 而不为主	All things subjected to Dao, but (Dao) not be master
09 可名为大	Can be named Great
10 以其终不自为大	Because Dao ultimately does not deem itself as great
11 故, 能成其大	Hence, can complete its greatness

Laozi's thinking

The great Dao is pervasive, flowing to the left and flowing to the right. L1,2
All things depend on Dao for existence, but Dao will not speak of this fact. L3
Hence, success achieves, Dao is not named and not given credit for the success. L4

Dao clothes and nourishes all things, but makes no claim to be their master. L5
Dao has no desires; hence, can be named Small. L6,7
All things submitted themselves to Dao, but Dao does not claim to be their master. L8
Hence, Dao can be named Great. L9

Because Dao till the end never consider itself as being great. L10
Hence, Dao's greatness is complete. L11

Comments:
Freedom, Dao is master of none (ch.34)

In Laozi's time, science has not been established to explain the many phenomena of nature.
The movement of stars, the sun, the moon, the day and night cycle, the four seasons cycle.
The volcanic eruptions, typhoons, earthquakes, tsunamis, floods, droughts, famines and such.
Laozi hypothesizes that Dao is the creator of all things, then observes that Dao is master of none.
All things in the universe have absolute freedom as Dao claims no ownership.
He sees no evidence of demand for worship from Dao, of things it created.
Hence, Daoism is not a religion, there is no god figure that claims ownership, control and worship.
It is remarkable that Laozi could conceive such thoughts in a time when superstition was rife.
Even today there is only a very tiny minority of us who can liberate ourselves as he did.

Laozi is truly a free-thinker, a seeker of truth, and Daoism is not a religion.

Dao De Jing

三十五章   Chapter 35

01 执大象	Uphold the great image (Dao)
02 天下往	The world will go (wherever Dao is)
03 往, 而不害	Go, and not be harmed
04 安平太	Peace, comfort and prosperity (will be found)
05 乐与饵	Music and food (also)
06 过客止	And passers-by stop
07 道之出口	Dao's emerging exit (of the bellows)
08 淡乎, 其无味	Dilute indeed, it has no smell
09 视之, 不足见	Look at it, not enough to see
10 听之, 不足闻	Listen to it, not enough to hear
11 用之, 不足既	Use it, not enough for a small-meal (very little substance)
(说文解字:小食也)	

Laozi's thinking
To the kingdom where Dao is upheld by the ruler, L1
The people of the world will go. L2
There they will experience no harm, L3
And only peace, comfort and prosperity are awaiting. L4
There are good music and good food, L5
And passers-by will be attracted to stop and to stay. L6

However, trying to find Dao, the principle in action from the exit (of the bellows), L7
Dao seems so dilute it cannot be smell. L8
Look for it and Dao cannot be seen. L9
Listen to it and Dao cannot be heard. L10
Use Dao and there seems to be not even enough for a tidbit-meal (with air from the bellows) L11

Comments
Dao, not detectable (ch.35)

In the land of Dao, there is no danger, only music and food that stop and retain passers-by.
There Dao has no smell, is invisible, inaudible, like air too thin and little for a meal.
Looks as he might, Laozi cannot find solid evidence of the existence of Dao by any sense.

To his credit, Laozi has never try to build a fantasy world around the concept of Dao.
He observes and when findings are negative, he is not afraid to say so.
When he does not know, he says he does not know.

With all his senses, Laozi is relentless in his effort to get physical evidence of Dao, the primal entity.

将欲取之
必固与之

Wishing to take it
Must first give it (bait)

(*Dao De Jing,* chapter 36)

Dao De Jing

三十六章   Chapter 36

01 将欲歙之, 必固张之   Wishing to shrink it, must first expand it
02 将欲弱之, 必固强之   Wishing to weaken it, must first strengthen it
03 将欲废之, 必固举之   Wishing to topple it, must first promote it
04 将欲取之, 必固与之   Wishing to take it, must first give it
05 是谓微明   This is said to be subtle enlightenment

06 柔弱, 胜刚强   Gentle and weak, triumph over strong and powerful
07 鱼, 不可脱于渊   Fish, cannot be separated from the deep sea
08 国之利器, 不可以示人   Nation's advanced instruments, cannot be shown to others

Laozi's thinking
The tender and weak can overcome the strong and powerful.
Wishing to shrink a rival nation, first one must yield to allow the rival to expand, L1
To become arrogant, to lower its guard, then it is time to reverse the situation and shrink it.
Wishing to weaken an opponent, one must first be weak to encourage opponent to win, L2
To have a false sense of strength, to lower its guard, then it is time to reverse the situation.
Wishing to ruin a rival nation, first promote the rival nation, L3
To divert its attention, to lower its guard, then it is time to reverse the situation and ruin it.
To catch a big fish, one first must offer a small fish as bait.
Similarly with humankind, wishing to take, one must first give to encourage a positive response. L4
This is said to be a subtle understanding of the nature of all things. L5

All of these soft and gentle tactics can be used to overcome the strong and powerful. L6
However, the fish must not leave the safety of the ocean depth and be exposed to danger. L7
Superior weapons of the nation must not be shown to others, else they could be rendered ineffective. L8

Comments
Triumph of the weak: strategies (ch.36)

To catch a fish, we must first offer a bait.
Business partners are entertained and showered with gifts in order to win big contracts.
Animal and human alike, our nature has not change down through the centuries.

Laozi is helping the weak with strategies to defend themselves from the strong and powerful.
He is certainly not instigating on how to scheme and to take advantage of others.
Else it is like using the standards of the evil to gauge the merits of the good.
But of course a sword is double-edged; it can be used for defense and for attack.

Laozi is a champion of the weak, certainly not an evil schemer as some might suggest.

Dao De Jing

三十七章   Chapter 37

01 道恒, 无为, 而无不为	Dao primal, without self-interest, then nothing will not do
02 侯王若能守之	Lords and Kings if can uphold Dao
03 万物将自化	All things will self-regulate (in accordance with Dao)
04 化, 而欲作	Regulated, then desires arise
05 吾将镇之, 以无名之朴	I shall stabilize it, with the nameless uncarved-wood (Dao)
06 无名之朴	The nameless uncarved-wood (Dao) (redundant?)
07 夫亦将不欲	Whoever also will not desire
08 不欲以靜	Not desiring is by quietude
09 天下将自定	The world will self-stabilized

Laozi's thinking
Dao primal takes on all tasks not for self-gain. L1
Hence, if lords and kings can emulate Dao and do likewise, L2
Then all things will self-regulate, following the good examples of their rulers. L3

After regulation, when desires reappear again to stir-up society, L4
I will stabilize with Dao's basic principles of anonymity and simplicity. L5,6
Then whoever again will have no desires. L7

By quietude, the leaders show they have no desires. L8
Not disturb by the demands and desires of the leaders, people follow their good examples.
Hence, the world will likewise be self-regulated and have no desires. L9

Comments
Be selfless in all actions (ch.37)

Laozi observes that Dao creates all things yet never proclaims itself the lord of the universe.
Dao always has this most important characteristic of being not selfish in all its actions.
Laozi therefore urges all rulers to do likewise and be not selfish in their rules.
The people will follow their good example and likewise be unselfish in all their actions.
When selfishness returns, control with repeat education in the humble principles of Dao.
Therefore, it is important that the rulers behave themselves in order to show the way to the people.

Today we certainly should promote this unselfish principle of Dao in people's hearts and minds.
Teaching pacific Daoism in school is the first step towards eradicating poverty in the world.
Through the combine effort of everyone behaving unselfishly and fairly to one another.
Correcting the attitude of individuals is the best medicine for curing society's ills.
Charity and huge donations are merely medicines for relieving the symptoms only.

Pacific Daoism in a nutshell: "Be unselfish in all our actions".

Dao De Jing

三十八章 Chapter 38

01 上德, 不德, 是以有德	High Virtue, not claiming virtue, hence has virtue
02 下德, 不失德, 是以无德	Low Virtue, not losing virtue, hence has no virtue
03 上德, 为之, 而无以为	High Virtue, takes action, and has no motive for action
04 下德, 为之, 而有以为	Low Virtue, takes action, but has motive for action
05 上仁, 为之, 而无以为	High Benevolence, takes action, but has no motive
06 上义, 为之, 而有以为	High Righteousness takes action, and has motive
07 上礼, 为之, 而莫之应	High Etiquette, takes action, and having no response
08 则攘臂而扔之	Will stretch arm to pull (people to comply)
09 故:	Hence:
10 失道, 而后德; 失德, 而后仁	Lost Dao, then comes Virtue; lost Virtue, then comes Kindness
11 失仁, 而后义, 失义, 而后礼	Lost Kindness, has Justice; lost Justice, has Etiquette
12 夫礼者, 忠信之薄, 而乱之首	This Etiquette entity, thin in Loyalty and Trust, it starts disorder
13 前识者, 道之华, 而愚之始	Above known entities, Dao's flowery-facets, they initiate stupidity
14 是以:	Therefore:
15 大丈夫居其厚, 不居其薄	Upright person dwell in thick (Trust), not dwell in thin (Etiquette)
16 居其实, 不居其华	Dwell in solid (Loyalty, Trust), not dwell in flowery (Etiquette)
17 故, 去彼取此	Hence, discard that (flowery-facets) and take this (Dao, Virtue)

Laozi's thinking
Person with high-Virtue does not claim virtue, hence has genuine virtue. L1
Person with low-Virtue wears virtue like a badge, hence has no genuine virtue. L2
Person with high-Virtue takes action and has no intention of showing off virtue. L3
Person with low-Virtue takes action but has intention of showing off virtue. L4
Person with high Benevolence takes action but has no intention of showing off Benevolence. L5
Person with high Righteousness takes action and has intention of showing off Righteousness. L6
Person with high Etiquette takes action and will not take no for an answer. L7
Person will stretch out arms and pull people in to make them comply. L8

When Dao is present, everything is naturally good and the world is in order.
Therefore: When Dao is lost, then Virtue is needed, and appears to put the world in order. L9,10
Likewise when Virtue is lost Benevolence, Righteousness and Etiquette will appear, in that sequence. L11
Thin in Loyalty and Trust, Etiquette is the beginning of disorder. L12
Benevolence, Righteousness and Etiquette mentioned above are Dao's flowery-facets. L13
Their appearance signify the beginning of stupidity. L13

Therefore: the gentleman will dwell in the thick solid facets of Dao, Loyalty, Trust and Virtue. L15-17
Not in the thin flowery-facets of Dao, Etiquette, Righteousness, and Benevolence. L15-17

Comments
Ranking of Virtues (ch.38)

In Dao's world, individuals are not selfish; there are no crimes and everyone is naturally self-sufficient. Therefore there is truly no need for Benevolence, Righteousness, and Etiquette. (elaborated in ch.18,19) Indeed their appearances signify disorder and the beginning of stupidity.

Benevolence, Righteousness and Etiquette are flowery-facets of Dao, not primal virtues.

Dao De Jing

三十九章   Chapter 39

01 昔之得一者:	In the past those that attain One (Dao):
02 天得一以清; 地得一以宁	Heaven attain One and be clear; Earth attain One and be quietened
03 神得一以灵; 谷得一以盈	Spirit attain One and be effective; Valley attain One and be filled
04 万物之得一以生	All matters attain One and be alive
05 侯王得一以为天下贞	Lords and Kings attain One and be world's finest (leaders)
06 其至之	All due to attaining Dao
07 天无以清, 将恐裂	Heaven unable to be clear, will fear splitting
08 地无以宁, 将恐废	Earth unable to be peaceful, will fear collapsing
09 神无以灵, 将恐歇	Spirit unable to be effective, will fear neglect
10 谷无以盈, 将恐竭	Valley unable to be filled, will fear drought
11 万物无以生, 将恐灭	All matters unable to survive, will fear extinction
12 侯王无以贵高, 将恐蹶	Lords, Kings unable to be grandiose, will fear downfall
13 故:	Hence:
14 贵以贱为本, 高以下为基	Nobility is based on the Commoners, High is founded on the Low
15 是以侯王自谓, 孤, 寡, 不穀	Thus, Lords' and Kings' self-designate Lonely, Lacking, Grainless
16 此非以贱为本耶？非乎？	Is this not with Humility as their base? Not at all?
17 故:	Hence:
18 至誉无誉	The highest honor is no honor
19 不欲琭琭如玉	Not wishing to be cut and polished like jade
20 珞珞如石	But be uncut and rough like stone

Laozi's thinking
In the past, those that had attained One (Dao) are: L1
Heaven attained Dao and be cleared; Earth attained Dao and be tranquil. L2
Spirit attained Dao and be effective; Valley attained Dao and be irrigated. L3
All things attained Dao and be alive; Lords and Kings attained Dao and be leaders. L4,5
All because they had attained Dao. L6

Heaven unable to clear will fear splitting; Earth unable to become quiet will fear collapsing. L7,8
Spirit unable to be effective will fear neglect; Valley unable to be irrigated will fear drought. L9,10
All things unable to live will fear extinction; Lords and Kings unable to be grandiose, fear downfall. L11,12

Hence: the nobility of Lords and Kings is based on the efforts of the commoners below. L13,14
The high towers are built on the lowly base foundations. L14
Lords and Kings assume self-salutation such as: Lonely, Lacking, Unproductive. L15
Is it not with Humility, that they understand their need for the support of the broad base of commoners? L16
Hence: Dao silently achieves the highest honor in enabling all creations, yet it claims no honor. L17,18
Emulating, the Daoist wishes not to be the polished jade but be the uncut stone. L19,20

Comments
Daoism is anonymity (ch.39)

Real achievements are accomplished unseen, unheard, unknown, unhonored, just like Dao.
The highest honor needs no honoring, no public acknowledgment.
Hence, the Daoist wishes not to be the polished jade but be the uncut stone; that is anonymity.

Laozi is the epitome of pacific Daoism and anonymity, a legendary unknown figure till this day.

Dao De Jing

四十章	**Chapter 40**

01 反者, 道之动 In cycles, Dao's action
02 弱者, 道之用 Weak and yielding, Dao's use

03 天下, 万物生于有 In the world, all things are created from You (Have)
04 有生于无 You (Have) is created from Wu (Have-not)

Laozi's thinking
Dao in motion, cyclical, like the stars, sun, moon, the four seasons, life and death, and others. L1
Dao in use, weak, like the yielding rain-water, sunshine, air and others, benefiting and not contending. L2

In the world all things are created from You (Have), the Mother-of-all things (ch.1). L3
And You (Have) is created from Wu (Have-not), the Beginning-of-Heaven-and-Earth (ch.1). L4

Comments
Dao, cyclical in action and gentle in use (ch.40)

Laozi first presents Dao, Wu (Have-not) and You (Have) to explain the existence of the universe (ch1).
These 3 hypothetical entities are the brave attempts by Laozi to explain the existence of the universe.

But today in our 21st century, modern science cannot find evidence to substantiate their realities.
So, it is inconsequential to try to understand how Anything can be created from Nothing!
Similarly, our present day theory on the beginning of the universe fares no better.
We are also unable to know what happen before the 'Big Bang'!

Dao may not be a reality, but Daoism founded on the perceived attributes of Dao is a beneficial realization.
Like the four seasons, Daoism is cyclical, changes from good-fortune to misfortune, and back to good-fortune.
Like water, Daoism is gentle in use, only benefiting and not contesting.

Indeed, the pacific principles of Daoism can only contribute to harmony and peace in our universe.

Dao De Jing

四十一章   Chapter 41

01 上士闻道, 勤而行之   The high scholar learns of Dao, diligently practice it
02 中士闻道, 若存若亡   The average scholar learns of Dao, like existing like not-existing
03 下士闻道, 大笑之   The lesser scholar learns of Dao, loudly laugh at it
04 不笑,不足以为道   Without laughing, not (silly) enough to be Dao

05 故, 建言有之: Hence, the 'Constructive Words' has these sayings:
06 明道若昧; 进道若退   Enlightened Dao like dim; advancing Dao like retreating
07 夷道若类; 上德若谷   Level path of Dao like uneven path; high Virtue like valley
08 大白若辱; 广德若不足   Great White (innocence) like humiliation; broad Virtue like not enough
09 建德若偷; 质德若渝   Building Virtue like theft; quality Virtue like worthless
10 大方无隅; 大器 晚成   Great Square has no border; great Project late (needs time) to complete
11 大音希声; 大象无形   Great Tone gives faint sound; great Image has no form

12 道隐, 无名   Dao invisible, has no name
13 夫唯道, 善始且善成   Indeed only Dao, good at starting also good at completing

Laozi's thinking
The top scholar understands when he hears of Dao and practice it diligently. L1
The average scholar cannot understand it fully, is perplexed and practices Dao with doubts! L2
The lesser scholar loudly laughs, and feels that if it is not laughable, it is not Dao!!! L3,4
Because Dao's attributes seem to be the reverse of accepted norms at best and senseless at worst.

The 'Constructive Words' has such sayings of wisdom: L5
Enlightened Way is like dim-witted as keeping low-profile is the style, is the wisdom; L6
Advancing Way is like retreating as not-contesting, the path of least resistance is favored. L6
Level Way is like uneven as not-contesting, perceived as weakness, hence can invite problems; L7
High Virtue is like the valley, occupying the lower ground as Daoist wishes to be humble. L7
Great Innocence is like guilt as Daoist feels the possibility that mistake has been made; L8
Broad Virtue is like not enough as Daoist's target for 100% coverage may not be met. L8
Building Virtue is like theft as Daoist is humble, not wishing to be seen doing good; L9
Quality Virtue is like worthless as Daoist is humble and unassuming, wishing anonymity. L9
Dao, like the Great Square has no borders as the universe has no borders; L10
Dao, like a Great Project is continuous with no completion time. L10
Dao, like the Great Tone that fills the universe only to give an inaudible sound; L11
Dao, like the Great Image that fills the universe, and hence, has no form to be seen. L11

Unseen and nameless, hence only Dao, is capable of success from beginning to ending. L12,13

Comments
Daoism is laughable!(ch.41)
Further to chapter 14, Laozi perceives more attributes of Dao.
These attributes are well expressed in the 'Constructive Words', and Laozi acknowledges quoting from it.
Laozi is fully aware of the controversial nature of his thoughts and sayings which seem negative.
These advices contrast with the accepted norms of society, appear silly and impractical.
Laozi expects the lesser scholar to laugh, even to feels that what is not silly enough is not Dao!
Liken it to the Greats (Square, etc) Laozi tries to explain why Dao is an inaudible, unseen, infinite success.

Pacific Daoism arises essentially from the Laozi's perceived attributes of Dao.

Dao De Jing

四十二章	Chapter 42

01 道生一；一生二 Dao created One; One created Two
02 二生三；三生万物 Two created Three; Three created All Matters
03 万物负阴，而抱阳 All things carry Yin (female energy), embrace Yang (male energy)
04 冲气以为和 Charge with energies (Yin and Yang) that harmonize

05 人之所恶 That which people dislike
06 唯孤，寡，不穀 Specifically The Lonely, The Lacking, The No-grain (Unproductive)
07 而王公以为称 Yet Kings, Lords use as self-salutations
08 故： Hence:
09 物或损之，而益 Things may be depreciated, to be benefited
10 或益之，而损 Or be benefited, to be depreciated

11 人之所教，我亦教之 Things that people teach, I also teach
12 "强梁者，不得其死" "The ruthless person, may not die a good death" (ancient maxim)
13 吾将以为教父 I will use as principle in teaching

Laozi's thinking
The formless Dao gives rise to One, (the first energy in the bellows, somehow); L1
One in turn give rise to the two energies, Yin (female) and Yang (male) (somehow); L1
Union of the two energies, Yin and Yang give rise to three, (the baby somehow); L2
The three together subsequently give rise to all things. L2
Thus all things carry Yin and embrace Yang, charge with the 2 energies, in harmony, and in balance. L3,4

The people dislike unfortunate words such as The Lonely, The Lacking, The No-Grain. L5,6
Yet Lords and Kings use them for self-salutations! L7
Hence: things may be depreciated in order to be benefited. L8,9
Or be benefited in order to be depreciated. L10

What people teach, I also teach. L11
There is this saying, "Whoever is violent will not die a natural death". L12
I shall use this maxim as the first principle in my teaching. L13

Comments
Daoism is harmony, humility and non-violence (ch. 42)

Many scholars find the 3 stanzas in this chapter quite disjointed.
Dao in creation, lords and kings with humble salutations and individuals be taught non-violence.
Nevertheless, the common concept in the 3 stanzas may be one of not-contesting.
Dao creates with harmony, lords and kings rule with humility, individuals live with non-violence.
In the 3rd stanza, Laozi acknowledges quoting an ancient maxim, hence, the *DDJ* is not an anthology.

Here Laozi hypothesizes that Dao creates the universe in a stepwise process, not in one "Big Bang".
This is just an academic observation as the concept of Dao is not supported by modern science today.

Pacific Daoism may be appreciated as Laozi's teaching of harmony, humility and non-violence.

Dao De Jing

四十三章	Chapter 43

01 天下之至柔　　　　The world's most gentle (Dao)
02 驰骋, 天下之至坚　　Rides about, in the world's hardest (such as melting bronze)
03 无有, 入无间　　　　Wu (Have-not) and You (Have) (or Dao), enter no space
04 吾是以知, 无为之有益　I therefore know that, without-motive does have benefits

05 不言之教　　　　　Teaching without saying (by examples)
06 无为之益　　　　　The benefits of no motive
07 天下希及之　　　　The world rarely can compare

Laozi's thinking
Dao formless, is the most gentle in the world. L1
Dao can move directly to engage with the toughest in the world. L2
Wu (Have-not) and You (Have) are both originated from Dao, thus together they are Dao. (ch.1) L3
Dao, invisible and formless, can enter where there is no space (from the bellows into bronze!). L3
Dao through Wu and You, subsequently give rise to all things.
Dao is the origin of the universe yet does not claim to be master of anything. (ch.34)
I therefore know from Dao the benefits of unselfish actions. L4

Dao teaches without verbalizing but by examples. L5
The benefits of acting unselfishly. L6
In the world, few can measure up to these two principles of Dao. L7

Comments
Daoism is unselfish and teaches by example (ch.43)

Stanza 1. Dao the gentlest in the world, can take on the hardest, like from the bellows into bronze, melting it.
　　　　Dao the formless is omnipresent; hence, I know the benefits of its actions without motives.
Stanza 2. Dao, none in the world can compare with its silent teaching and its unselfish actions.

In stanza 1, Laozi alluded to the omnipotence of Dao entering no space!
This of course we cannot substantiate for him today.
In Stanza 2, Laozi suggests that we can all learn two principles from Dao.
Firstly, teach not with verbal criticisms, but with good examples set by ourselves.
Secondly, unselfish acts that benefit.
None in the world can compare with Dao on these 2 scores.

Laozi appreciates Dao's perceived attributes, urges emulation thus spawning pacific Daoism.

Dao De Jing

四十四章	Chapter 44

01 名与身, 孰亲？　　　　Name (fame) versus body (life), which is dearer ?
02 身与货, 孰多？　　　　Body versus goods, which is more (important) ?
03 得与亡, 孰病？　　　　Gain versus loss (death), which is sick ?

04 是故:　　　　　　　　Therefore:
05 甚爱, 必大费　　　　　Much love, certainly big expenses
06 多藏, 必厚亡　　　　　Much hoarding, certainly much loss

07 知足, 不辱　　　　　　Know contentment, not be disgraced
08 知止, 不殆　　　　　　Know the limit, not be endangered
09 可以长久　　　　　　　Can be long and lasting (in survival)

Laozi's thinking
Fame versus life, which is dearer? L1
Life versus wealth, which is more important? L2
Gaining fame and wealth versus loss of life, which is sick? 3

Therefore: L4
Much obsessive love for things certainly will incur big expenses. L5
Much hoarding of goods will certainly incur more losses. L6

Knowing contentment and not pushing for more will avoid being disgraced. L7
Knowing when to stop and not pushing over the limit will avoid being endangered. L8
Then can be long and lasting in survival. L9

Comments
Life -survival vs Fame-wealth (ch.44)

Laozi is penetrating in identifying the common social ills such as greed for fame and wealth.
His recommended treatments are: be contented and know your limits.

Pursuing fame and wealth is dangerous; Laozi advises, knows one's limits and be contented to be safe.

Dao De Jing

四十五章   Chapter 45

01 大成, 若缺	Great success, seems deficient
02 其用, 不弊	Its use, not flawed
03 大盈, 若沖	Great fullness, seems charging (like air from bellows)
04 其用, 不穷	Its use, not exhaustible
05 大直, 若屈	Great straightness, seems bent
06 大巧, 若拙	Great skill, seems clumsy
07 大辩, 若讷	Great debater, seems inarticulate
08 躁胜寒	Exercise overcomes coldness
09 靜胜热	Quietude overcomes hotness
10 清靜, 为天下正	Clear-minded inactivity (no wars), enables the world be balanced

Laozi's thinking
Dao's great success seems deficient but its use is not flawed. L1,2
Dao's great fullness, like charging air from the bellows, its use is inexhaustible. L3,4
Great archer's arrow appears bend as it arches towards hitting the target. L5
Artisans great skill seems clumsy as the task is easily and effortlessly done. L6
Great debater seems inarticulate as only the right simplest choice of words are used. L7
Like Dao, true greatness in life, does not have to appear great.

When cold, we exercise to warm-up. L8
When hot, we stop activity to cool-down. 9
Lords and Kings likewise by quietude clear their mind and stop the incessant warring activities; L10
Thus allowing the world to normalize and to achieve the right balance. L10
Hence, Lords and Kings can likewise be great for achieving peace and prosperity.

Comments
Paradoxes of greatness (ch.45)

Laozi shows with 5 examples where true greatness paradoxically do not appear great.
Laozi suggests that rulers can do likewise and be truly great.
That they can paradoxically achieve greatness by quietude, not by great conquests.
By stopping the fighting and let states of the world achieve great prosperity in peace.

Urging quietude behavior of rulers, Laozi speaks again for the benefit of common people.

四十六章　　　　　Chapter 46

01 天下有道　　　　The world has Dao
02 却走马以粪　　　Walk horses with manure (to fertilize the fields)
03 天下无道　　　　The world has no Dao
04 戎马生于郊　　　War horses give birth in the country-side

05 祸,莫大于不知足　Disaster, none greater than not knowing contentment
06 咎,莫大于欲得　　Crime, none greater than desire to possess

07 故:　　　　　　　Hence:
08 知足之足　　　　Knows contentment of the contented
09 恒足已　　　　　Always contented indeed

Laozi's thinking
When the world has Dao, peace pervades the land. L1
And horses carry manure to fertilize the field. L2
When the world has no Dao, wars overrun the land. L3
And war horses give birth in the country-side. L4

Lords and Kings who do not embrace Dao, are not contented, and they embark on expansionism.
Wishing to enhance their status, they start wars to expand their territories and to enhance their wealth.
Therefore, of disasters, none greater than not knowing contentment. L5
And of crimes, none greater than greed. L6

Hence: L7
Knowing contentment and its sufficiency. L8
Shall always be contented indeed. L9

Comments
Be contented (ch.46)

Stanza 1. Contrasting images of life when Dao is present in peace and when Dao is absent in war.
Stanza 2. Identifying the root causes of the disaster of war as discontentment and greed.
Stanza 3. Hence, the solution lies in really knowing contentment and being contented.

The first stanza depicts the devastation seen in wars.
The second stanza gives reasons for wars, the greed for power and wealth of Lords and Kings.
The third stanza suggests the solution, everlasting contentment when true contentment is understood.

Contentment is one of the pillar principle of Laozi's pacific Daoism..

Laozi: Quest for the Ultimate Reality

不出戶	Without stepping-out the door
知天下	Knows the world

(Dao De Jing, chapter 47)

Dao De Jing

四十七章   Chapter 47

01 不出戶, 知天下	Without stepping-out the door, knows the world
02 不窺牖, 见天道	Not looking out the window, sees Heaven's way
03 其出弥远	Whoever goes even farther
04 其知弥少	Whoever knows even less
05 是以:	Therefore:
06 圣人不行, 而知	The Sage does not travel, but knows
07 不见, 而名	Does not see, but names (understands)
08 不为, 而成	Does not act, but is accomplished (with study)

Laozi's Thinking
The records of history documented events and reasons for the ups and downs of past dynasties.
Basic human nature down through the generations never changes.
Hence, the world may be known without stepping-out the door. L1
Records of astronomy, studies of the cyclical changes of the seasons, the sun, moon, and stars.
Hence, Heaven's way can be known without looking out the window. L2

The archives are accumulated knowledge of many individuals written over hundreds of years.
Whereas the individual traveler may have only personal experience from one life-time.
Hence, whoever goes even farther for knowledge may be more exhausted and knowing less. L3,4

Hence: the Sage by studying the archives, and by thinking, knows without travels. L5,6
Understands without seeing, and has knowledge without "action" (traveling and seeing). L7,8

Comments
Power of the written archives (ch.47)

Stanza 1. Records enable one to study and know the world and Heaven's way without stepping out the door.
Stanza 2. Without study and thinking, just traveling far and wide for knowledge is less efficient.
Stanza 3. Hence, the Sage knows, understands, and has knowledge without direct action.

This chapter does not mean the Sage is deriving supernatural powers from the Dao!
Stanza 2 lamented the inefficiency of traveling far to seek knowledge.
Laozi is not actually talking about supernatural powers and the likes of it.
Without mentioning, Laozi is referring to the vast archive of knowledge and its empowering influence.
Without looking out the window, one knows there is a full-moon in the sky on a mid-autumn night.

Civilization really took off with the invention of the written language.

Dao De Jing

四十八章　　　　　　　Chapter 48

01 为学, 日益	Take-up learning, daily gain (of knowledge, desire)
02 为道, 日损	Practice Dao, daily reduction (of desire)
03 损之又损	Reducing it yet reducing
04 以至于无为	To reach till no motive (unselfish)
05 无为, 而无不为	Not selfish, then no (task) not actionable
06 取天下, 恒以无事	Take the world, always with no agenda .
07 及其有事	If there is an agenda
08 不足以取天下	Not able to take the world

Laozi's thinking
In learning, daily we gain knowledge and desires. L1
In practicing Dao, daily we reduce our desires. L2
Gradually, we reach the state of having no selfish desires. L3,4
Not for personal desire and gain, we can undertake any task for the common good of all. L5

King Tang founded Shang Dynasty only by eliminating the last tyrant King Jie of the Xia Dynasty.
King Wu founded Zhou Dynasty only by eliminating the last tyrant King Zhou of the Shang Dynasty.
Hence, the world is often taken with no selfish agenda but for the liberation of the country and its people. L6
When there is an agenda of self-interest only, then the world cannot be taken. L7,8

Comments
Daoism is unselfishness (ch.48)

Knowledge increases desires; hence Laozi urges practice of Daoism to reduce desires daily
When unselfishness is achieved, then can take on any task.
With unselfish agenda, even the world can be taken; this is impossible with a personal agenda!

Pacific Daoism in a nutshell: not just for self gain, but for the common benefit of all, one can take any action.

Dao De Jing

四十九章   Chapter 49

01 圣人无恒心	The Sage has no absolute heart (wishes)
02 以百姓心为心	But takes the people's heart (wishes) for self
03 善者, 吾善之	With a good person, I am good
04 不善者, 吾亦善之, 德善	With a no-good person, I am also good, virtuous goodness
05 信者, 吾信之	With a trust-worthy person, I will trust
06 不信者, 吾亦信之, 德信	With a trust-unworthy person, I will also trust, virtuous trust
07 圣人在天下, 歙歙焉	The Sage in the world, profile low indeed
08 为天下, 浑其心	For the world, blend-in own heart (wishes)
09 百姓, 皆注其耳目	The people, all focus their ears and eyes
10 圣人, 皆孩之	The Sage, treats all like own children

Laozi's thinking
The Sage has no personal wishes. L1
But embraces the people's wishes for self. L2

With a good person I shall be good. L3
With a no-good person I shall also be good, virtuous goodness. L4
With a trustworthy person I shall trust. L5
With a trust-unworthy person I shall also trust, virtuous trust. L6

The Sage in the world takes a low-profile. L7
And for the world's sake blends in all wishes and be one with the world. L8
Hence, the people all focus their eyes and ears on the Sage with trust and submission. L9
And the Sage treats them well, like own children. L10

Comments
Salvation, universal (ch.49)

The wishes of the people is also the wishes of the Sage.
The Sage is kind to the unkind, trusting the trust-unworthy (with due precaution taken!).
That is, the Sage tries to help everyone and rejects nobody.
This idea of rejecting nobody is revisited in chapter 63, "Repay grievance with kindness".

Pacific Daoism is universal salvation.

Dao De Jing

五十章　　　　　　　　　　Chapter 50

01 出生, 入死	Emerge in birth, bury in death
02 生之徒, 十有三	Those who live long, 3 out of 10
03 死之徒, 十有三	Those who die early, 3 out of 10
04 人之生, 动之死地, 亦十有三	Those who live long, but move to ground of death, also 3 of 10
05 夫何故? 以其生生之厚	Why is this so ? Because of living thick (in excesses)
06 盖闻: 善摄生者	Ever heard of: individuals good at preserving life
07 陵行, 不遇兕虎	Walking in the hills, not meet with rhino and tiger
08 入军, 不被甲兵	In the army, not get hurt by weapon
09 兕, 无所投其角	Rhino, finds nowhere to trust its horn
10 虎, 无所措其爪	Tiger, finds nowhere to place its claws
11 兵, 无所容其刃	Soldier, finds nowhere to put-in the blade
12 夫何故?	Why is this so ?
13 以其无死地	Because they avoid ground of death

Laozi's thinking
In birth we emerge into this world. L1
In death we are buried into the earth. L1
Those who live long, there are 3 out of 10. L2
Those who die young, there are 3 out of 10. L3
Those who can live long but have move into harms way; L4
And die young, there are also 3 out of 10. L4
Why is this so? L5
Because they have indulge in the excesses of life. L5
Such as over eating, excessive drinking, womanizing, lack of exercise, etc.

We have heard of individuals who are good at survival. L6
They walk in the hills and do not meet with rhino, or tiger. L7
They enlist in the army and do not get hurt by weapon. L8
For rhino finds no place to thrust its horn. L9
The tiger finds no place to apply its claws. L10
The soldier finds no place to run-in the blade. L11
Why is this so? L12
Because such individuals know, how not to get into harm's way. L13
For example, walking in the hills, they travel in large group, and in broad daylight.

Comments
Life and Death, do not go into harm's way (ch.50)

A third have long life, a third have short life, and a third prematurely kill by unhealthy life-style.
Laozi's use of colorful images in the 2rd stanza has led to mystified interpretation of this chapter.
But in reality, survivors merely take precautions, take no risks, and avoid entering grounds of death.

Today in the 21st century, thousands die on the road each year.
If only pedestrians can take extra precautions and avoid getting into harm's way.
Laozi's warning of life-style is still relevant today; premature death from obesity, alcoholism, and smoking.

Laozi has insights, analyzing the reasons and chances of survival, and premature death.

Dao De Jing

五十一章   Chapter 51

01 道生之, 德畜之	Dao creates them, Virtue nurtures them
02 物形之, 势成之	Matter forms them, Momentum completes them
03 是以:	Therefore:
04 万物, 莫不尊道而贵德	All things, none do not respect Dao and value Virtue
05 道之尊, 德之贵	The respecting of Dao, the valuing of Virtue
06 夫, 莫之命, 而恒自然	Indeed, are never decreed, but are always naturally so
7 故:	Hence:
8 道生之, 德畜之	Dao creates them, Virtue nurtures them
9 长之, 育之	Grows them, develops them
10 亭之, 毒之	Protects them, cares for them
11 养之, 覆之	Feeds them, shelters them
12 生, 而不有	Creates, but does not possess
13 为, 而不恃	Achieves, but not presumptuous
14 长, 而不宰	Has seniority, but does not control
15 是谓玄德	This is termed primal Virtue

Laozi's thinking
Dao creates all things, Virtue nurtures all things. L1
Matter forms all things, Momentum completes all things. L2

Therefore, all things respected Dao and valued Virtue. L3,4
The respecting of Dao and the valuing of Virtue, L5
Are not decreed by Dao but are natural expressions of gratitude from all things. L6

Hence, Dao creates them and Virtue nurtures them. L7,8
Grows, develops, protects, cares, feeds and shelters them. L9-11
Creates, and has no ownership of them. L12
Achieves, but does not become presumptuous. L13
Leads, but does not control them, or lord over them. L14
This is termed primal Virtue. L15

Comments
Primal Virtues, total Freedom (ch.51)

Laozi has conceived of Dao, the ultimate entity, to explain the existence of the universe.
He conceives that Dao creates and cares for all things, not for self-glorification.
To his credit, Laozi is not awed by Dao's power of creation.
He has not degraded himself to superstitious beliefs and worship based on the 'supernatural power' of Dao.
Laozi states that Dao has not decreed that respect is due from all its creations.
Rather, the primal virtue of Dao claims no ownership and exert no control over all its creations.

Daoism is freedom for all things; hence, is a pacific philosophy, not a religion.

Dao De Jing

五十二章   Chapter 52

01 天下有始, 以为天下母   The world began with You (Have), which is mother of the world
02 既得其母, 以知其子   Since we have the mother, so we know the son
03 既知其子, 复守其母   Since knowing the son, back to upholding the mother
04 沒身不殆   Till end-of-life no danger

05 塞其兑, 闭其门   Block the portals, close the doors (to desires)
06 终身, 不勤   Life-long, no labor (no hardship)
07 开其兑, 济其事   Open the portals, promote the affairs (of desires)
08 终身, 不救   Life-long, not be saved

09 见小曰明, 守柔曰强   See Small (Dao) is enlightened, uphold gentleness is strong
10 用其光, 复归其明   Use the light (of Dao), again return to its enlightenment
11 无遗身殃, 是谓习常   No legacy of personal disaster, this is practicing Dao (principles)

Laozi's thinking
The world has a beginning in You (Have), and all things created are traced back to this Mother. L1
Thus having Dao (the Mother), we know all the things created (the sons). L2
And knowing all the things created (the sons), we go back to upheld Dao (the Mother). L3
Then till death will not have danger. L4

Shut-out desires, life-long trouble-free. L5,6
Open-up to indulgences, life-long no salvation. L7,8

Seeing the Small (Dao) is enlightenment. L9
Upholding gentleness is strength. L9
Using the light of Dao to return to enlightenment. L10
Then there will be no personal legacy of disaster. L11
This is practicing the principles of Dao. L11

Comments
Salvation, self-discipline (ch.52)

Laozi suggests that we know Dao through all the things created, hence we should embrace Dao.
Be self-disciplined, shut-out all desires and be trouble-free life-long.
Else open the door to desires and have no salvation life-long.
Be enlightened through the lights of Dao, upheld gentleness and has no legacy of problems in life.

Pacific Daoism is self-discipline, shut out desires and has a trouble-free life.

Dao De Jing

五十三章	Chapter 53
01 使我介然有知：	By my natural limits of knowledge:
02 行于大道	Traveling on great highway (Dao)
03 唯施是畏	Only banner-signs are feared
04 大道甚夷	The highway of Dao is very flat
05 而民好徑	But people love walk-paths (by-paths)
06 朝甚除	Palace steps very high (grand building)
07 田甚芜	Crop fields very overgrown (with grass)
08 仓甚虚	The granary nearly empty
09 服文采	Cloth in finery (Lords and Kings)
10 带利剑	Carry sharp swords
11 厌饮食	Over-indulge in food and wine
12 财货有余	Wealth and goods possession in excess
13 是谓盗夸	They are chiefs of robbers
14 非道也哉！	Not in accord with Dao indeed

Laozi's thinking
With my little knowledge, I do know this: on the highway of practicing the principles of Dao. L1,2
I should fear being lead astray by signs of temptation for power and wealth. L3
The highway of Dao is very flat and easy to follow. L4
However, people loves short-cuts and are easily led astray. L5

Look at the Lords and Kings in great power and who have great wealth.
They build grand palaces, while the crop-fields are over-grown with grass. L6,7
The granary stores are near empty while they cloth in finery. L8,9
They carry fine swords and over-indulge in fine food and fine wine. L10,11
They possess wealth and goods in excess; they are in reality heads of robbers. L12,13
They have strayed from the principles of Dao indeed! L14

Comments
Beware of Temptation (ch.53)

Laozi observes that the path of life according to Dao is flat and easy to follow.
Yet people love to take by-paths to wealth and power and are lead astray.
Especially Lords and Kings who can be found to live in grand palaces.
Clothe in fineries, indulge in food and wine, and possess wealth in excess.
While the crop fields are left in neglect and granaries left empty.
In reality, Lords and Kings are chiefs of robbers.
Their conduct and behavior are not in accordance with Dao
Here Laozi once again speaks up for the common people.

Chastising the Lords and Kings, Laozi's warning of temptation also speaks to all individuals. .

Dao De Jing

五十四章 Chapter 54

01 善建者, 不拔	Person good at building (virtue), will not uproot
02 善抱者, 不脫	Person good at embracing (virtue), will not let-go
03 子孫以祭祀不輟	Progeny will observe rites without fail
04 修之于身, 其德乃真	Cultivate it in self, the virtue is real
05 修之于家, 其德乃余	Cultivate it in family, the virtue is more
06 修之于乡, 其德乃长	Cultivate it in village, the virtue is multiplied
07 修之于邦, 其德乃丰	Cultivate it in nation, the virtue is abundant
08 修之于天下, 其德乃普	Cultivate it in world, the virtue is universal
09 故:	Hence:
10 以身, 观身	From self, observe other selves
11 以家, 观家	From family, observe other families
12 以乡, 观乡	From village, observe other villages
13 以邦, 观邦	From nation, observe other nations
14 以天下, 观天下	From the world, observe other worlds
15 吾何以知天下然哉？	How do I know the world's nature indeed ?
16 以此	With this (method)

Laozi's thinking
Person good at building virtue will not dismantle it. L1
Person good at embracing virtue will not lose it. L2
And progeny will observe these traditions without fail. L3

Virtue cultivated in self is real, in family is more, in village is multiple. L4-6
Virtue cultivated in the nation is abundant, in the world is universal. L7,8

Hence: L9
From the self observes other selves, from the family observes other families. L10,11
From village observes other villages, from nation observes other nations. L12,13
From the world observes other worlds. L14
This way, I learn of the world. L15,16

Comments
Cultivating virtues start with self (ch.54)

Cultivating virtues starts with self, is then extended to family, village, state and finally world-wide. It is fair to say that when one do not cultivate virtues in oneself, one do not know the virtues in others. Then there is no point talking about cultivating virtues in family and levels beyond.

It makes sense to start with self in cultivating virtues and knowing the world.

Dao De Jing

五十五章　　　　　　　　　　Chapter 55

01 含德之厚, 比于赤子	Contained virtues that are thick, comparable to the naked baby
02 毒虫不螫, 猛兽不据	Poisonous insects don't sting, fierce beasts don't paw
03 攫鳥不搏	Teloned birds don't claw
04 骨弱, 筋柔, 而握固	Bones weak, sinews tender, yet grip is strong
05 未知牝牡之合, 而朘作	Not knowing female male in union, yet phallus erect
06 精之至也	Life-essence is present indeed
07 终日號, 而不嗄	Whole day howling, yet not hoarse,
08 和之至也	Harmony is present indeed
09 知和曰常; 知常曰明	Knows harmony is Constant; knows Constant is enlightened
10 益生曰祥; 心使气曰強	Beneficial living is good-fortune; heart controlling breath is strong
11 物壮则老	Matters prime will age
12 谓之不道, 不道早已	Says this is not Dao, not Dao soon ends

Laozi's thinking
Imbibing in virtue thick, none can compare with the naked baby. L1
In its glorious innocence, it is one with the universe.
Wearing not a shred of hostility or tension, absolutely not a threat to anyone
Chance upon it, poisonous insects will not sting, fierce beasts and teloned birds will not attack. L2,3

Bones may be weak and sinews tender but its grip is strong. L4
Not knowing the significance of sexual union, it phallus erect, for life-essence is present. L5,6
Howling the whole day for food and not be hoarse; harmony is present not anger and frustration. L7,8

Knowing harmony is knowing Constant (Dao), knowing Constant (Dao) is enlightened. L9
Beneficial living is good-fortune; L10
Benevolent heart feeling in control over breathing of hot-air of aggression is strength. L10

When matters prime, the aging starts. L11
Hence, pushing the limit is not in accordance with Dao and will lead to an early demise. L12

Comments:
Harmony is Dao (ch. 55)

Here, the benefits of harmony is highlighted and exemplified with the image of the innocent naked baby.
It is plausible that a poisonous snake glide harmlessly pass a baby who, in its innocence, shows no tension.
Whereas passing by a fearful, knowing adult, the snake senses danger and attacks.
These images of immunity to attack have led to interpretation of the mystical power of Dao by some scholars.

"Matters primed will age" seems another odd proposition from Laozi.
But it is like reaching the summit; the next step is downhill.
It is like the day of birth is also the first day in a journey towards death.
Hence, there is no rush to push for early peaking.
Because that means early decline and this is natural.

Here Laozi is really promoting the benefits of Daoist harmony, not Daoist mysticism

Dao De Jing

五十六章   Chapter 56

01 知者不言; 言者不知	Whoever knows does not speak, whoever speaks does not know
02 塞其兑, 闭其门	Blocks its opening (to desires), close the door (to desires)
03 挫其锐, 解其纷	Blunts its edges (not hurting), resolves its disputes (peace-loving)
04 和其光, 同其尘	Harmonizes its light (low-profile), unites with its dust (blend-in)
05 是谓玄同	This is primal union
06 故:	Hence (person with Dao):
07 不可得而亲, 亦不可得而疏	Cannot be had and be intimated, cannot be had and be distanced
08 不可得而利, 亦不可得而害	Cannot be had and be benefited, cannot be had and be harmed
09 不可得而贵, 亦不可得而贱	Cannot be had and be honored, cannot be had and be debased
10 故:	Hence:
11 为天下贵	Valued by the world (person with Dao)

Laozi's thinking
A person who knows Daoism, does not declare possession of Dao and does not speak of possessing Dao; L1
A person who does not really know Daoism, declares possession of Dao and speak of having Dao. L1
The Daoist, a person with Dao:
Will block all openings, and close all doors to desires. L2
Will blunt all edges in the personality and be non-confrontational. L3
Will resolve all disputes and be peace-loving. L3
Will not dazzle but harmonize with the light, keeping profile low in appearance. L4
Will blend in with the dust of the ambience and be inconspicuous. L4
Altogether in primal union and be one with the Dao. L5

Hence (person with Dao): L6
May not be associated intimately or distanced; may not be benefited or harmed. L7,8
May not be honored or debased. L9

Hence: L10
The Daoist is valued by the world. L11

Comments
Daoist cannot be influenced (ch.56)

The Daoist has no desire and is not confrontational.
The Daoist keeps a low-profile, harmonizes with the light and unites with the dust, just like Dao.
The Daoist cannot be intimated, distanced, corrupted, honored or debased
That is, the Daoist cannot be influenced either way, for good or for evil.

When every individual in the world knows and embraces Dao.
With behaviors and conducts as described above, not contesting and incorruptible.
All individuals will not harm one another but rather help each other in need.
Then everybody is safe, self-sufficient and prosperous.
Only when each and every one of us is a willing participant, living the principles of Dao.
Then there will be no suffering in the world, but paradise on earth.
For this is primal union of all humankind.

The Daoist has no desires, at peace with society, is incorruptible, and is valued by the world.

五十七章　　　　　　　　　　Chapter 57

01 以正, 治国	With honesty, governs nation
02 以奇, 用兵	With surprises, deploys army
03 以无事, 取天下	With no agenda, takes the world
04 吾何以知其然哉？	How do I know this is true?
05 以此：	By this:
06 天下多忌讳, 而民弥贫	The world with more prohibitions, citizens are poorer
07 人多利器, 国家滋昏	People with more sharp weapons, the nation is more confused
08 人多伎巧, 奇物滋起	People with more skills and ingenuity, exotic things often arise
09 法物滋彰, 盗贼多有	Laws and materials proliferate, robbers/thieves numbers increase
10 故圣人云：	Hence the Sage said:
11 我无为, 而民自化	I have no motive, and citizens will self-develop
12 我好静, 而民自正	I love quietude, and citizens will self-regulate
13 我无事, 而民自富	I have no agenda, and citizens will self-prosper
14 我无欲, 而民自朴	I have no desires, and citizens will self-humble

Laozi's thinking
With honesty govern a nation, for many failed states are due to corrupt government. L1
With surprises deploy an army, for such tactics are always useful to overcome the enemy. L2
With no personal agenda take the world. L3
For by good leadership, other states will join in alliance without a fight.

How do I know these are true? L4
Through the following observations. L5
If the world has more prohibitions, citizens are poorer. L6
If the people have more weapons, the nation is more confused and chaotic. L7
If the people have more skill and ingenuity, exotic things proliferate. L8
When the land is flooded with laws and materials, there are more robbers and thieves. L9

Hence, the Sage King with Dao will govern and says: L10
I have no motive for self-glorification with projects, so the citizens have time and resources to develop. L11
I love quietude and do not lightly issue laws and rules, so citizens develop self-discipline. L12
I have no agenda for conquests, so the citizens have time to express themselves and prosper. L13
I have no desire for lavish living, so citizens can emulate, be humble, and not be wasteful. L14

Comments
Daoist government (ch. 57)

Preceding chapter shows an individual embracing the attributes of Dao, and be a person the world valued. This chapter shows a government embracing Daoism so that citizens are free to pursue their own prosperity. Good leaders have no personal desires, no agenda, no extra rules and laws to burden the citizens.

Daoist in government is not self-serving; rather, citizens are free to pursue their own dreams.

Dao De Jing

五十八章　　　　　　　Chapter 58

01 其政闷闷, 其民淳淳	The government is boring and dull, the people are simple and humble
02 其政察察, 其民缺缺	The government is alert and discerning, the people are broken and lacking
03 祸兮, 福之所倚	Misfortune indeed, where good fortune depends
04 福兮, 祸之所伏	Good-fortune indeed, where misfortune lurks
05 孰知其极?	Who knows the limit?
06 其无正	There is no normal
07 正复为奇, 善复为妖	Normal back to be abnormal, good back to be evil
08 人之迷, 其日固久!	People's confusion, such days have been many!
09 是以:	Therefore:
10 圣人方, 而不割	The Sage gathers together, but not cut-away (abandon)
11 廉, 而不刿	Incorruptible, but not injuring
12 直, 而不肆	Straight and direct, but not unruly
13 光, 而不耀	Bright, but not dazzle

Laozi's thinking
When the government seems dull, not initiating wars or grand projects. L1
People are not disturbed in their livelihoods, and are therefore humble and peaceful. L1
When the government seems alert and discerning, initiating conquests and building palaces. L2
People are disturbed in their livelihoods, are broken and are lacking. L2

Misfortune breeds good-fortune, and in good-fortune lurks misfortune. L3,4
Who knows the limits? There is no answer. L5,6
Normal can become abnormal, and good can become evil. L7
People have long been confused by the cycles of good-fortune and misfortune. L8

Hence: to help the people, the Sage keeps all together and never abandon anyone. L9
Incorruptibly sharp but never injure anyone. L11
Is straight and honest, but never behave in an unruly manner to anybody. L12
Is bright and smart but dazzles no one. L13

Comment
Cycles of good-fortune and misfortune, (ch.58)

Stanza 1 seems more appropriate to be included in preceding chapter, Dao in government.
Stanza 2 correctly observes that cycle of changes in the world are uncertainties and long puzzle the people.
Stanza 3 suggests that Sage ruler can help by being honest and low-profile, and staying compassionate.

Face with the confusion of cycles of changes, Laozi gives logical and pragmatic suggestions.
Laozi has not added to the confusion by invoking help from some mystical power of Dao.

Face with uncertainties of life, Laozi advises honesty, a low-profile, and compassion.

Dao De Jing

五十九章

Chapter 59

01 治人, 事天　　　　　Manage people, serve Heaven
02 莫若啬　　　　　　None like Thrift

03 夫唯啬　　　　　　Indeed only with Thrift
04 是以早服　　　　　Hence early application
05 早服, 谓之重积德　　Early application, is called serious accumulating virtues
06 重积德, 则无不克　　Serious accumulating virtues, then nothing cannot be overcome
07 无不克, 则莫知其极　Nothing cannot be overcome, then none knows the limit
08 莫知其极　　　　　None knows the limit
09 可以有国　　　　　Can then have nation
10 有国之母　　　　　Having nation's mother (principle of government, Thrift)
11 可以长久　　　　　Can be long and lasting
12 是谓, 深根, 固柢　　This is called, deep roots, firm roots
13 长生, 久视, 之道　　Long existence, lasting vision, this way

Laozi's thinking
In the management of people and serving Heaven, L1
None better than with Thrift. L2

And with Thrift, there is early application. L3,4
With early application, there is great accumulation of great Virtue (and wealth). L5
The nation becomes strong and there is nothing that cannot be overcome. L6
And none will know the limit in the development of this nation. L7
Hence, in this way, the Sage can build and have a strong nation. L8,9
With this great principle of Thrift, the nation can last long. L10,11
For the roots of nation-building are deep and firm. L12
This is the way to build a nation that will have a long existence and a lasting vision. L13

Comment
Thrift for nation building (ch.59)

Here Laozi expounds the first principle for nation building, Thrift.
Indeed the practice of Thrift can be the strong foundation for building a nation.
No wastage on wars, extravagant palaces, and exotic gardens for the privileged few.
The people can enjoy a peaceful livelihood with low taxes.
There is no need to fight wars or build grand projects.
There is time to develop and to increase production.
And to innovate for better living experiences on earth.

Teaching Thrift to rulers, Laozi is pragmatic, and far from being a mystical or a spiritual thinker.

Dao De Jing

六十章   Chapter 60

01 治大国, 若烹小鲜	Governing big nation, like cooking small fish
02 以道莅天下	With Dao prevailing in the world
03 其鬼不神	The ghosts not powered
04 非其鬼不神	Not that ghosts not powered
05 其神不伤人	Their powers not hurting people
06 非其神不伤人	Not that their powers not hurting people
07 圣人亦不伤人	The Sage also not hurting people
08 夫, 两不相伤	Indeed, both not hurting (the people)
09 故, 德交归焉	Hence, virtues interact and return indeed (to the people)

Laozi's thinking
Governing a big nation is like cooking a small fish. L1
It is this easy, provided that the principles of Dao are established. L2

When Dao prevails in the world, everyone is taken care of and gets a fair share in all things.
The people are not burdened with high taxes, conscription for conquests, or conscription for building palaces.
There is prosperity and happiness over the land and everybody is contented.
Hence, evil elements, and their powers will not be effective in hurting the people. L3-5
Besides them, the Sage also will not hurt the people. L6,7
Indeed, both do not hurt the people. L8
Hence, their virtues interact and return to benefit the people. L9

Comment
Daoism makes governing easy as cooking a small fish (ch. 60)

Daoism is government for the benefits of people, not for the benefits of leaders and their cronies.
With Daoism prevailing, there will be harmony, peace, and prosperity in the world.
In such a happy environment, the ghosts and the Sage are powerless in hurting the people.
Indeed, governing a big nation can be as easy as cooking a small fish when Daoism prevails over the land.

Laozi urges use of Daoism for effective and easy government in the world.

Dao De Jing

六十一章 Chapter 61

01 大国者, 下流	Whatever big nation, be low flowing (humble)
02 天下之牝	Be the world's female
03 天下之交	Be the place where the world meet
04 牝恒以靜胜牡	The female always by quietude triumphs over the male
05 以靜为下	By quietude be low (humble)
06 故:	Hence:
07 大国, 以下小国	Big nation, be humble to small nation
08 则取小国	Then gains (allegiance of) small nation
09 小国, 以下大国	Small nation, be humble to big nation
10 则取大国	Then gains (alliance from) big nation
11 故:	Hence:
12 或下以取	Or be humble to gain allegiance
13 或下而取	Or be humble to gain alliance
14 大国, 不过欲兼畜人	Big nation, only wish to extend leadership-care over people
15 小国, 不过欲入事人	Small nation, only wish to enter to serve people
16 夫, 兩者, 各得所欲	Indeed, both nations, separately get what each wishes
17 大者, 宜为下	Big nation, appropriate to initiate humility

Laozi's thinking
For big nation, be humble; be like the mother of the world. L1,2
Be where the nations of the world meet and be the kind and loving leader. L3
Be like the female which often triumphs over the male with quietude and humility. L4,5

Hence: L6
By being humble, big nations gain the allegiance of small nations. L7,8
And by being humble, small nations gain alliances with big nations. L9,10

Hence: L11
Gain allegiance by humility, and gain alliance by humility. L12,13
Big nations only wishes to extend their leadership, and small nations only wishes to be of service. L14,15
This is a win-win situation and it is proper that the big nations take the initiative for such an alliance. L16,17

Comment
Humility for diplomacy (ch. 61)

Here Laozi simply urges nations to behave with humility to avoid conflicts with each other.
Big and small nation can achieve peaceful co-existence which benefits both parties.
Being dominant, it is appropriate for the big nation to be humble, and to take the initiative.

Daoism urges humility in diplomacy for harmony among nations and peace on Earth.

六十二章 / Chapter 62

01 道者, 万物之奥	Dao, the refuge of all things
02 善人之宝	Treasure of good people
03 不善人之所保	Protector of no-good people
04 美言可以市	Nice words can win respect in the market place
05 尊行可以加人	Honorable conduct can be bestowed on people
06 人之不善	People being no-good
07 何弃之有？	How can they be abandoned ?
08 故:	Hence:
09 立天子	Crowning the emperor
10 置三公	Appointing the 3 senior ministers
11 虽有拱璧以先驷马	Though have Jade Seal preceding the 4-horse chariot
12 不如坐进此道	Not comparable to sitting-in (installing) this Dao
13 古之所以贵此道者何？	What is the ancient's reason for valuing this Dao ?
14 不曰: 求以得	(Is it) not saying: appeal and be given
15 有罪以免邪？	Have guilt will be forgiven ?
16 故为天下贵	Hence (Dao) is treasured by the world

Laozi's thinking
Dao is the ultimate origin of all things.
Hence in Dao, all things can take refuge and be saved. L1
Dao is the treasure of the good people. L2
Dao is the protector of the no-good people. L3
Nice words can win respect in the market place. L4
Honorable conduct can be bestowed on other people. L5
Hence with no-good people, L6
How can they be abandoned and not be helped ? L7

Hence: crowning the emperor and appointing the 3 senior ministers. L8-10
With the ceremonial Jade Seal preceding the 4-horse chariot procession. L11
These pomps are not comparable to establishing Dao in government. L12

What was the reason, and why did the ancients value this Dao ? L13
Well, it has been said, "Appeal and be given, have guilt will be forgiven." L14,15
That is, Dao abandons nobody.
Hence, Dao is treasured by the world. L16

Comment
Daoism is refuge for all things (ch.62)

Laozi conceives Dao as the ultimate origin of all things.
Hence, he conceives that Dao has absolute compassion and is also the ultimate refuge for all things.
He urges leaders to govern with the principles of Dao, giving people chance to repent and be forgiven.

Daoism for government, abandons nobody.

六十三章　　　　　　　　　　Chapter 63

01 为无为　　　　　　　　　　Act not for self-purpose
02 事无事　　　　　　　　　　Serve not for self-affair
03 味无味　　　　　　　　　　Taste not for self-indulgence
04 大小, 多少　　　　　　　　Big or small, more or less (injustice)
05 报怨以德　　　　　　　　　Repay injustice with virtue (reconciliation)

06 图难于其易; 为大于其细　　Plan for difficulty when it is easy; do the big when it is small
07 天下难事, 必作于易　　　　The world's difficult affairs, should be done when it is easy
08 天下大事, 必作于细　　　　The big affairs in the world, should be done by starting small
09 是以:　　　　　　　　　　Therefore:
10 圣人终不为大, 故能成其大　The Sage till the end does not do it big, hence can achieve it big

11 夫, 轻诺, 必寡信　　　　　Indeed, lightly promise, certainly lack trust
12 多易, 必多难　　　　　　　More easiness (early), certainly more difficulties (later)
13 是以:　　　　　　　　　　Therefore:
14 圣人犹难之　　　　　　　　The Sage treat (all tasks) as difficult
15 故终无难已　　　　　　　　Hence ultimately no difficulties indeed

Laozi's thinking
Take action not for self-gain but for the common benefit of all. L1
Manage affair not for self-gain but for the common benefit of all. L2
And taste not for self-indulgence. L3
Big or small injustice, more or less injustice, L4
Respond to all grievances with kindness to break the vicious cycles of revenge and retaliation. L5

Tackle difficulty where it is easy; do the big project when it is small. L6
The world's difficult tasks, should be tackle early, when it is easy. L7
The world's big projects, should be tackled from small, and to build up gradually. L8
Therefore: the Sage never attempts big, hence, can achieve it big, by accumulated small efforts. L9,10

Indeed, promises that are lightly made often fail, resulting in lack of trust. L11
Taking it easy in the early stage, often results in more difficulties later. L12
Therefore: L13
The Sage prepares for difficulties from the beginning. L14
Hence, will ultimately experiences no difficulties indeed. L15

Comment
Repay injustice with kindness; Be prepared for difficulties (ch.63)

Here, two pieces of great advice from Laozi.
Firstly, be selfless like Dao, respond to grievance with reconciliation to break the vicious cycles of hatred.
Secondly, if you are prepared for difficulties, then it is easy to nip them in the bud.

The depth of wisdom is shown when Laozi advises reconciliation to grievances suffered.
The extent of pragmatism is shown when Laozi advises, "be prepared for difficulties".

Laozi: Quest for the Ultimate Reality

千里之行　　Journey of thousand miles,
始于足下　　Starts beneath the feet

(*Dao De Jing,* chapter 64)

Dao De Jing

六十四章 — Chapter 64

01	其安易持; 其未兆易谋	Things stable is easy to maintain; no sign (of problem) is easy to prevent
02	其脆易破; 其微易散	Brittle is easy to break; micro is easy to scatter
03	为之于未有; 治之于未乱	Action before it (problem) exists; manage it before turmoil (manifest)
04	合抱之木, 生于毫末	Trees of large girth, grow from micro seed
05	九层之台, 起于累土	Tower of 9-stories, rise from accumulated earth
06	千里之行, 始于足下	Journey of thousand miles, starts beneath the feet
07	为者败之	Whoever attempts will fail it
08	执者失之	Whoever holds on will lose it
09	是以:	Therefore:
10	圣人无为, 故, 无败	The Sage has no self-agenda, hence, no failure
11	无执, 故, 无失	No holds-on, hence, no loss
12	民之从事	The people working on a project
13	恒于几成, 而败之	Often near finishing, then fail it
14	慎终如始	Careful at finish as at beginning
15	则无败事	Then no fail project
16	是以:	Therefore:
17	圣人欲不欲, 不贵难得之货	The Sage desires to not-desire, not valuing hard to get goods
18	学不学, 复众人之所过.	Learn to not learn, not repeating mistakes of the people
19	以辅万物之自然, 而不敢为	To help all things in their nature, so dare not act

Laozi's thinking

Things that are stable are easy to maintain; before signs of trouble, it is easy to plan prevention. L1
What is brittle is easy to break and what is micro is easy to scatter. L2
It is easy to take preventives and act before a problem exists; and easy to manage before turmoil starts. L3

Large trees grow from tiny seeds and tall towers rise from building up bricks of earth. L4,5
Journey of a thousand miles starts beneath the feet with the first step. L6
Hence, great things can be achieved progressively, starting small, from the bottom-up and stepwise.

Great success is the cumulative effort of many; hence, individual claiming credit will fail, and lose it. L7,8
Therefore, working for the common good, the Sage has no personal agenda; hence, no personal failure. L9-11

People working on projects often fail before finishing as they are careless towards the end. L12,13
Hence, be careful at the beginning till the end, then there will be no failed projects. L14,15
The Sage desires not to have desires like the people, hence, does not value rare goods. L17
The Sage learns not to learn the short-cuts of the people, so as not to repeat their mistakes. L18
Also, to help all things in their natural development, the Sage dares not act upon them in any way. L19

Comments
Journey of a thousand miles starts beneath the feet (ch.64)
Stanza 1. Cautions against difficulties, hence seems more appropriate to belong to preceding chapter 63.
Stanza 2. Gives 3 examples of great successes: humbly starting small, from bottom up and done stepwise.
Stanza 3. Warns that individual desiring credit will fail, hence the Sage has no desires, no failure. (see ch.29)
Stanza 4. Warns of failure as people are careless, not being vigilant from beginning till end of projects.
Stanza 5. The Sage desires not, hence, allows all things to develop naturally without imposing upon them.

Great successes are built in small steps; and one must be vigilant from start to finish.

Dao De Jing

六十五章   Chapter 65

01 古之善为道者	Ancient person good at practicing Dao
02 非以明民	Not by enlightening the people
03 将以愚之	But by keeping them ignorant
04 民之难治	People are difficult to manage
05 以其智多	Because they have much cleverness
06 故以智治国, 国之贼	Hence using cleverness to govern a nation, is nation's thief
07 不以智治国, 国之福	Not using cleverness to govern a nation, is nation's fortune
08 知此两者亦稽式	Know these two principles are also contrasting models
09 恒知稽式	Always know the contrasting models
10 是谓玄德	Is said to be primal Virtue
11 玄德深已, 远已	Primal Virtue deep indeed, far-reaching indeed
12 与物, 反已	With things, the reverse (of norm) indeed
13 然后乃至大顺	There after then till great order (establishes)

Laozi's thinking
The ancient Sage good at practicing Dao, L1
Does not enlighten the people, but will provide for them. L2,3
Because people are difficult to govern when they have too much cleverness. L4,5

Hence, using cleverness to govern a nation, is a nation's thief. L6
Not using cleverness to govern a nation, is a nation's good fortune. L7

These two principles are contrasting models of government. L8
Often, knowing these contrasting models of government means having primal Virtue. L9,10

Such primal Virtue is deep indeed, far-reaching indeed, the reverse of norms. L11,12
In the end, this will lead to the great experience of human life when everything works like a breeze. L13

Comments
Govern not with cleverness (ch.65)

Stanza 1. The ancient Daoist does not enlighten the people, else they are difficult to govern.
Stanza 2. Hence, one who govern with cleverness is a thief, else one is a national blessing.
Stanza 3. Knows the contrasting government models is a primal Virtue.
Stanza 4. Govern not with cleverness is the reverse of norms but can building a paradise on earth.

Here against the norms, Laozi advises not enlightening the people for easy government.
May be 2,500 years ago, universal education for all citizens is hard to imagine.
This is one of the few fallacies in the text where I cannot agree with Laozi.
The unenlightened may be simple and honest, easy to govern and not likely to rebel.
However, they are also at the same time susceptible to manipulation by the unscrupulous.
In fact, ideally, every individual should be as educated and empowered as Laozi himself.
Then the chance of creating a paradise on earth will be much higher.

"To govern, but not to educate the citizens" is a step backward, not acceptable in pacific Daoism.

Dao De Jing

六十六章   Chapter 66

01 江海, 所以能为百谷王者	Rivers and seas, reason for being kings of the hundred valleys
02 以其善下之	For they are good at being subservient
03 故能为百谷王	Hence can be kings of the hundred valleys
04 是以:	Therefore:
05 圣人, 欲上民	The Sage, wishing to be above citizens (as leader)
06 必以言下之	Must with language be subservient to them
07 欲先民	Wishing to be ahead of the citizens
08 必以身后之	Must with body be behind them
09 是以:	Therefore:
10 圣人居上, 而民不重	The Sage sitting on high, and citizens not burdened
11 居前, 而民不害	Leading up-front, and citizens not harmed
12 是以:	Therefore:
13 天下乐推, 而不厌	The world is happy to recommend, and not be tired
14 以其不争	For the Sage does not contest
15 故, 天下, 莫能与之争	Hence, in the world, none can contest with the Sage

Laozi's thinking

Rivers and seas are kings of the hundred valleys. L1
Reason is they are good at being subservient as they occupy the lower positions. L2
Serving the valleys with irrigation for agriculture and drainage of floods. L3

Therefore: the Sage wishing to be above the citizens as leader, must speak humbly in service. L4-6
Wishing to be ahead of the citizens as leader, must be behind in priority for benefits. L7,8

Therefore: the Sage sitting on-top as leader, citizens feel no burden. L9,10
Leading up-front, citizens feel no danger. L11

The world is happy to recommend and not be tired of the Sage. L13,14
Hence, not-contesting, yet none in the world can contest with the Sage. L15

Comments
To rule is to serve (ch.66)

Stanza 1. Laozi takes cue from the low-lying rivers and seas as kings of the hundred valleys.
Stanza 2. And expounded that likewise, the Sage be humble in speech and behind in priority for benefits.
Stanza 3. Humility of the Sage is genuine not hypocritical, for the citizens are not burdened or harmed.
Stanza 4. The Sage does not contest, is liked by the citizens and recommended for continued leadership.

Scholars have accused Laozi of hypocrisy, practicing humble speech while eying for the role of leadership.
Clearly Laozi is speaking of genuine humility, no hypocrisy in the Sage, for good government.

Daoist rule is to serve, putting oneself last.

Dao De Jing

六十七章   Chapter 67

01 天下皆谓我道大, 似不肖	The world all say my Dao is Great, seems no resemblance (of Greatness)
02 夫唯大, 故似不肖	Indeed because it is Great, hence seems no resemblance (of Greatness)
03 若肖, 久已其细也夫!	If resembles, long then Dao is small indeed!
04 我有三宝, 持而保之	I have got 3 Treasures, hold and keep them
05 一曰慈, 二曰俭	First is Love, second is Thrift
06 三曰不敢为天下先	Third is Not-dare-be-world's-first
07 慈, 故能勇	Love, hence can be brave
08 俭, 故能广	Thrift, hence can be far-reaching
09 不敢为天下先	Not daring to be the world's first
10 故能成器长	Hence can become the world's leader
11 今舍慈, 且勇	Now abandon Love, yet is still brave
12 舍俭, 且广	Abandon thrift, yet is still far-reaching
13 舍后, 且先, 死已	Abandon following, yet be first, death then
14 夫慈, 以战则胜, 以守则固	With Love, for war will triumph, for defense will be solid
15 天将救之, 以慈卫之	When Heaven is saving it, with Love to protect it

Laozi's thinking
All the world say my Dao is Great, but it does not appear to be so. L1
Because Dao is truly Great, it does not show Greatness. L2
If it shows Greatness, then it will long be considered small and insignificant indeed. L3

I have 3 treasures to upheld and to keep: Love, Thrift and Not-dare-be-world's-first. L4-6
Govern with Love, the nation will have brave citizens. L7
Govern with Thrift, the nation will have a surplus to help all citizens in a time of crisis. L8
With Not-dare-be-world's-first, the nation starts no war and can be leader among nations. L9,10

Now if Love, Thrift and Not-dare-be-world's-first are abandoned. L11-13
And leaders act brave, over-reached and attack first in conquests, then death for the nation. L13
Hence, governing with love, the nation is brave, triumphant in war and solid in defense. L14
The Heaven in helping the nation, uses Love to protect the nation. L15

Comments
The three treasures: Love, Thrift and Not-dare-be-world's-first (ch.67)

Laozi says the world does not see Greatness in his Dao is precisely because Dao is truly great.
If Dao needs to show its Greatness, then Dao is truly small and insignificant. (Stanza 1)

Laozi has 3 treasures namely, Love, Thrift and Not-dare-be-world's-first. (Stanza 2)
Laozi urges that leader use them to build a nation which is brave, prosperous and a leader among nations.

Else abandoning them in building a nation means death of the nation. (Stanza 3)
Love, will triumph in war, solid in defense, that even the Heaven uses to save and protect.

These down-to-earth treasures reflect Laozi's pragmatism; he is not a mystic or spiritual philosopher.

Dao De Jing

六十八章　　　　　　Chapter 68

01 善为士者, 不武	Whoever good at being a scholar, not violent
02 善战者, 不怒	Whoever good at fighting-wars, never angry
03 善胜敌者, 不与	Whoever good at overcoming the enemy, never engage
04 善用人者, 为之下	Whoever good at employing people, be humble
05 是谓, 不争之德	This is termed, the Virtue of not contesting
06 是谓, 用人之力	This is termed, employing the people's strength
07 是谓, 配天	This is termed, matching Heaven's (Ways)
08 古之极	The ancients' ultimate (wisdom)

Laozi's thinking
Whoever is good at being a scholar is never militant, solving problems by peaceful means. L1
Whoever is good at fighting-wars is never angry as in anger mistakes are easily made. L2
Whoever is good at overcoming the enemy never engages directly, but uses strategy. L3
Whoever is good at engaging people will be humble and respect their different talents. L4
This is called the Virtue of not contending. L5
This is called employing people's different areas of strength. L6
This is called heavenly matching. L7
This is the ultimate wisdom of the ancients. L8

Comments
Respect for Talents (ch.68)

People with talent as a scholar, a warrior and a strategist have the common virtue of not contending.
Whoever is good at deploying people has humility, respect people for their talents, hence also not contending.
People with different talents should be deployed where their strengths are best utilized.

Noted: talents that Laozi identifies are down-to-earth, never supernatural or mystical.

Dao De Jing

六十九章　　　　　　　Chapter 69

01 用兵有言：	Warfare strategist has a saying:
02 "吾不敢为主，	" I do not dare be the master (aggressor),
03 而为客；	But be the guest (defender);
04 不敢进寸，	Not dare to advance an inch (attack),
05 而退尺。"	But retreat a foot (in defense)."
06 是谓，行无行	This is called, marching the no-march (as not attacking)
07 攘无臂	Raise no arm (as not attacking)
08 执无兵	Hold no weapon (as not attacking)
09 扔无敌已	Overcome no enemy indeed (as not attacking)
10 祸，莫大于轻敌	Disaster, none bigger than underestimating the enemy
11 轻敌，几丧吾宝	Underestimating the enemy, nearly lost my treasure (army, nation)
12 故，抗兵相加	Hence, opposing armies confronting each other
13 哀者胜已	The compassionate one triumphs indeed

Laozi's thinking
In warfare strategy there is this saying, L1
"I dare not be the aggressor, but rather be the defender ; L2,3
I dare not advance an inch to attack, but rather retreat a foot to defend". L4,5

This is to say that in defense, there is no marching to attack, no raising of arms to strike. L6,7
No holding of weapon to fight, no enemy to over-run. L8,9

Of all disasters, there are none bigger than underestimating the enemy. L10
Underestimating the enemy nearly lost me, my army and my nation. L11

When opposing armies confront each other, the army with compassion will triumph indeed. L12,13

Comments
Wars, only for defense (ch.69)

Quoting a saying of warfare strategists, Laozi advises waging wars only in defense. (Stanza 1)
Therefore, no marching is needed, no fighting, no deaths of enemies. (Stanza 2)
Laozi also warns of disastrous consequences for underestimating the enemy. (Stanza 3)
But Laozi firmly believes that a compassionate army will be triumphant. (Stanza 4)

Clearly, Laozi is not speaking of some supernatural powers of Dao for fighting wars.
In fact, he even warns against underestimating the enemy with dire consequences.

Fight only in defense, is true to the spirit of the not-contesting principle of Daoism.

Dao De Jing

七十章   Chapter 70

01 吾言, 甚易知, 甚易行   My words, very easy to know, very easy to do
02 天下, 莫能知, 莫能行   The world, none able to know, none able to do

03 言有宗   Words had origins
04 事有君   Affairs had masters
05 夫唯无知   Indeed especially not knowing
06 是以不我知   Therefore know me not
07 知我者希   Whoever know me are rare
08 则我者贵   Whoever understand me are precious (rarer)

09 是以: Therefore:
10 圣人被褐, 而怀玉   The Sage wears coarse-jacket, but bosom-held jade (Dao)

Laozi's thinking
My words are very easy to know and very easy to do. L1
However, in the world, none can understand and none can implement. L2

Words have origins and affairs have masters or ownerships. L3,4
However, people have no knowledge of my sayings; hence know me not. L5,6
Those who know me are rare. L7
Those who understand me are rarer still. L8

Therefore: L9
The Sage is humble, wears coarse-jacket outside, and remains unnoticed. L10
However, inside, the Sage holds Dao to his heart, practicing the principles of Dao quietly. L10

Comments
Laozi's sayings are easy to know, easy to practice (ch.70)

It is easy to know humility, unselfishness, not-contesting and such are admirable Daoist principles.
And it is within our ability to practice them if we so choose.
Yet in our daily life, how many of us can successfully and consistently put them into practice.
Laozi's teachings are easy to know and to practice, yet none in the world can fulfill them. (St.1)
Laozi laments that few know him for his teachings; even rarer are those who really understand him. (St.2)
Laozi sees himself as the Sage, unknown, wearing a coarse-jacket, who at heart, embraces Daoism. (St.3)

Self-interest is often perceived to be equivalent to self-survival to a large extent.
By instinct, our first choice is therefore to act in our own self-interest, rather than for common interests.
However, in a world where everyone acts only in self-interest, there can only be chaos.
Hence, Laozi advises us to emulate Dao and work for the common good which includes ourselves.
Then there will be peace, harmony, and prosperity in our world.

Daoism is easy to know and to practice, but in reality, it is truly not easy to fulfill.

Dao De Jing

七十一章　　　　　　　　Chapter 71

01 知不知, 上　　　　　　Knows not knowing, high
02 不知, 知, 病　　　　　Not knowing, (acts) knowing, sick

03 圣人, 不病　　　　　　The Sage, is not sick
04 以其病, 病　　　　　　As the Sage is sick of, this sickness
05 是以, 不病　　　　　　Therefore, (the Sage) is not sick

Laozi's thinking
When we know that we don't know, we are honest. L1
When we don't know, yet pretend that we know, we are sick. L2

The Sage is not sick. L3
The Sage is wise and is sick of this sickness of self-denial. L4
Hence the Sage is not sick. L5

Comments
Not knowing acts knowing, sick (ch.71)

Ignorance does not present us with a favorable image.
We tend to hide it from others by pretending to know what we do not know.
Here, Laozi suggests that it is wise to acknowledge our own ignorance.
To pretend to know what we don't know is a sickness of self-denial, and to be avoided. (St.1)
The Sage understands and is sick of all pretensions to know, hence, is not sick. (St.2)

Often, it is shame and pride that prevent us from acknowledging our ignorance.
But really, it is no sin to be ignorant.
Therefore, it is good to acknowledge the truth and have the stress relieved.
Once free, we will then have all the energy we need to improve ourselves and be ignorant no more.

Self-denial often prevent us from acknowledging this common sickness in ourselves.

Dao De Jing

七十二章	Chapter 72
01 民, 不畏威	Citizens, not afraid of power (oppression)
02 则, 大威至	Then, great power (rebellion) is here
03 无狎, 其所居	No intrusion, into people's dwellings
04 无厌, 其所生	No oppression, of people's livelihood
05 夫, 唯不厌	Indeed, because not oppressing (the people)
06 是以, 不厌	Therefore, no oppression (by the people)
07 是以:	Therefore:
08 圣人自知, 不自见	The Sage is self-aware, but not self-centered
09 自爱, 不自贵	Self-loving, but not self-aggrandizing
10 故, 去彼, 取此	Hence, discard that, embrace this

Laozi's thinking
When oppression push people to the cliff, they become not afraid of power. L1
Then the greater power of rebellion is here. L2
Leaders should not intrude into people's dwellings. L3
Nor oppress the people's livelihood. L4
Indeed because the leaders do not oppress the people, L5
They will in turn not be oppressed by the people. L6

Therefore: L7
The Sage is self-aware but not self-important; hence, does not initiate conquests. L8
Self-loving but not self-aggrandizing; hence, does not build grand palaces and gardens. L9
Therefore, discards self-importance and self-aggrandizing, embraces self-awareness and self-love. L10
Then there is no need for high taxes, no conscription for wars, and no conscription for building projects.
Hence, if there is no oppression of the people, there is no rebellion by the people.

Comments
Rebellion arises from oppression (ch.72)

Leaders are warned not to oppress the people.
Pushed to the limit, people have nothing to lose.
They have no choice but to rebel for a chance of survival. (Stanza 1)

With no conquests, no grand building schemes, no high taxes, the people will live in peace and prosperity.
Hence, the solution is for leaders to discard self-importance and self-glorification with conquests. (Stanza 2)

Laozi analyzes rebellion and suggests solutions to leaders; he is truly the people's philosopher.

Dao De Jing

七十三章 Chapter 73

01 勇于敢, 则杀	Brave to dare, then get kill
02 勇于不敢, 则活	Brave to not-dare, then survive
03 此兩者	This two entities
04 或利, 或害	May be beneficial, may be harmful
05 天之所惡	What Heaven dislike
06 孰知其故？	Who knows the reasons ?
07 天之道	Heaven's way
08 不爭, 而善勝	Not contesting, but good at winning
09 不言, 而善應	Not voicing, but good at responding
10 不召, 而自來	No solicitation, but self-coming (the people)
11 繟然, 而善謀	Unhurried and natural, but good at accomplishing
12 天網, 恢恢	Heaven's net, vast and vast
13 疏, 而不失	Widely-meshed, but do not leak

Laozi's thinking
Have the courage to contest, get kill. L1
Have the courage not to contest, will survive. L2
These two choices may have advantages or disadvantages. L4
What Heaven likes or dislikes, nobody knows why. L5,6

These are Heaven's way: L7
Not contesting but good at winning. L8
Not voicing but good at responding. L9
No solicitation but the people come on their own in submission. L10
Unhurried and naturally, but good at accomplishing. L11
Hence, we should have confidence in Heaven to behave properly, and to respond fairly.

Heaven's net of justice and retribution is far-spread and invisible. L12
The mesh seems loose and wide but it never leaks. L13
Retribution are meted out in due course; the bad and evil will be punished.
For it is true, sow goodwill gets goodwill, sow ill-will gets ill-will.

Comments
The Retribution net of Heaven does not leak (ch.73)

Laozi observes that life is unpredictable, be killed or survive, we know not Heaven's dislikes. (St.1)
But we should have confidence, as Heaven is not contesting, is silent, good and accomplished. (St.2)
As the retribution net of Heaven never fails, justice will be meted to the evil doers in due course. (St.3)

Laozi believes retribution from Heaven never fails, for we harvest what we sow.

Dao De Jing

七十四章   Chapter 74

01 民, 不畏死	The citizens, do not fear death
02 奈何, 以死惧之？	Then why, use death to threaten them？
03 若使民, 恒畏死	If can cause citizens, to constantly fear death,
04 而, 为奇者	Then, whoever commits strangeness (a crime)
05 吾得执而杀之, 孰敢？	I will catch and execute, then who dares？
06 恒, 有司杀者, 杀	Always, have executioners, to execute
07 夫, 代司杀者, 杀	Indeed, whoever substitutes for the executioner, to execute
08 是谓, 代大匠, 斫	This is called, substituting for master-carpenter, to chop
09 夫,代大匠斫者	Indeed, whoever substitutes for master-carpenter to chop
10 希有, 不伤其手已	Rarely has, not injured own hand indeed

Laozi's thinking
With bad government, taxes are high and citizens are conscripted to fight and die in wars.
Or are conscripted for dangerous projects such as to build the Great Wall of China.
In such dire circumstances, citizens' life are very cheap and they no longer fear death. L1
Then why use death to threaten them? L2
On the other hand good government in practice, taxes are low and there are no wars.
When citizens are well fed, safe, and happy, they want the good life and will fear death. L3
When someone commits a crime, I will catch and execute, then who dares? L4,5

Often there are executioners doing the necessary executions. L6
Whoever substitutes for the executioner is like substituting for the master-carpenter. L7,8
Unskilled, whoever substitutes for the master-carpenter to chop will likely to self-injure. L9-10
Hence, leaders and citizens are not qualified to take justice into their own hands.
Heaven will punish the bad and evil in due course.

Comments
Retribution from society risks miscarriage of justice (ch. 74)

In the preceding chapter, Laozi promises retribution from Heaven without fail.
Probably Laozi has seen much miscarriage of 'justice' by the Lords and Kings on their subjects.
Here Laozi warns rulers of wanton 'judicial killings' that can back fire on them.

Fearing miscarriage of justice, Laozi frown upon society meting out judicial punishment.

Dao De Jing

七十五章   Chapter 75

01 民之饥	The people's hunger
02 以其上食税之多	Because their rulers tax too much
03 是以，饥	Hence, the hunger
04 民之难治	The citizens being difficult to govern
05 以其上之有为	Is because their rulers have action (ambitions)
06 是以，难治	Hence, the difficulty to govern
07 民之轻死	The citizens' taking death lightly
08 以其上求生之厚	Is because their rulers wanting to live life lavishly
09 是以，轻死	Hence, taking death lightly
10 夫，唯无以生为者	Thus, the leader not living lavishly
11 是贤于贵生	Is more virtuous than the leader living lavishly

Laozi's thinking

The citizens are hungry because their rulers tax them too much. L1-3

The citizen are being difficult to govern because the rulers have these ambitious desires. L4-6
They started wars to expand their territories and conscript citizens to fight for them.
Citizens who are conscripted may never return from war alive, hence, they are hard to control.

The citizens take death lightly and rebel, because their rulers live lavish lifestyles. L7-9
They are conscripted to build grand palaces, gardens, and hunting grounds.
Leaving behind their families and farms, their own livelihoods are completely upset.

Thus leaders who act not for lavish living are wiser than those who indulge in grandiose life-style. L10,11

Comments
Hunger arises from high taxes (ch.75)

The citizens are hungry; they are unruly, rebellious, and do not fear death.
Laozi correctly place the reasons for all these problems squarely at the palace gate.

Such problems still exist today in our 21st century.
Like the top general of a ruling junta, married off daughter in lavish style.
While the majority of the population still live below the poverty line.

The causes of hunger and rebellion are taxes, expansionism and extravagance of rulers.

七十六章　　　　　　　　Chapter 76

01 人之生也, 柔弱	People when living, are gentle and weak
02 其死也, 坚強	When dead, are hard and stiff
03 草木之生也, 柔脆	Grass and trees when living, are gentle and fragile
04 其死也, 枯槁	When dead, are dry and shrivel
05 故, 坚強者, 死之徒	Hence, the hard and strong, path to death
06 柔弱者, 生之徒	The gentle and weak, path to life
07 是以:	Therefore:
08 兵強, 則不胜	Army strong, will not triumph
09 木強, 則折	Wood strong, will break
10 強大, 居下	Strong and big, rank low
11 柔弱, 居上	Gentle and weak, rank high

Laozi's thinking

When alive, the human body is supple and soft. L1
When dead, the body is hard and stiff. L2
Similarly, with grass and trees, the living are supple and fragile. L3
Whereas the dead are dry and shrivel. L4
Hence, whatever are hard and stiff, are moving towards death. L5
And whatever are supple and weak, are moving towards life. L6

Therefore: L7
An army standing strong and inflexible, can be destroyed. L8
Trees standing strong and rigid against a storm, can break. L9
Clearly the strong and big rank low. L10
The gentle and weak rank high. L11

Comments
Gentle path to life, rigid path to death (ch. 76)

Laozi observes suppleness of the living and rigidity of death in both plant and human life. (Stanza 1)
Hence, he infers that the gentle and weak are superior to the rigid and hard which is breakable. (Stanza 2)

These observations of the living and the death besides his observation of water impress Laozi.
Be gentle and weak, yielding and flexible; the path to life.
Be hard and strong, unyielding and be broken; the path to death.

Daoism is to follow Laozi down the gentle path of life.

Dao De Jing

七十七章   Chapter 77

01 天之道	Heaven's way
02 其犹张弓也？	Is it not like stretching a bow calmly?
03 高者, 抑之	If high, press it (down)
04 下者, 舉之	If low, raise it (up)
05 有余者, 损之	Have-excess (string), reduce it
06 不足者, 补之	Not-enough (string), supplement it
07 天之道	Heaven's way
08 损有余, 而补不足	Reduce Have-excess, to supplement Not-enough
09 人之道, 则不然	People's way however, is not so
10 损不足, 以奉有余	Reduce Not-enough, to offer Have-excess
11 孰能有余, 以奉天下？	Who can have excess, to offer the World ?
12 唯有道者	Only whoever has Dao (the Daoist)
13 是以:	Therefore :
14 圣人为, 而不恃	The Sage acts, and not be presumptuous
15 功成, 而不居	Success achieved, and not claim
16 其不欲见贤	As not wishing be seen virtuous

Laozi's thinking

Heaven's way is like stretching a bow calmly to hit the target. L1,2
If the aim is high, press down a little to adjust. L3
If the aim is low, raise up a little to adjust. L4
If the string is too much and lax, reduce it. L5
If the string is too little and tight, supplement it. L6

Heaven's way, reduce the Have-excess to supplement the Not-enough. L7,8
People's way, however, is to reduce the Not-enough to offer to the Have-excess. L9,10

So who has excess to offer to the world? L11
Only whoever has Dao can do this. L12

Hence: L13
The Sage accomplishes, but is not presumptuous of capability. L14
When success is achieved, no credit is claimed. L15
As the Sage does not wish to be seen as virtuous. L16

Comments
Heaven's way: like adjusting the bow to hit target (ch.77)

People's way is to take from the Not-enough to offer to the Have-excess.
By analogy with adjustment needed to stretch and aim a bow to hit the target.
Laozi shows that people's way is wrong and will never hit the target.

Who can have excess to offer to the world? The Daoist.

103

七十八章　　　　　　　　　　Chapter 78

01 天下, 莫柔弱于水	In the world, none gentler and weaker than water
02 而攻坚强者, 莫之能胜	But attacking the hard and strong, none can surpass
03 以其, 无以易之	For this, none can replace water
04 弱之胜强	The weak triumph over the strong
05 柔之胜刚	The gentle triumph over the hard
06 天下, 莫不知	In the world, none do not know
07 莫能行	None can implement
08 是以, 圣人云 :	Therefore, the Sage said :
09 "受国之垢,	"Whoever bears the nation's dirt,
10 是谓社稷主;	Is hailed master of society;
11 受国不祥,	Whoever bears the nation's misfortune,
12 是谓天下王."	Is hailed king of the world."
13 正言若反	Positive sayings seem negative

Laozi's thinking
Water can disintegrate hard iron and torrential rain can bring down mountains, trees and boulders.
Hence, in the world, none gentler and weaker than water. L1
But attacking the hard and strong, none can surpass and none can replace water. L2,3

The weak triumphs over the strong and the gentle triumphs over the hard. L4,5
In the world, none do not know but none can implement such principle. L6,7

Besides, water benefits and not contesting, it carries all the dirt and takes the lowest position.
Then sublimates and rises as clouds to return once again, purified as rain to nourish the land.
Hence, the Sage says whoever bears the nation's dirt, is hailed as the master of society. L8-10
Whoever bears the nation's misfortune is hailed as king of the world. L11-12

Bearing dirt and suffering misfortune may seem negative.
But such actions reflect positive results for the people.
Such good leaders take responsibilities and put the people first.
Hence, positive sayings seem negative. L13

Comments
Triumphs of the Weak and Gentle (ch.78)

Water, weak and gentle, flows everywhere, accesses the inaccessible.
Water takes the lowest position and washes away all the dirt.
"The weak triumphs over the strong" may sound paradoxical and few realize the potential.
Highlighting the triumph of water, Laozi actually gives hope and encouragement to the weak and gentle.

Daoism is like water, though weak and gentle, will triumph.

Dao De Jing

七十九章   Chapter 79

01 和大怨	Resolving great grievance
02 必有余怨	There must remain residual grievance
03 安可以为善？	How can this be good ?
04 是以:	Therefore :
05 圣人执左契, 而不责于人	The Sage holds the left contracts, and does not demand of others
06 有德, 司契	Has virtues, administers contracts
07 无德,司彻	Without virtues, administers taxes
08 天道无亲	The Heaven's way has no favoritism
09 恒与善人	Always helps the good people

Laozi's thinking
After resolving big grievances, there must have residual grievances. L1,2
How can this be good? L3
Therefore, better to sow no grievances in the first instance.

Hence: L4
The Sage holding the left portion of loan contracts make no demand for repayment. L5
Whoever with virtue is like the Sage, administering contracts and giving out loans. L6
Whoever without virtue is like the tax-collector, always demanding payments. L7

Heaven's way may show no favoritism. L8
But Heaven will always help whoever is good. L9
Because, more often than not, goodwill begets goodwill.

Comments
Salvation, sow no grievances (ch.79)

Laozi rightly observes that there remains residual grievances after resolving great grievances.
So it is best to sow no grievances; if one sows goodwill, one will receive goodwill.

Pacific Daoism is: sow goodwill, not grievences.

Dao De Jing

八十章   Chapter 80

01 小国, 寡民	Small nation, with few citizens
02 使有什伯之器, 而不用	Cause to have many varied equipments, and not using
03 使民重死,而不远徙	Cause citizens to take death seriously, and not go far-away
04 虽有舟舆, 无所乘之	Though have boats and vehicles, no need to ride them
05 虽有甲兵, 无所陈之	Though have armored army, no need to display them
06 使民复结绳, 而用之	Cause citizens to knot ropes, to use them (for recording)
07 甘其食; 美其服	Enjoyment in their food; beautiful in their clothing
08 安其居; 乐其俗	Safe in their dwellings; happy in their traditions
09 邻国相望	Neighboring nations mutually in sight (of each other)
10 鸡犬之声相闻	Sound of chickens and dogs mutually be heard (from both sides)
11 民至老死, 不相往來	Citizens till old and die, do not mutually come and go (contact)

Laozi's thinking
The ideal state is a small nation with few citizens, so that there is enough resources for everyone. L1
Citizens need not resort to use of equipments to fight or to migrate. L2
Citizens are safe and happy; they fear death and do not want to go far away. L3
Hence, though they have boats and vehicles, there are no reasons for using them. L4
Though they have armored armies, there is no need to deploy them for conquests. L5

The citizens are encouraged to returned to the ancient tribal society. L6
Where ropes are knotted to keep records of things. L6
Where citizens enjoy their food, and be beautiful in their fine clothes. L7
Be safe in their dwellings and happy in their traditional practices. L8
Neighboring nations are in sight of each other and sounds of chickens and dogs can be mutually heard. L9,10
However, their citizens till old and die, never interact with each other. L11
In this way there are no frictions, and no wars between nations.

Comments
Small nation, few citizens, back to basics (ch.80)

In Laozi's ideal world, nations are small with few citizens, happy in tribal life, never counter-attacking.

Now in our 21st century world, with huge populations, we use much equipments for increased productivity.
Heavy uses of machinary cause much contamination of the environment on land, in the air, and in the seas.
Deforestation, depletion of mineral and energy resources, global warming and the extinction of species.
Fast transport across the globe has caused the fast spread of diseases among humans and animals.
Mass migration of rural populations are over-stretching city amenities.

Laozi's back-to-tribal society with few citizens, may not be a bad idea to save our planet, today!

Dao De Jing

八十一章	Chapter 81

01 信言, 不美	Trustworthy words, are not beautiful
02 美言, 不信	Beautiful words, are not trustworthy
03 善者, 不辩	Whoever is good, does not argue
04 辩者, 不善	Whoever argue, is not good
05 知者, 不博	Whoever is well-known, is not knowledgeable
06 博者, 不知	Whoever is knowledgeable, is not well-known
07 圣人不积	The Sage does not accumulate (for self)
08 既以为人, 己愈有	With working for people, self will have more
09 既以与人, 己愈多	With giving to people, self is more bountiful
10 天之道	Way of Heaven
11 利, 而不害	Benefiting, and not harming
12 圣人之道	Way of the Sage
13 为, 而不争	Acting, but not-contesting

Laozi's thinking
Trustworthy words need not be beautified for deception and to gain acceptance. L1
Untrustworthy words are beautified to deceive in order to gain acceptance. L2
Whoever is good need not argue and whoever argue is not good. L3,4
Whoever keeps low profile and is not known for his knowledge, is knowledgeable. L5
Whoever keeps a high profile and makes known his knowledge, is not knowledgeable. L6

The Sage does not accumulate for the self. L7
Having acted for the people, the Sage possesses more from the returned goodwill. L8
Having given to people, the Sage gains more from returned gratitude. L9

The way of Heaven, benefiting, and not harming. L10,11
The way of the Sage, taking action but not-contesting. L12,13

Comments
Heaven's way is benefiting and not harming (ch.81)

In the 1st Stanza, Laozi warns of the common pitfalls in real life.
That is, un-trustworthiness that hides behind beautiful words.
Clever arguments use to cover bad intentions.
A high-profile display of apparent knowledge in the place of true ignorance.

2nd Stanza suggests that we need not be selfish.
Helping others, giving to others, one will invariably be rewarded with more from returned goodwill

3rd Stanza aptly and succinctly summarizes his whole philosophy of pacific Daoism:
Heaven benefits and does not harm; the Sage acts and does not contest.

Pacific Daoism may be summarized as benefiting and not harming, contributing without contesting.

108	**DISCUSSION**
109	Dating the *Dao De Jing* (Dao and Virtue Classic)
110	Authorship
111	Is Laozi writing for the rulers?
112	Is Laozi a mystic?
113	Is Laozi religious?
114	Is Laozi a philosopher?
115	Is Laozi a scientist?
116	Is Laozi a pessimist?
117	Is Laozi laughable?
118	The Chinese Bellows
119	Concept of Dao (道, the Primal Entity)
120	Concept of De (德, the Primal Virtue)
121	Concepts of Wu (无, Have-ot) and You (有, Have)
122	Concept of Naming
123	Concept of Correlatives
124	On Benevolence, Righteousness and Etiquette
125	On Contentment
126	On Fame and Wealth
127	On Fears and Crises
128	On Femininity appreciated
129	On Freedom
130	On Greatness
131	On Happiness of the Daoist
132	On Honesty
133	On Human Desires and Failings
134	On Humility
135	On Life-Death, Survival
136	On Meditation
137	On Not-Contesting
138	On Paradoxes
139	On Problems and Difficulties
140	On Purpose of Life
141	On Retribution
142	On Salvation
143	On Self-Understanding and Cultivation
144	On Success and Failure
145	On Triumph of the Weak
146	On Trust
147	On Uncertainties of Life
148	On Wars
149	On WuWei (无为)
150	On WuWei, WuBuWei (无为,无不为)

Discussion

Dating the *Dao De Jing* (*DDJ*)

绝圣, 弃智	End sage-hood, abandon intelligence
民利百倍	Citizens benefit 100-fold
绝仁, 弃义	End benevolence, abandon righteousness
民复孝慈	Citizens return to filial love (ch.19)

Such declarations in the *DDJ* have been interpreted as attack on Confucian ethics.
As such, are advanced as evidence that the *DDJ* was written after Confucius (551-479 BCE).
If the *DDJ* can be dated before Confucius, the theory of its anti-Confucianism cannot stand.
Hence, dating the *DDJ* is important in itself as in its interpretation.

Zhuangzi (369-286 BCE) often presented Laozi as a teacher instructing Confucius (551-479 BCE).
In the *Shi Ji*, Sima Qian (145-86 BCE) refers to Laozi as an elder contemporary of Confucius.
These writings suggest, the *DDJ* was written in the Spring Autumn period (770-476 BCE).

Two copies of *Laozi* written on silk, were recovered from a Han tomb at Mawangdui, Changsa, Hunan, 1973.
The tombs date back to 200 BCE; hence, the *DDJ* is written before the 2nd century BCE.
Latest recovery was in 1993 - the Guodian *Laozi* from a tomb of the State of Chu.
Brushed on bamboo slips, the text material matches 24 chapters of the present-day *DDJ*.
The tomb dates back to 350 BCE, thus placing the *DDJ* firmly in the 4th century BCE.

The *Yi Jing* or *Book of Change* is an ancient classic consulted for its philosophical advice.
It is purportedly initiated by Fuxi (2852 BCE) and completed by King Wen (1143 BCE) and son.
Confucius (551-479 BCE) loved the *Yi Jing*, studied it, edited it and added explanatory notes.
The *Shi Jing (Book of Poems)* was also purportedly collected and edited by Confucius.
These poems are from the various states of the Zhou Dynasty (1066-221 BCE).
The *DDJ* text is in short, terse verse form, much in the style of the *Yi Jing* and *Shi Jing*.
Hence, it seems reasonable to accept that the *DDJ* is from a period closer to the *Yi Jing* and *Shi Jing*.

The *DDJ* mentions no proper names for persons or events that may help in dating it.
However, the *DDJ* often refers to rulers as both Lords and Kings.
Lords and Kings are vassal-state rulers in the Spring Autumn period of the Zhou Dynasty.
But in the Warring States period (475-221 BCE), power are concentrated in the Kings.
Thus, the *DDJ* is likely a product of the earlier Spring Autumn period (770-476 BCE).

道恒, 无为, 而无不为	Dao primal, without self-interest, then Nothing will not do
侯王若能守之	Lords and Kings if can uphold Dao
万物将自化	All things will self-develop (in accordance with Dao) (ch.37)
侯王得一以为天下贞	Lords & Kings attain One and be world's finest (leaders) (ch.39)

Without solid evidence to the contrary, we shall continue to accept the traditional wisdom.
Laozi, legendary author of the *DDJ* is an elder contemporary of Confucius (551-479 BCE).

Arguably, the DDJ was written during Confucius time in the Spring Autumn period, about 2500 BCE.

Discussion

Authorship of the *Dao De Jing* (*DDJ*) (first known as the *Laozi*)

Is the *Dao De Jing* an anthology, a collection of wise sayings among the population?
That the *Laozi* is an anthology is never an option with Sima Qian (145-87BCE), and scholars before him.
Furthermore, writing in the first person, I (吾, 21x; and 我, 19x) has been quite insistent in the *Laozi* text.

Before the Qin Dynasty (221-206 BCE), books of philosophy are named after their authors.
Books with name such as the *Mozi*, the *Zhuangzi* and the *Hanfeizi* imply single authorship.
Unlike books of known collective authorship such as the *Yi Jing* and the *Book of Poems*.
First known as the *Laozi*, the *DDJ* seems no exception and its single authorship is recognized early.
By the end of the Han Dynasty, the *Laozi* is revered and formed part of the official curriculum.
It was elevated to classical status and given the name, *Dao De Jing (The Primal and Virtue Classic)*.

The single authorship of the *Laozi* has been accepted by authors in the pre-Qin era.
In the *Zhuangzi*, quotes match well the current *DDJ* and precedes with "Laozi says,.."
Hence, Zhuangzi (369-286 BCE) clearly acknowledges Laozi as the author of the *DDJ*.
Hanfeizi (280-233 BCE) in his book *Hanfeizi* devotes 2 chapters to explaining the *Laozi* specifically.
Sima Qian (145-86 BCE) in his *Historical Records (Shi Ji)* puts up 3 alternative names for authorship.
Even in doubt, Sima Qian has not suggested collective authorship for the *DDJ*.

Ideas like 'triumph of the weak', 'play the female role', 'use of emptiness' are common in the *DDJ*.
Such unorthodox concepts are not in the writings then and were likely unknown amongst the people.
Even today, such controversial thoughts are hardly common among the general population.
The author on an quest for the truth of the universe, without a spiritual or mystical bias, is uniquely rare.
Furthermore, the consistency of Daoist pacific principles is seen throughout the whole book.
These are indirect evidences to suggest that the *DDJ* is not an anthology of popular quotes.

In the written text, the *DDJ* is consistent in the style of terse, short expression.
In thought, the *DDJ* is consistent with that of a single individual.
The *DDJ* reads like the quest of a rare individual seeking to know the truth of the universe.
The author even claims personal ownership of the text and its sayings:

吾言甚易知, 甚易行	My sayings very easy to know, very easy to implement
天下莫能知, 莫能行	The world none able to know, none able to implement
言有宗, 事有君	Words had origins, affairs had masters
夫唯无知, 是以不我知	Indeed especially not knowing, therefore know me not
知我者希, 则我者贵	Whoever know me are rare, whoever understand me are precious (ch.70)

Furthermore the author does acknowledge when quoting from outside sources:

用兵有言:	Warfare strategist has a saying:
"吾不敢为主, 而为客"	" I not dare be master (aggressor), but be the guest (defender)" (ch.69)

On bamboo slips, the Guodian *DDJ* is written in the Chu version of the Da Zhuan script.
Down the centuries, the *DDJ* had been transcripted in the Xiao Zhuan script of Qin Dynasty.
In the Li Shu script of Han Dynasty and then in the Standard script, all copied by hand.
Over the millennium, transcript errors, missing bamboo slips, and misplacement of slips may had occured.
And even intentional insertion of new text for clarification may have corrupted the ancient text.
Nevertheless, the *DDJ* text still read consistent and uniquely like the work of an individual.
Establishing the single authorship of the *DDJ* has been difficult.
Establishing the identity of the individual author is next to impossible.
The name Laozi literally means "Old Teacher"; it is possibly a reverend salutation, not a name.

On balance, the evidence is not in favor that the Laozi or Dao De Jing is an anthology.

Discussion

Is Laozi writing for the rulers?

Laozi is not a philosopher of the ruling class but a spokesperson for the common people.

A product of his time, Laozi accepts that the King has the mandate to rule from Dao.
域中有四大	In this universe there are 4 Greats
而王居其一焉	And King occupies one of them indeed (ch.25)

For ease of control, Laozi's ideal state is small with few citizens who are kept ignorant with no desires.
Thus Laozi has been suspected to be writing for the ruling class against the commoners and slaves.
恒使民无知, 无欲	Constantly causes citizens not to know, not to desire (ch.3)
非以明民	Not by enlightening the people
将以愚之	But keeps them ignorant. (ch.65)

But in reality, Laozi is for the commoners, chiding rulers for oppression that gives rise to rebellion.
And accusing them of causing hunger and poverty with high taxes
无狎, 其所居	No intrusion, into people's dwellings
无厌, 其所生	No oppression, of people's livelihood (ch.72)
民之饥	The people's hunger
以其上食税之多	Because their rulers tax too much (ch.75)

Also, he warns the ruling class against the disastrous crime of expansionism that brings wars and misery.
祸, 莫大于不知足	Disaster, never greater than not knowing contentment
咎, 莫大于欲得	Crime, never greater than desire to possess (ch.46)

In fact, good rulers are to have no personal agenda but the agenda of the citizens.
That is, to rule is to serve, and not to be served
圣人无恒心	The Sage has no absolute heart (wishes)
以百姓心为心	But embraced the people's heart (wishes) for self (ch.49)

Also rulers are advised to set good examples themselves, not to exalt and enrich themselves.
Else citizens will be confused and do likewise, resort to fighting and robbery for glamor and wealth.
我无为, 而民自化	I have no motive, and citizens will self develop
我好静, 而民自正	I love quietude, and citizens will self regulate
我无事, 而民自富	I have no agenda, and citizens will self prosper
我无欲, 而民自朴	I have no desires, and citizens will self humble (ch.57)
圣人自知, 不自见	The Sage is self-aware, but not self-important
自爱, 不自贵	Self-loving, but not self-aggrandizing (ch.72)
为无为	Act not for self-interest (not selfish)
则无不治	Then none not governable (ch.3)

Laozi lived in the time of slavery and feudal society of the Zhou dynasty about 2500 BCE.
He is still trapped in the traditional belief that the ruling class has a mandate from Heaven to rule.
But his learning makes him see the excesses of the ruling class and the suffering of the commoners.
He observes that ruling is made easy if rulers act not just for themselves but also for the people.

On balance, the Dao De Jing shows that Laozi is essentially a philosopher of the common people.

Is Laozi a mystic?   **Discussion**

A mystic believes in insight into mysteries, transcending ordinary human knowledge. (Random House, 1984)
On first reading, Laozi does use words of a mystic nature in the *DDJ*.
However, at closer examination, he is not really a mystic.

天地之间	Heaven and Earth, the space in-between
其犹橐龠乎？	Is it not like the bellows (barrel and plunger) ?
虚而不屈	Empty but not yielding
动而愈出	Move (plunger), yet more come out (air, feeding the fire) (see ch.5)

Laozi observes the bellows of a space between Heaven and Earth and postulates Dao is in it.
However, he does not ascribes any fanciful, supernatural, and mystical power to Dao.

谷神不死	Valley spirit (of fertility) never dies
是谓玄牝	Is said to be the mysterious female
玄牝之门	The mysterious female's doorway
是谓天地根	Is said to be foundation of Heaven and Earth (see ch.6)

In his ancient time, how is he to describe the female and male involvement in procreation?
Hence, Valley spirit and vague terms, but no flight into the mystical, supernatural powers of Dao!

不出戶, 知天下	Without stepping-out the door, knows the world
不窥牖, 见天道	Not looking out the window, sees Heaven's way (see ch.47)

These are no mystical utterance of Laozi, only the power of the written words of the archives.
Without looking out of the window, one knows there is a full moon on the 15th day of every lunar month.

至虚极	Reach emptiness at its limit (clear the mind)
守静笃	Hold stillness seriously (maintain the clear mind)
万物并作	The myriad things simultaneously in action
吾以观复	This I have observed repeatedly
夫物芸芸	Indeed all things like evergreen grass
各复归其根	Each again return to its root (in cycles of life and death) (see ch.16)

This verse just registers the observation that all things, living and non-living, have a life-death cycle.
Laozi's strong words like 'Reach emptiness at its limit' is for emphasis, but in no way mystify the message.

兕无所投其角.	Rhino finds nowhere to trust its horn
虎无所措其爪	Tiger finds nowhere to place its claws
兵无所容其刃	Soldier find nowhere to put-in the blade
夫何故？	Why is this so ?
以其无死地	Because they avoid ground of death (see ch.50)

"Do not get into harms way", the last line de-mystified the 3 preceding situations of mystical impossibilities.

下士闻道, 大笑之	The lesser scholar learn of Dao, loudly laughs at it
不笑, 不足以为道	Without laughing, not (silly) enough to be Dao (see ch.41)

The 'emptiness' of Dao in the bellows heightens Laozi's awareness for the negative aspects of things.
Laozi is fully aware of his unconventional observations and counter-intuitive thinking.
Hence, he expects misunderstanding and admits that his teachings may seem laughable to the un-initiated.

Laozi's words may mystify, but he is no mystic and his message is certainly not mysticism.

Is Laozi religious?   **Discussion**

Religion is a set of beliefs concerning the cause, nature and purpose of the universe and a superhuman creator.
Religion can be a system of worship involving devotional and ritual observances.
Religion often have a moral code for the conduct of human affairs. (Random House, 1984)

Laozi the archivist of the court of Zhou has full access to all the written knowledge of his world.
Tracing back in time, he knows there was nothing at the beginning, no written history, no creator.

无，名天地之始	Wu (Have-not), to name the beginning of Heaven and Earth (ch.1)

However, Laozi observes that the space between Heaven and Earth is like a huge bellows.
The bellows looks empty, yet resists applied pressure, and its air keeps the fire burning without depleting!

天地之间	Heaven and earth, the space in-between
其犹橐龠乎？	Is it not like the bellows (barrel and plunger) ?
虚而不屈	Empty but not yielding
动而愈出	Move (plunger), yet more come out (air, feeding the fire) (ch.5)

Inspired, Laozi postulates that before Heaven and Earth, there exists a primal entity, which he named Dao.
He further postulates that Dao subsequently give rise to all things, and hence, can be mother of the universe

有物浑成	There are matters that mixed and formed
先天地生	Created before Heaven and Earth
周行而不殆	Moving in cycles and not in danger (of stopping)
可以为天下母	Can be the mother of the World (Universe)
吾不知其名，字之曰道	I do not know its name, in word call it Dao (ch.25)

All things rely on Dao for their existence, but Dao never demand ownership; hence, all things are free.

衣养万物，而不为主	Clothes and nourishes all things, but Dao will not be their master (ch.34)

All things have complete freedom, but on their own accord, naturally respect Dao and value De.
And Dao, with perceived primal Virtues, demands no possession, claims no credit, and exercises no control.

万物，莫不尊道而贵德	All things, none do not respect Dao and value Virtue
道之尊，德之贵	The respecting of Dao, the valuing of Virtue
夫，莫之命，而恒自然	Indeed, are never decreed, but are always natural
生，而不有	Creates, but does not possess
为，而不恃	Achieves, but not presumptuous
长，而不宰	Has seniority, but does not control
是谓玄德	These are termed primal Virtues (ch.51)

Laozi concludes that Heaven's (or Dao's) way, only benefiting and not harming.

天之道	Way of Heaven
利而不害	Benefit and not harming (ch.81)

Tracing backward in the archives, Laozi finds nothing at the beginning of time, no written history, no creator.
However, to explain the universe, he postulates Dao, the primal entity that exists before Heaven and Earth.
Laozi also perceives that Dao does not claim ownership, does not demand respect from the things it created.
Hence, Daoism is not a religion, there is no system of worship that involves devotional and ritual observances.
Daoism is a pacific philosophy best summarizes in the principle of benefiting and not harming.

Laozi may be a scientist and a philosopher, but certainly not a religious man.

Discussion

Is Laozi a philosopher?

Philosophy is the rational inquiry of the truths and principles of being, knowledge, or conduct.
Philosophy is a system of principles for guidance in practical affairs.
Philosophy is associated with mental calmness, or stoic attitude. (Random House, 1984)

Laozi is inspired by the working of the 'empty' bellows that charges the furnace fire without depleting.
And he has not fail to observe that the space between Heaven and Earth is like an all-pervasive bellows.

天地之间	Heaven and earth, the space in-between
其犹橐龠乎？	Is it not like the bellows (barrel and plunger) ?
虚, 而不屈	Empty, but not yielding
动, 而愈出	Move (plunger), yet more come out (air, feeding the fire) (ch.5)

Laozi believes a primal entity exists in the all-pervasive space to provide the vital energy for all creations.
He postulates a primal entity, that exists before Heaven and Earth, and named it Dao.
He perceives that Dao subsequently creates all things, and hence, can be the Mother of the World.

有物浑成, 先天地生	There are matters that mixed and formed, created before Heaven and Earth
寂兮, 寥兮, 独立而不改	Silent indeed, rarefied (formless) indeed, alone stand and not change
周行而不殆	Moving in cycles and not in danger (of stopping)
可以为天下母	Can be the Mother of the World
吾不知其名, 字之曰道	I do not know its name, in word call it Dao (ch.25)

In addition, Laozi perceives many primal Virtues of Dao, attributes that we can practice in our daily lifes.

生, 而不有	Creates, but does not possess
为, 而不恃	Achieves, but not presumptuous
长, 而不宰	Has seniority, but does not control
是谓玄德	These are termed primal Virtues (ch.51)

Laozi also praises water for benefiting and not contending, and for its humility in taking lowly positions.

上善若水	High goodness like water
水善, 利万物, 而不争	Water good, benefits all things, yet not contending
处众人之所恶	Resides where all people will hate (bottom)
故几于道	Hence is rooted in Dao (ch.8)

Laozi urges that we practice Daoism daily, to attain the ultimate state of "being unselfish in all our actions".

为道, 日损, 损之又损	Practice Dao, daily reduction (of desire), reducing it yet reducing
以至于无为	To reach till no motive (unselfish)
无为, 而无不为	Not selfish, then no task not actionable (ch.48)

In summary Laozi suggests that we emulate Heaven's way, benefit and not harming.

天之道	Way of Heaven
利而不害	Benefit and not harming (ch.81)

Laozi ponders on the truths and principles of being of the universe, and postulates the existence of Dao.
Impressed by the perceived attributes of Dao (not selfish in all actions), his thoughts spawn pacific Daoism.
This philosophy is, creates but claim no credit, acts but not in contest, and such advices in practical affairs.
Pacific Daoism is a philosophy conducive to mental calmness, or stoic attitude for effective actions.
Dao and its creation of the universe may never be proven, but pacific Daoism remains a practical philosophy.

By all 3 counts, Laozi is indeed a great philosopher.

Discussion

Is Laozi a scientist?

The writing format of the *Dao De Jing* is like that of a scientific thesis.
Everywhere are connecting words like "hence" (故), "therefore" (是以) and "then" (则).
Connecting an observation of the world or a thought with an inference or conclusion.

In the *Dao De Jing* "hence" (故) is used 65 times, "therefore" (是以) 37 times and "then" (则) 32 times.

不自见, 故明	Not self-centered, hence enlightened (ch.22)
是以, 圣人终日行不离辎重	Therefore, the Sage on the move stray not from the baggage wagon (ch.26)
为无为, 则无不治	Act not for self-interest (not selfish), then none not governable (ch.3)

He does not plagiarized; he quotes his sources if they are not his own words.
古之所谓「曲则全」者　　The ancient saying, "Bend and be preserved whole" (ch.22)

When he does not know, he acknowledges his ignorance.
吾不知谁之子　　I don't know whose child (Dao is)
象帝之先　　Preceding Emperor of Forms (Dao is formless) (ch.4)

In fact, he condemns as sickness, the pretension to knowledge when one does not know.
知不知, 上　　Knows not knowing, high
不知, 知, 病　　Not knowing, yet (acts) knowing, sick (ch.71)

He is not dogmatic; he often queries first, then thinks and uses reasoning to find an answer.
何谓贵大患若身?　　Why says take seriously big trouble because of self?
吾所以有大患者　　The reason that I have big trouble
为吾有身　　Is because I have a body (self)
及吾无身　　When I have no body (willing to sacrifice self)
吾有何患?　　What trouble do I have? (ch.13)

Laozi is acutely observant of nature and human society.
合抱之木, 生于毫末　　Trees of large girth, grow from micro seed (ch.64)
民之饥, 以其上食税之多　　The people's hunger, because their rulers tax too much (ch.75)

He identifies correlatives as natural pairs, hence, advises no prejudice against one or the other.
故, 有无相生　　Hence, You (Have) and Wu (Have-not) are correlatives in creations
难易相成　　Difficulty and easiness are correlatives in manifestations
长短相形　　Long and short are correlatives in forms (ch.2)

He also observes that naming is not absolute, like Dao, it is only a hypothesis for further investigation.
道可道, 非恒道　　Dao can be described, not absolute Dao
名可名, 非恒名　　Name can be named, not absolute name (ch.1)

Laozi is acutely observant of nature and human society, a thinker seeking to understand the universe.
He is investigative, honest and truthful; he humbly acknowledges his ignorance.
He is always pragmatic in his approach to all matters and never dogmatic in his writing.

Laozi is an ideal scientist in his ancient setting.

Discussion

Is Laozi a pessimist?

Not-contesting in world affairs, retreating for defense in wars and such ideas make Laozi seems pessimistic. But these pacific actions that Laozi prefers are as relevant and effective as their confrontational alternatives.

Laozi is capable of not claiming credit for achievement, yet be optimistic that the credit due will not be lost!
为而不恃, 功成而不居　　Accomplishes but is not presumptuous, success achieves but takes no credit
夫唯不居, 是以不去　　　Only when does not take credit, then (credit) does not go away (ch.2)

If only rulers are not selfish, Laozi is optimistic that all people are governable!
為無為　　　　　　　　Act for no self-interest (not selfish)
則無不治　　　　　　　Then none not governable (ch.3)

Laozi will bend and bear incrimination upfront, optimistic that affairs will straighten and be whole again.
曲则全　　　　　　　　Bend and be whole (preserved)
枉则直　　　　　　　　Incriminated and be straightened (vindicated) (ch.22)

Laozi is able to trust the trust-unworthy and is hopeful that he will win trust in return.
不善者吾亦善之, 德善　　With a no-good person I am also good, virtuous goodness
不信者吾亦信之, 德信　　With a trust-unworthy person I will also trust, virtuous trust (ch.49)

Laozi is able to respond to grievances with reconciliation, hopeful he will break the vicious cycle of hatred.
大小多少　　　　　　　Big or small, more or less (injustice)
报怨以德　　　　　　　Repay injustice with virtue (kindness) (ch.63)

Laozi shows confidence of making the journal of a thousand miles with the first step beneath his feet.
千里之行, 始于足下　　　Journey of thousand miles, starts beneath the feet (ch.64)

Laozi is confidence anyone can govern a big nation when Daoism prevails, for everybody is self-disiplined.
治大国, 若烹小鲜　　　　Governing big nation, like cooking small fish
以道莅天下　　　　　　With Dao prevailing in the world (ch.60)

And even in misfortune, Laozi sees the possibility for good fortune
祸兮, 福之所倚　　　　　Misfortune indeed, where good fortune depends (ch.58)

In fact Laozi is such an optimist that he declares, "Only the Daoist has excess to help the world"!
孰能有余以奉天下？　　　Who can have excess to offer the World ?
唯有道者　　　　　　　Only whoever has Dao (the Daoist) (ch.77)

Laozi's philosophy may be summed up with the following: WuWei, ErWuBuWei.
无为, 而无不为　　　　　Not selfish, then no tasks not actionable (ch.48)

Thus, far from being a pessimist, Laozi is a great optimist.

Discussion

Is Laozi laughable?

Search the internet for Laozi and you will find website that suggest this is so!
Indeed Laozi knows full well that his thoughts are counter-intuitive, and often laughably unconventional.

Laozi even suggests that if the less scholar does not find it silly enough to laugh, it is not Daoism. (line3,4)

上士闻道, 勤而行之	The high scholar learn of Dao, diligently practice it
中士闻道, 若存若亡	The average scholar learn of Dao, like existing like not existing
下士闻道, 大笑之	The lesser scholar learn of Dao, loudly laugh at it
不笑不足以为道	Without laughing, not (silly) enough to be Dao
故建言有之:	Hence the 'Constructive Words' has these sayings:
明道若昧, 进道若退	Enlightened Dao like dim, advancing Dao like retreating
夷道若类, 上德若谷	Level path of Dao like uneven path, high Virtue like valley
大白若辱, 广德若不足	Great White (innocence) like humiliation, broad Virtue like not enough
建德若偷, 质德若渝	Building Virtue like stealing, quality Virtue like worthless
大方无隅, 大器 晚成	Great Square has no border, great Project late (needs time) to complete
大音希声, 大象无形	Great Tone gives faint sound, great Image has no form
道隐无名	Dao invisible, has no name
夫唯道, 善始且善成	Indeed only Dao, good at starting also good at completing (ch.41)

This is because as Laozi has also noted, often positive sayings sound negative.

是以, 圣人云:	Therefore, the Sage said :
"受国之垢,	" Whoever bears the nation's dirt,
是谓社稷主;	Is hailed master of society;
受国不祥,	Whoever bears the nation's misfortune,
是谓天下王."	Is hailed King of the World."
正言若反	Positive sayings seems negative (ch.78)

Sometime, Laozi is made laughable because of mis-interpretation by scholars who come after.

为无为	Act <u>not selfish</u>
则无不治	Then none not governable (ch.3) (this study)

Contrast with the following:

为无为	Act in accordance with this principle of <u>inaction</u>
则无不治	And the world will be kept in order everywhere (ch.3) (Gu, 1995)

Also, there are some horrible mis-interpretation when he is taken out of context.

绝圣弃智	<u>End</u> sage-hood, abandon intelligence
民利百倍	Citizens benefit 100-fold (ch.19) (this study)

Contrast with the following:

绝圣弃智	<u>Slaughter</u> the talented (suggests Lao Zi)
民利百倍	And everybody will benefit (ch.19) (Merkin, 2008)

Laozi's teachings may seem 'dark' and 'pessimistic' on first reading.

进道若退	Advancing Dao like retreating

However, retreating to a better position for defense may be the best form of attack!

View under the proper light, Laozi's teachings are in reality, no laughing matters.

Laozi's Concepts

The Chinese Bellows

Large artifacts excavated showed that the Shang Dynasty had advance technique in bronze metallurgy.
The humble Chinese bellows is important in providing the fire power needed for these heavy metal works.

Living in the Zhou Dynasty that followed, Laozi certainly is impressed by the "fire-power" of the bellows.
Searching for Dao the primal entity to explain existence of the universe, he believes he found it in the bellows!

道冲	Dao charges (out from the bellows)
而用之或不盈	Yet use it, may not be depleted
渊兮	Deep indeed
似万物之宗	Seems to be the ancestor of all things (ch.4)

He extends the "bellows" image to the space between heaven and earth.
Hence, Dao is pervasive in the whole of the universe, befitting Dao as the primal entity.

天地之间	Heaven and earth, the space in-between
其犹橐龠乎？	Is it not like the bellows (barrel) ?
虚而不屈	Empty but not yielding
动而愈出	Move (plunger), yet more come out (air, feeding the fire) (ch.5)

However at the exit of the bellows, he finds Dao tasteless, invisible, inaudible and too little in substance!

道之出口	Dao's emerging exit (from the bellows)
淡乎, 其无味	Dilute indeed, it has no smell
视之, 不足见	Look at it, not enough to see
听之, 不足闻	Listen to it, not enough to hear
用之, 不足既 (说文:小食也)	Use it, not enough for a small-meal (very little substance) (ch.35)

Yet weak and gentle in the bellows, Dao in the fire seems able to move into the bronze metal, and melting it.

天下之至柔	The most gentle in the world (Dao)
驰骋天下之至坚	Rides (move) in and out into the hardest in the world
无有入无间	Wu (Have-not) and You (Have) (or Dao) enter no space (ch.43)

Laozi perceives, Dao in the Chinese bellows, enables a strong fire to make all kinds of metal instruments.
And subsequent manufacturing and building activities will produce the physical universe as we see it.
Of course, now we know why the bellows work, and it is because of the oxygen in the air.
Hence, today, Dao as the physical primal entity is dead.
But as an inspiring philosophical entity, it will continue to thrive in pacific Daoism.

The Chinese Bellows seems to have fascinated Laozi, and initiated his concept of Dao, the primal entity.

Laozi's Concepts

Concept of Dao (道, the Primal Entity)

The word Dao (means 'path' or 'way'), for naming the primal entity, is first used in the *Dao De Jing*.
Laozi conceives that Dao creates all things to account for the existence of the universe.
From observations of nature, Laozi philosophically associates Dao with many gentle attributes.

This is how Laozi describes the birth of Dao before Heaven and Earth.
有物浑成	There are matters that mixed and formed
先天地生	Exist before Heaven and Earth (ch.25)

He does not know its name, hence arbitrary calls it Dao.
吾不知其名	I do not know its name
字之曰道	In word call it Dao (ch.25)

He perceives Dao exists in the bellows of space between Heaven and Earth
天地之间	Heaven and earth, the space in-between
其犹橐籥乎？	Is it not like the bellows (barrel and plunger) ?
虚, 而不屈	Empty, but not yielding
动, 而愈出	Move (plunger), yet more come out (air, feeding the fire) (ch.5)

Laozi believes Dao is in the female for procreation
谷神不死	Valley spirit (Dao) never dies
是谓玄牝	Is said to be the primal female (ch.6)

He thinks he finds the substance of Dao in the semen of the male in procreation.
道之为物, 惟恍惟惚	Dao itself as substance, all vague all elusive
惚兮恍兮, 其中有象	Elusive indeed vague indeed, within there is image
恍兮惚兮, 其中有物	Vague indeed elusive indeed, within there is substance
窈兮冥兮, 其中有精	Faraway indeed dim indeed, within there is essence (semen) (ch.21)

Hence, he conceives that stepwise, Dao in the harmonious fusion of the female and male creates all things.
道生一, 一生二	Dao created One, One created Two
二生三, 三生万物	Two created Three, Three created All Matters (ch.42)

Dao can be said to be formless, the image of nothing!
是谓无状之状	This is called the formless form
无物之象	The image of nothing (ch.14)

Thus Laozi admits he can describe Dao, but cannot describe the primal Dao.
道可道, 非恒道	Dao that can be described, is not primal Dao (ch.1)

Today in our 21st century, science cannot substantiate the existence of Laozi's Dao.
Similarly, the 'Big Bang' theory of our scientists also remains like Dao, just a concept.
So we have not done better than Laozi in explaining the existence of the universe.
In search of the universal truth, Laozi has left a most important legacy with us.

The spirit of 'Dao' may yet unite all humankind in the quest for the Ultimate Reality.

Laozi's Concepts

Concept of De (德, the Primal Virtue)

De (means 'virtue') is the second topic explored in Laozi's book; hence, the classic name, *Dao De Jing*. Traditional virtues like Benevolence and Righteousness are regarded as curses of humankind (ch.19). Counter-intuitively, Laozi suggests primal virtues like Nurturing, Humility and Not-contesting.

Primal virtues are Nurturing, Not-possessive, Not-presumptuous, Not-dictatorial.
生之畜之	Create it nourish it
生而不有	Create and not possessing
为而不恃	Accomplish but not presumptuous
长而不宰	Senior but not controlling (life and death)
是谓玄德	These are called primal virtues (ch.10)

Primal virtues also include Humility by taking the female role in support.
By taking responsibility for the prevention of errors, and bearing the disgrace from mistakes made
知其雄, 守其雌	Knowing the male (role), hold the female (role)
知其白, 守其黑	Knowing the white (right), hold the black (wrong)
知其荣, 守其辱	Knowing the honor, hold the disgrace (ch.28)

Virtuous acts should not have ulterior motives, else such actions have no genuine virtue.
上德不德, 是以有德	High Virtue, not claiming virtue hence has virtue
下德不失德, 是以无德	Low Virtue, not losing virtue hence has no virtue (ch.38)

Virtue in respond to injustice is suggested to break up the vicious cycle of revenge and retaliation.
报怨以德	Repay injustice with virtue (kindness) (ch.63)

Not-contesting is a virtue that is common among all who are good in their own capacity in life.
Be it the scholar, the warrior, the winner, the employer, and so on.
善为士者, 不武	Whoever good at being a scholar, not violent
善战者, 不怒	Whoever good at fighting-wars, never angry
善胜敌者, 不与	Whoever good at overcoming the enemy, never engage
善用人者, 为之下	Whoever good employing people, be humble
是谓不争之德	This is termed the Virtue of not contesting (ch.68)

And Thrift is observed to be a most powerful virtue in the management of people.
治人事天, 莫若啬	Manage people, serve Heaven, none like Thrift (ch.59)

Conventional virtues like Benevolence and Righteousness make demands on the charity of others. They are not our inherent rights and are outside our control; hence, they are not dependable. Whereas Dao's primal virtues like Nurturing, Humility, Not-contesting are demands of ourselves. These are our inherent capabilities and within our control; hence, can be depended upon. Cultivation of virtues starts with self, then extends outward to family, the nation and the world.

De's demand of self-discipline from each individual, forms the basis of pacific Daoism.

Laozi's Concepts

Concepts of Wu (无, Have-not) and You (有, Have)

Besides Dao and De, Laozi defines 2 more entities to help explain existence of the universe.

The beginning of Heaven and Earth is Wu (Have-not) and the mother of all things is You (Have)!
Laozi bravely declares they are derivatives of Dao, to be examined to understand the universe!

道可道, 非恒道	Dao can be described, not absolute Dao
名可名, 非恒名	Name can be named, not absolute name
无, 名天地之始	Wu (Have-not), to name the beginning of Heaven and Earth
有, 名万物之母	You (Have), to name the mother of all things
故恒无, 欲以观其妙	Hence, absolute Wu (Have-not), if wishes to observe wonders of Dao
恒有, 欲以观其徼	Absolute You (Have), if wishes to observe manifestations of Dao
此两者, 同出而异名	These 2 entities, same source but differently named
同谓之玄	Both said to be mysterious
玄之又玄	Mystery upon mystery
众妙之门	Door-way to all wonders (ch.1)

These 2 concepts are correlatives, showing a mutually exclusive relationship

有无相生	You (Have) and Wu (Have-not) are correlatives in creation (ch.2)

Laozi clearly states here that all things of the universe are created by the entity You (Have)!
That You (Have) can be created from Wu (Have-not)!

天下万物生于有	In the world, all things are created from You (Have)
有生于无	You (Have) is created from Wu (Have-not) (ch.40)

That Wu (Have-not) and You (Have) combined is (Dao) which can go into all things!

无有入无间	Wu (Have-not) and You (Have) (equal Dao) enter no space (ch.43)

That the universe begins with You (Have), which, hence, is the mother of the universe!

天下有始, 以为天下母	The world begins with You (Have), is mother of the world (ch.52)

Laozi is probably correct to say that in the beginning there is Wu (Have-not).
Laozi observes that from the 'empty' bellows, 'something' is pushed out to work the fire.
But he has not clarified exactly how Wu (Have-not) can be transformed to You (Have)!
Admittedly, Wu and You are rather crude derivative concepts that Laozi uses to construct the universe.
When Dao, the source, cannot be substantiated, it is rather hopeless trying to substantiate its derivatives

Wu (Have-not) and You (Have) are improbable derivative concepts of Dao for constructing the universe.

Concept of Naming

In the Chinese tradition, names are not just vocal utterance, but have attached meanings.
Sun, moon, flower, righteousness, humility, any word can be used as a name.
King Liu Bang from the land of Han, named his imperial dynasty, Han, when he became emperor.

Laozi postulates formation of the primal entity, then agonizes in naming it.
Arbitrarily he calls it Dao (meaning 'path'), then the next moment suggests calling it Big.

有物浑成	There are matters that mixed and formed
先天地生	Created before Heaven and Earth
寂兮寥兮	Silent indeed rarefied (formless) indeed
独立而不改	Alone stand and not change
周行而不殆	Moving in cycles and not in danger (of stopping)
可以为天下母	Can be the mother of the World
吾不知其名	I do not know its name
字之曰道	In word call it Dao
强为之名曰大	Force to naming it, call it Big (ch.25)

Laozi cannot see Dao, hear it or hold it.
And he wonders whether to call it Unseen, Rarefy or Micro!

视之不见, 名曰夷	Look at it (Dao) and see not, name it Unseen
听之不闻, 名曰希	Listen to it and hear not, name it Rarefy
搏之不得, 名曰微	Grasp it and hold not, name it Micro (ch.14)

Laozi perceives that Dao has no desires, hence Dao can also be named Tiny.
Clothes and nourishes all things, yet Dao is master of none; hence, Dao may be named Great.

衣养万物, 而不为主	Clothes and nourishes all things, but Dao will not be their master
恒无欲	Dao have no desires
可名于小	Can be named Tiny
万物归焉,而不为主	All things subjected (to Dao), but Dao will not be their master
可名为大	Can be named Great (ch.34)

Dao is invisible; hence, may be named Nameless.

道隐无名	Dao invisible, has no name (ch.41)

In recognizing the uncertainty of naming, Laozi recognizes the hypothetical nature of Dao.
This is clearly declared in the first 2 lines of his *Dao De Jing*.

道可道, 非恒道	Dao can be described, not primal Dao
名可名, 非恒名	Name can be named, not primal name (ch.1)

The many names Laozi has considered for Dao reflect the many perceived attributes of Dao.
Naming is Laozi's way of expressing investigation of the nature of Dao through its many manifestations.

Through the uncertainty of naming, Laozi is really trying to convey the hypothetical nature of 'Dao'.

Concept of Correlatives

Correlative, adj. So related that each implies or complement the other.
Correlative, noun. Either one of two things, as two terms that are correlatives (Random House)
Laozi highlights correlative pairs as naturally occurring common phenomena.

When one comments that this is Beauty, the idea of what is not-Beauty must exist at the same time.
Similarly, when one has the concept of what is good, then what is not-good has already been conceived.

天下皆知美之为美	The world all know beauty as beauty
斯恶已	Therefore not-beauty is known
天下皆知善之为善	The world all know goodness as good
斯不善已	Therefore not-good is known (ch.2)

And correlatives occur in creation, in work, in forms, in inclinations, in harmony, in sequence, etc.
Correlatives are naturally occurring and are abound in life wherever we turn to.

故, 有无相生	Hence, You (Have) and Wu (Have-not) are correlatives in creations
难易相成	Difficulty and easiness are correlatives in manifestations
长短相形	Long and short are correlatives in forms
高下相倾	High and low are correlatives in inclinations
音声相和	Tone and sound are correlatives in harmony
前后相随	Front and back are correlatives in sequence (ch.2)

Hence, Laozi philosophizes that we manage tasks with no bias against the long or short, high or low, etc.
That we create and not possess, achieve and not claim, for credit due will not be lost.

是以, 圣人处无为之事	Therefore, the Sage without bias manages tasks
行不言之教	Do non-verbal teaching (set good examples)
万物作而不辞	All things in action but makes no comment
生而不有	Creates but does not possesses
为而不恃	Achieves, but not presumptuous
功成而不居	Success achieves but takes no credit
夫唯不居	Only when does not take credit
是以不去	It (credit) does not go-away (ch.2)

In correlatives, Laozi highlights the many prejudices in our conduct of life.
However, correlatives are naturally occurring phenomena and are common in all spheres of human life.
Each member of a correlative pair is a natural consequence of the other.
Thus, Laozi philosophizes that we should not have prejudice against the beautiful or the not-beautiful.

Correlatives have inspired Laozi to make "Respect for all", a great principle of pacific Daoism.

Laozi's thoughts

On Benevolence (Ren, 仁), Righteousness (Yi, 义), Etiquette (Li, 礼)

Benevolence, Righteousness and Etiquette are traditional values establish long before Laozi.
They are extolled in older books like the Yi Jing (**易 经**), Book of History (尚书) and Book of Poems (诗经).

Hence Laozi's disapproval of these core values of ancient times is not an attack on Confucianism.
Furthermore, Laozi and the *DDJ* arguably predates Confucius and Confucianism.

绝圣弃智	End sage-hood abandon intelligence
民利百倍	Citizens benefit 100-fold
绝仁弃义	End benevolence abandon righteousness
民复孝慈	Citizens return to filial love (ch.19)

Here, Laozi gives his reason for rating the primal virtue of Dao higher.
It is because Benevolence, Righteousness and Etiquette are practiced with ulterior motives.

上德, 不德, 是以有德	High Virtue, not claiming virtue, hence has virtue
下德, 不失德, 是以无德	Low Virtue, not losing virtue, hence has no virtue
上仁为之, 而无以为	High Benevolence takes action, but has no motive
上义为之, 而有以为	High Righteousness takes action, and has motive
上礼为之, 而莫之应	High Etiquette takes action, and having no response
则攘臂而扔之	Will stretch arm to *pull* (people to comply) (ch.38)

When Dao is lost, Benevolence, Righteousness and Etiquette are promoted.
Laozi thinks that having to promote them signals the beginning of chaos and stupidity.
For their practice depend on the charity of others and are opened to bias and abuse.

故, 失道, 而后德	Hence, lost Dao, then comes Virtue
失德, 而后仁	Lost Virtue, then comes Benevolence
失仁, 而后义	Lost Benevolence, then comes Righteousness
失义, 而后礼	Lost Righteousness, then comes Etiquette
夫礼者, 忠信之薄	This Etiquette entity, thin in loyalty and trust
而乱之首	The beginning of disorder
前识者, 道之华	The preceding known *entities*, Dao's flowery-facets
而愚之始	The beginning of stupidity (ch.38)

Therefore, Laozi prefers the primal virtues of Dao, such as humility, less-selfishness, and less-desires.

见素, 抱朴	Show plainness, embrace original-self
少私, 寡欲	Lessen selfishness, reduce desire (ch.19)

Benevolence, Righteousness, and Etiquette are demands of individuals to help others out of charity.
These are secondary virtues not easy to control, and abuses are common in charity works.
Benevolence, righteousness and etiquette are just symptomatic treatment of social failures.
Whereas Laozi is recommending Daoism; primal virtues that basically produce no illnesses of society.
In the perfect world of Dao, there is no need for Benevolence, Righteousness, and Etiquette.
Cultivating humility, less selfishness, less desires are all within control of the individuals.
The individuals practicing Daoism will be self sufficient and need make no demands of others.

Laozi promotes self-discipline and self-reliance, rather than Benevolence, Righteousness, and Etiquette.

Laozi's thoughts

On Contentment

The contented person is a happy person.
Hence, much unhappiness among us may be avoided when we stop seeking ever more.

Laozi rightly says, whoever is contented has abundant wealth.
Ambition may be pursued without losing sight of ethical direction and we can survive long.
Long after one's physical death, when remembered for good deeds done, one has true longevity.

知足者富	Whoever knows contentment has abundant wealth
强行者有志	Whoever who forces action has ambition
不失其所者久	Whoever has not lost life-direction will last long
死而不亡者寿	Whoever is dead but not forgotten is long-lived (ch.33)

Laozi warns the individual of the danger of chasing glory and wealth to the detriment of health and life.
Know contentment and when to stop in our pursuit of glory and wealth to avoid disgrace and danger.

名与身孰亲？	Name (fame) versus body (life), which is dearer ?
身与货孰多？	Body versus goods which is more (important) ?
得与亡孰病？	Gain versus loss (of life) which is sick ?
是故:	Therefore:
甚爱必大费	Much love certainly big expenses
多藏必厚亡	Much hoarding, certainly much loss
知足不辱	Know contentment, not be disgraced
知止不殆	Know the limit, not be endanger
可以长久	Can be long and lasting (in survival) (ch.44)

Laozi warns of the disastrous consequences when rulers are not contented and started expansionism wars.
He declares, no disaster is greater than being not contented, and no crime is greater than the desire to possess.

天下有道	The world has Dao
却走马以粪	Walk horses with manure (to fertilize the fields)
天下无道	The world has no Dao
戎马生于郊	War horses give birth in the country-side
祸莫大于不知足	Disaster never greater than not knowing contentment
咎莫大于欲得	Crime never greater than desire to possess
故:	Hence:
知足之足	Knowing contentment in the truly contented
恒足已	Always contented indeed (ch.46)

To individuals, Laozi warns of danger in their incessant pursuit of glory and wealth.
To rulers, he warns of the disastrous consequences of wars in their desire to possess more by expansionism.

On Fame and Wealth

To gain fame and wealth is almost the universal wish of all individuals, and hence, needs no encouragement. So what is needed is a reminder that there is danger in the blind pursuit of fame and wealth.

For it is not possible to guard and keep great wealth even if you can acquire it.
金玉滿堂	Gold and jade filling the hall
莫之能守	None who can guard it (ch.9)

Hence contentment is key to stopping our insatiable desires for more.
知足者富	Whoever knows contentment has abundance (ch.33)

Laozi has not failed to warn of the danger to life and property if one knows no limit in such pursuits.
名与身孰亲？	Name (fame) versus body (life), which is dearer ?
身与货孰多？	Body versus goods which is more (important) ?
得与亡孰病？	Gain versus loss which is sick ?
是故:	Therefore:
甚爱必大费	Much love (fame) certainly big expenses
多藏必厚亡	Much hoarding, certainly much loss
知足不辱	Know contentment, not be disgrace
知止不殆	Know the limit, not be endanger
可以长久	Can be long and lasting (in survival) (ch.44)

Laozi also warns of the disastrous consequences when rulers seek fame through expansionism and wars.
天下有道	The world has Dao
却走马以粪	Walk horses with manure (to fertilize the fields)
天下无道	The world has no Dao
戎马生于郊	War horses give birth in the country-side
祸, 莫大于不知足	Disaster, never greater than not knowing contentment
咎, 莫大于欲得	Crime, never greater than desire to possess (ch.46)

He chastises rulers as heads of robbers for enjoying excesses, while neglecting the welfare of their people.
朝甚除	Palace steps very high (grand building)
田甚芜	Crop fields very grass-overgrown
仓甚虚	The granary nearly empty
服文采	Cloth in finery (lords and kings)
带利剑	Carry sharp swords
厌饮食	Over-indulge in food and wine
财货有余	Wealth and goods possession in excess
是谓盗竽	They are chiefs of robbers
非道也哉！	Not in accord with Dao indeed (ch.53)

Laozi warns, relentless pursuit of fame and wealth is dangerous for both rulers and individuals.

Laozi's thoughts

On Fears and Crises

With all the insecurity of life, it is important that we are prepared to handle fears and crises.
We certainly welcome advice from the *Dao De Jing* on this matter.

Our greatest fear is personal safety, when faced with life and death situations.
If we are ready to sacrifice our lives, then what problem is there?

吾所以有大患者	The reason that I have big trouble
为吾有身	Is because I have a body (self)
及吾无身	When I have no body (willing to sacrifice self)
吾有何患？	What trouble do I have ? (ch.13)

Hence, to minimize worry of our own safety, we should not contest in all actions and antagonize nobody.
夫唯不争, 故无尤　　Indeed only not contesting, hence no rivalry (ch.8)

In confrontational situations, we should yield first to preserve ourselves, and survive to fight another day.
曲则全　　Bend and be whole (preserved)
枉则直　　Incriminated and be straightened (vindicated) (ch.22)

Long-term, we should be contented and know when to stop our desires for glory and wealth to avoid danger.
祸, 莫大于不知足　　Disaster, never greater than not knowing contentment ,
咎, 莫大于欲得　　Crime, never greater than desire to possess (ch.46)

If we indulge in our desires without limit, then we are doomed for life
开其兑, 济其事　　Open the portals, promote the affairs (of desires)
终身, 不救　　Life-long, not be saved (ch.52)

Furthermore, if we are to be arrogant in our plenty, we are sowing the seed of our own downfall.
富贵而骄　　Rich and noble but arrogant
自遗其咎　　Self-bequeath own destruction (ch.9)

We should tackle our problems in the beginning when they are small and easy.
We should be careful from beginning till end to ensure no failure
图难于其易, 为大于其细　　Plan for difficult when it is easy, do the big when it is small (ch.63)
慎终如始, 则无败事　　Careful at finish as at beginning, then no fail project (ch.64)

When disaster strike, we should have hope that there is always something good coming out of it.
祸兮, 福之所倚　　Misfortune indeed, where good fortune depends (ch.58)

The *Dao De Jing* has not only given instruction for action to take in time of crisis.
It also advice not-contesting, minimal desires as a way of life to pre-empt crises.
Furthermore, when misfortune has struck, it offers hope that something good will come out of it!

Laozi's advices for facing fears and handling crises are pragmatic, not supernatural.

Laozi's thoughts

On Femininity Appreciated

Laozi is highly appreciative of femininity.

He observes the never ending part play by the female in reproduction.
Hence, he salutes woman as "the foundation of Heaven and Earth'.

玄牝之门	The mysterious female's doorway
是谓天地根	Is said to be foundation of Heaven and Earth (ch.6)

Laozi hypothesizes the self-existence of Dao and its creation of the universe.
Saying, Dao has taken the role of a mother for the world.

周行而不殆	Cyclical in progress and not in danger (of stopping)
可以为天下母	(Dao) Can be the mother of the World (ch.25)

Laozi also observes that woman often in quietude is more level-headed than man.

牝恒以靜胜牡	The female always by quietude triumphs the male
以靜为下	By quietude be low (humble) (ch.61)

Hence, he asks if we can embrace femininity and not be confrontational in world affairs.

天门开阖	Heaven's door open and close (affairs of the world)
能为雌乎？	Possible to assume the female (mother role)? (ch.10)

The dominant male should also be as gentle as the female, unobtrusive like the little stream.
In today's language, everyone can appreciate a boss who does not boss people around.
But rather be like a mother who takes good care of the staff.

知其雄	Knowing the male (dominant position)
守其雌	Hold the female (support position)
为天下谿	Be the world's creek (small stream) (ch.28)

The selfless care and devotion of a mother to her children.
The gentle traits of woman are preferred to the macho behaviors of man.
These are positive attributes of femininity that Laozi observes and appreciates.

Appreciaiton of femininity shapes Laozi's philosophy of gentleness and non-violence.

Laozi's thoughts

On Freedom

Freedom is the sacred inherent right of all individuals and of all things in the universe.
Is Freedom respected under Dao and Daoism as Laozi perceives and has written in the *Dao De Jing*?

Laozi observes that Dao creates and nurture, but claims no ownerships.
That is, freedom of all things are inherent from Dao, the hypothetical primal entity.

万物恃之, 而生而不辞	All things depend on Dao to exist, but Dao will not speaks of it
衣养万物, 而不为主	Clothes and nourishes all things, but Dao will not be their master
万物归焉, 而不为主	All things subjected to Dao, but Dao will not be their master (ch.34)

Laozi insists that nobody can succeed ruling the world like it is one's own private property.
Implying that the freedom of the world and all things is sacred.

将欲取天下而为之	Wishing to take the world and govern it
吾见其不得已	I see that cannot be done
天下神器	The world a sacred instrument
不可为也	Cannot be manage indeed
为者败之	Whoever tries will fail it
执者失之	Whoever holds on will lose it (ch.29)

The Sage has no personal agenda but the citizens' agenda.
Hence, to govern is to serve.

圣人无恒心	The Sage has no absolute heart (wishes)
以百姓心为心	But embraced the people's heart (wishes) for self (ch.49)

And the Sage says that only one who cares and takes responsibility is qualified to rule.

受国之垢, 是谓社稷主	Whoever bears nation's dirt, is hailed master of society
受国不祥, 是谓天下王	Whoever bears nation's misfortune, is hailed King of the world (ch.78)

Laozi likewise advises the individual to meditate and cultivate selflessness for the conduct of world affairs
That is, all individuals should respect the inherent freedom of others and all things

爱民治国	Love the citizen and manage the state
能无为乎?	Possible without self-agenda?
天门开阖	Heaven's door open and close (affairs of the world)
能为雌乎?	Possible to assume the female (mother role)?
明白四达	Clear understanding in 4 corners (of the world)
能无知乎?	Possible not aware of knowledge (its power for self gain)? (ch.10)

Clearly as perceived by Laozi, all things are free under Dao, the primal entity.
There is no suggestion of worshiping Dao thereby turning Daoism into a religion.
The Sage and rulers are there to serve the people, and to respect the inherent freedom of all things.
Individuals are encouraged to meditate and cultivate the perceived traits of Dao, or pacific Daoism.

Total freedom for all individuals and all things are inherent in pacific Daoism.

Laozi's thoughts

On Greatness

Everything aspires to be great, as perceived "Greatness" can win admiration, fame and wealth. However, the "true Greatness" lauded in the *Dao De Jing* seems quite the opposite kind.

Dao's Greatness: it creates all things, but master of none, and never claim greatness.

万物归焉, 而不为主	All things subjected to Dao, but Dao will not be their master
可名为大	Can be named Great
以其终不自为大	Because Dao ultimately does not deem itself as Great
故, 能成其大	Hence, can complete its greatness (ch.34)

天下皆谓我道大, 似不肖	The world all say my Dao is great, seems no resemblance (of Greatness)
夫唯大, 故似不肖	Indeed because it is great, hence, seems no resemblance (of Greatness)
若肖, 久已其细也夫!	If resembles, long then Dao is small indeed! (ch.67)

Universe's Greatness: in the dark outer-space, its vastness knows no boundary, no sound, and no form.

大方无隅	Great Square has no border
大音希声	Great Tone gives faint sound,
大象无形	Great Image has no form (ch.41)

Society's Greatness: similarly, are not seen, heard or felt.
For example, great skill seems deceptively clumsy, and great debater seems deceptively inarticulate.

大成, 若缺; 其用, 不弊	Great success, seems deficient; its use, not flawed
大盈, 若冲; 其用, 不穷	Great fullness, seems charging (air from bellows); its use, not exhaustible
大直, 若屈	Great straightness, seems bent
大巧, 若拙	Great skill, seems clumsy
大辩, 若讷	Great debater, seems inarticulate (ch.45)

The Sage never try to be great, but through multiple small tasks done well, ultimately achieve Greatness.

图难于其易, 为大于其细	Plan for difficulty when it is easy, do the big when it is small
天下难事, 必作于易	The world's difficult affairs, should be done when it is easy
天下大事, 必作于细	The big affairs in the world, should be done by starting small
是以:	Therefore:
圣人终不为大, 故能成其大	The Sage till the end does not do it big, hence can achieve it big (ch.63)

In the *Dao De Jing*, true Greatness is never about self glorification and self gain.
Emulating Dao, Greatness is all about contributing and working for the common good of all.
Hence, everyone has a chance to achieve "true Greatness" by using our individual talent for the common good.
While by conventional standard, few can achieve "Greatness" by amassing great individual wealth and glory.

In pacific Daoism, true Greatness is about contributing to the common good, not about individual glory.

Laozi's thoughts

On Happiness of the Daoist

Every individual desires happiness, and nothing is wrong with this desire.
The *Dao De Jing* teaches pacific Daoism.
So the Daoist finding pacific Daoism must be a happy individual.
How happy is the Daoist?

The Daoist conduct is inscrutable, but is ever-prepared, careful, and considerate of others.
Dignify in appearance, gentle in manner, honest, broad-minded, common, mixing-in with the crowd.

古之善为道者	In ancient time, persons good at practicing Dao
豫兮若冬涉川	Prepared indeed like in winter crossing a river
犹兮若畏四邻	Hesitant indeed like fearful of the neighbors
俨兮其若客	Dignify indeed like the guest
涣兮其若冰之将释	Gentle indeed like ice on the verge of melting
敦兮其若朴	Sincere indeed like the simpleton
旷兮其若谷	Open-minded indeed like the valley
浑兮其若浊	Flow-together indeed like muddy (ch.15)

The Daoist seems dull and unexciting, lonely and at a loss with the self.
However, the Daoist, with minimal desires is carefree, floating, relaxed as at sea or riding free on the wind.

众人熙熙	All the people talking happily
如享太牢	Like enjoying a sacrificial feast (of cattle, goat and pig)
如春登台	Like ascending the viewing tower of spring
我独泊兮其未兆	I alone park (at water-edge) with no sign (of celebration)
众人皆有余, 而我独若遗	The people all have surplus, but I alone like at a loss
俗人昭昭, 我独昏昏	Common people are most clear-minded, I alone am most dim-witted
俗人察察, 我独闷闷	Common people are most discerning, I alone am most boring
澹兮其若海, 飘兮若无止	Floating indeed like on open sea, riding on wind indeed like no limit
众人皆有以, 而我独顽似鄙	The people all have purpose, but I alone am stubborn and lowly (ch.20)

The Daoist cannot be intimated or distanced; cannot be corrupted, honored or debased.

不可得而亲	Cannot be had and be intimated
不可得而疏,	Cannot be had and be distanced
不可得而利	Cannot be had and be benefited
不可得而害	Cannot be had and be harmed
不可得而贵	Cannot be had and be honored
不可得而贱	Cannot be had and be debased (ch.56)

In the traditional sense, happiness is manifested in having great feast and party celebrations.
In reality, the expression of happiness is related to the set of values that the individual has.
Shutting out undesirable wants it appears that happiness of the Daoist is quite unconventional.
The Daoist prefers quietude, floating relaxed on the waves at sea or riding free with the winds in meditation.
Happiness is achieving inner peace with the self and harmony with the world.

The Daoist's happiness is inner peace and harmony, not power and advantages over others.

On Honesty

To be honest, to own up to one's ignorance and mistake, often require great courage.
In quest for the Ultimalte Reality, truthfullness is most valued, and Laozi is certainly not lack of it.

Laozi honestly declares that he cannot describes the primal Dao in the very first line of the *Dao De Jing*.
道可道, 非恒道　　　　　　If Dao can be described, it is not the primal Dao (ch.1)

And truthfully, Laozi repeatedly declares his ignorance about this primal entity that he has conceived.
吾不知谁之子　　　　　　I don't know whose child (Dao is)
象帝之先　　　　　　　　Preceding Emperor of Forms (Dao is formless) (ch.4)

吾不知其名, 字之曰道　　I do not know its name, addressing it call Dao
强为之, 名曰大　　　　　Force to do it, name and call it Great (ch.25)

So very often, with his other thoughts, he is not dogmatic, but honestly discuss and asks, " Is this not so?"
贵以贱为本, 高以下为基　　The Nobility is based on the Commoners, High is founded on the Low
是以侯王自谓, 孤, 寡, 不榖　Hence the Lords' and Kings' self-salutations, Lonely, Lacking, Grainless
此非以贱为本耶？非乎？　　Is this not with Humility as their base? Not at all? (ch.39)

Facing the uncertainties of Life and Nature, time and again, Laozi admits he cannot know the future.
祸兮, 福之所倚　　　　　Misfortune indeed, where good fortune depends
福兮, 祸之所伏　　　　　Good-fortune indeed, where misfortune lurks
孰知其极？　　　　　　　Who knows the limit? (ch.58)

天之所恶　　　　　　　　What Heaven dislike
孰知其故？　　　　　　　Who knows the reasons ? (ch.73)

Laozi calls pretension to knowledge when one is ignorant, lying, and it is a sickness.
知不知, 上　　　　　　　Knows not knowing, high
不知, 知, 病　　　　　　Not knowing, acts knowing, sick
圣人, 不病　　　　　　　The Sage, is not sick
以其病, 病　　　　　　　As the Sage is sick of, this sickness
是以, 不病　　　　　　　Therefore, (the Sage) is not sick (ch.71)

Finally, he warns that those who profess to know, really do not know!
知者, 不博　　　　　　　Whoever is well-known, is not knowledgeable
博者, 不知　　　　　　　Whoever is knowledgeable, is not well-known (ch.81)

Laozi has been truly honest and transparent with his ignorance and incompleteness of knowledge.
This cannot be said of our world today, especially of our financial and banking world.
The near melt-down of the financial system of the world had happened insideously in the year 2008.
And to date, there is no clear explanation, and there is nobody who has been held to account!

Rightly, Laozi regards honesty above all, and calls lying, a sickness to be avoided.

Laozi's thoughts

On Human Desires and Failings

Laozi says, indulgence of the senses is harmful.
五色, 令人目盲	Five colors, cause people's eyes blindness
五音, 令人耳聋	Five tones, cause people's ears deafness
五味, 令人口爽	Five flavors, cause people's mouths tasteless (ch.12)

Laozi says, self-promotion can be counter-productive
企者, 不立	Whoever is on tip-toe, cannot stand (firm)
跨者, 不行	Whoever is standing astride, cannot move (forward) (ch.24)

Laozi says, frivolity can have serious consequences, especially if your are the emperor.
奈何万乘之主	It is inexplicable why the master of ten thousand chariots
而以身轻天下？	Will in person slight the world (with frivolity)? (ch.26)

Laozi says, extravagances show you up as the Head, leading a bunch of robbers and thieves.
朝甚除, 田甚芜	Palace steps very high (grand building), crop fields very grass-overgrown
仓甚虚, 服文采	The granary nearly empty, cloth in finery (Lords and Kings)
带利剑, 厌饮食	Carry sharp swords, over-indulge in food and wine
财货有余	Wealth and goods possession in excess,
是谓盗夸	They are chiefs of robbers (ch.53)

Laozi says, ignorant of one's ignorance is a sickness.
知不知, 上	Knows not knowing, high
不知, 知, 病	Not knowing, acts knowing, sick (ch. 71)

Laozi says, rich and arrogant will only lead to self destruction.
富贵而骄,	Rich and noble but arrogant,
自遗其咎	Self bequeath own destruction (ch. 9)

Laozi says, obssessions and hoardings are expensive and can lead to great losses.
甚爱, 必大费	Much love, certainly big expenses
多藏, 必厚亡	Much hoarding, certainly much loss (ch.44)

Laozi says, the greatest disaster is discontentment and the greatest crime is the desire to possess.
祸,莫大于不知足	Disaster, never greater than not knowing contentment
咎,莫大于欲得	Crime, never greater than desire to possess (ch.46)

Laozi says, taking things easy and lightly promises will only bring problems to oneself later.
夫, 轻诺, 必寡信	Indeed, lightly promise, certainly lack trust
多易, 必多难	More easiness (early), certainly more difficulties (later) (ch.63)

Laozi says, the anti-dotes are:
见素, 抱朴	Show plainness, embrace original-self
少私, 寡欲	Lessen selfishness, reduce desire (ch.19)
圣人去甚, 去奢, 去泰	The Sage discards excesses, extravagance, extremes (ch.29)

On Humility

The embrace and practice of humility is certainly a corner-stone of pacific Daoism.

Beside not-contesting, Laozi admires the humility of water, in its willingness to occupy lowly positions.

上善若水	High goodness like water
水善, 利万物, 而不争	Water good, benefits all things, yet not contending
处众人之所恶	Resides where all people will hate (bottom)
故, 几于道	Hence, is rooted in Dao (ch.8)

Laozi also favours the humble female role in support, like the small stream, flowing low, irrigating the land.

知其雄, 守其雌	Knowing the male (role), hold the female (role)
为天下豀	Be the world's creek (small stream) (ch.28)
牝恒以静胜牡	The female always by quietude triumphs over the male
以静为下	By quietude be low (humble) (ch.61)

And he appreciates that with humility, big nations can peacefully gain the allegiance of small nations.

大国, 以下小国	Big nation, be humble to small nation
则取小国	Then gains (allegiance of) small nation
大者, 宜为下	Big nation, appropriate to initiate humility (ch.61)

Because they are low lying, the rivers and seas collect all water of the land.
Hence, Laozi urges rulers to do likewise, to rule with humility and gain the support of all their citizens.

江海, 所以能为百谷王者	Rivers and seas, reason for being kings of the hundred valleys
以其善下之	For they are good at being subservient
故能为百谷王	Hence can be kings of the hundred valleys
是以:	Therefore:
圣人, 欲上民	The Sage, wishing to be above citizens (as leader)
必以言下之	Must with language be subservient to them
欲先民	Wishing to be ahead of the citizens
必以身后之	Must with body be behind them (ch.66)

Between individuals, Laozi also observes that humility creates harmony and get things done.

善用人者, 为之下	Whoever good at employing people, be humble
是谓, 不争之德	This is termed, the Virtue of not contesting
是谓, 用人之力	This is termed, employing the people's strength (ch.68)

Humility harmonizes all human relationships, between individuals, and among nations.

Laozi's thoughts

On Life, Death & Survival

The issues of life, death and survival are matters of immediate concern in our daily life.
It should be enlightening to see what Laozi has to say about them.

Like little evergreen grass, the cycle of life-death goes on constantly and never ceases.
Life seems like a mission, and death seems like reporting back after mission has been accomplished.

夫物芸芸	Indeed all things like evergreen grass
各复归其根	Each again return to its root (in cycles of life and death)
归根曰静	Returned to its root is called Stillness
是谓复命	This is called fulfilling Destiny (ch.16)

Laozi observes that longevity, early death and premature death, each account for a third of all lives.
And premature deaths are due to living in excesses and risky behavior that gets one into harm's way.

生之徒十有三	Those who live long, 3 out of 10
死之徒十有三	Those who die early, 3 out of 10
人之生动之死地, 亦十有三	Those who live long but move into ground of death, also 3 out of 10
夫何故？	Why is this so ?
以其生之厚	Because of living in excesses
盖闻善摄生者	Have heard of individuals good at preserving life
陵行不遇兕虎	Walking in the hills, not meet with rhino, tiger
入军不被甲兵	In the army not get hurt by weapon
以其无死地	Because they avoid ground of death (ch.50)

When there are grave risks and danger, which is more important, life, or fame, or wealth?
Laozi would rather be contented and knows his limit, so as to achieve a sustainable life.

名与身孰亲？	Name (fame) versus body (life), which is dearer ?
身与货孰多？	Body versus goods (wealth) which is more (important) ?
得与亡孰病？	Gain versus loss which is sick ?
知足不辱	Know contentment, not be dishonor
知止不殆	Know the limit, not be endanger
可以长久	Can be long and lasting (in survival) (ch.44)

Laozi thinks that we have big worries because we have our lives, reputation and wealth to protect.
If we are selfless with no big ego and no excess wealth, then we have no worry, we relax and survive.

何谓贵大患若身？	Why says take seriously big trouble because of self?
吾所以有大患者	The reason that I have big trouble
为吾有身	Is because I have a body (self)
及吾无身	When I have no body (ready to sacrifice, selfless)
吾有何患？	What trouble do I have? (ch.13)

Laozi observes that life-death is cyclical and death awaits for all things at the end.
That premature death is preventable if people avoid excessive lifestyles and avoid unnecessary risks.
So be contented, know the limits and do not endangered yourself by chasing fame and hoarding wealth.

Glory and wealth endanger; rather, be contented and enjoy the carefree life of a daoist.

On Meditation

In Laozi's time, people received guidance from asking questions of the Book of Change (易经 Yijing). In addition, Laozi himself seems to get his inspiration and revelation through meditative thinking.

Compose body and mind, breath like a child and banish all supernatural thoughts.
Then cultivate the mind with thoughts of love for people and country with unselfish motives.
With thoughts of discharging worldly affairs with the feminine touch of support and care.
With thoughts of using knowledge for the common good, unaware of its facility for self-gain

载营魄抱一	Compose body & mind to embrace One (Daoism)
能无离乎？	Possible not to stray away (from Dao) ?
专气至柔	Focus on the breath till gentleness (achieve)
能如婴儿乎？	Possible to be like the baby ?
涤除玄览	Wash and remove mysterious visions (supernatural thoughts)
能无疵乎？	Possible without blemishes ?
爱民治国	Love the citizen and manage the state
能无为乎？	Possible without self-agenda?
天门开阖	Heaven's door open and close (affairs of the world)
能为雌乎？	Possible to assume the female (mother role) ?
明白四达	Clear understanding in 4 reaches (all knowledgeable)
能无知乎？	Possible not aware of knowledge (its power for self gain)? (ch.10)

Meditating with absolute clarity of mind in an extremely quiet ambience.
Revelation of the life & death cycle is repeatedly realized.
Knowledge of the inevitability of death causes the experience of closure with one's life.
Causes one to mature, to mellow; causes one to be accommodating and to be fair in all of one's actions.

至虚极	Reach emptiness at its limit (clear the mind)
守静笃	Hold stillness seriously (maintain the clear mind)
万物并作	The myriad things simultaneously in action
吾以观复	This I have observed repeatedly
夫物芸芸	Indeed all things like evergreen grass
各复归其根	Each again return to its root (in cycles of life and death)
归根曰静	Returned to its root is called Stillness
是谓复命	This is called fulfilling Destiny
知常容	Knowing Death-inevitable, will be accommodating
容乃公	Being accommodating, will be fair (ch.16)

The 3-steps technique describes by Laozi for meditation is simple.
First, find a quiet place to compose the body and mind.
Second, breath like a child who is absolutely relaxed, free of all worldly cares.
Third, clear the mind of all desires and supernatural thoughts.
These are effective steps I use to calm myself when awaken in a cold sweat and fear at night.
These are effective steps I take to de-distress and stop any panic attacks I may have in daily life.
With this release of tension, perceived threats are not so big and problems not so difficult.

Relax in meditation, let good ideas flow; action is directed and crisis resolved.

Laozi's thoughts

On Not-Contesting (不争)

It is conventional wisdom to encourage contesting to win, to be leaders.
It is counter-intuitive to advise not-contesting as a way to success and happiness.

Laozi clearly sees that contesting starts when there is more to be gained.
Hence, he advises that the talented not to be exalted (i.e., overly rewarded).

不尚贤	Not valuing the virtuous-talented
使民不争	Causes citizens not to contest (ch.3)

Water nourishes and benefits all things, yet is yielding and not contesting in nature.
Likewise in human society, Laozi observes that those not-contesting have less frictions with others.

水善利万物而不争	Water good benefits all things yet not contesting
夫唯不争, 故无尤	Indeed only not contesting, hence no differences (rivalries) (ch.8)

Self-effacing the Sage has no stress or pressure to live up to unnecessary high standards.
Not contesting, the Sage meets with no contest to his leadership.

不自见, 故明	Not self-centered, hence enlightened
不自是, 故彰	Not self-righteous, hence illustrious
夫唯不争	Indeed because not contending
故天下莫能与之争	Hence in the world none can engage in contention with (ch.22)

The reason is, the rule of the self-effacing Sage does not burden or harm the citizens.

圣人居上而民不重	The Sage sitting on high and citizens not burdened
居前而民不害	Leading up-front and citizens not harmed (ch.66)

The good scholar, the good warrior, the good winner and the good employer.
Their best is brought out by their common virtue of not-contesting.

善为士者, 不武	Whoever good at being a scholar, not violent
善战者, 不怒	Whoever good at fighting-wars, never angry
善胜敌者, 不与	Whoever good at overcoming the enemy, never engage
善用人者, 为之下	Whoever good employing people, be humble (ch.68)

Significantly, the last 2 words in the *Dao De Jing* is not-contesting.

为而不争	Action but not contesting (ch.81)

Contesting is rather brutal, it creates a zero sum game where there is a loser for every victor!
Conventional wisdom may perceive not-contesting as weakness, and it may even be despised.
However, non-aggression is not weakness, for a pacifist can be fearless - but only in defense.
The most important advantage in not-contesting, is that one is not stressed and the mind is clear.
One is calm and relaxed, at peace with self, with others, and with the world.
The best result may yet be achieved under this ideal stress-free condition for performance.
It is better to gain by new creations, than by contesting others for what is already created.
When all individuals accept and practice not-contesting, there will be paradise on earth.

Not-contesting is indeed a pillar of principles in pacific Daoism.

Laozi's thoughts

On Paradoxes

A Paradox is a statement seemingly self-contradictory or absurd but expressing a possible truth.
Paradoxes abound in the *DDJ*, recording realities in life that are unconventional and counter-intuitive.

"Bend and be whole", such paradoxical statements make sense when one pauses to think a little bit more.
Like yielding to robbers to preserve lives on the spot, then report them to authority to get them punished.

曲则全	Bend and be whole (preserved) (ch.22)

"Without stepping out, knows the world", such paradoxical statement are defensible.
By studying the written archive, an individual may know about a country even before visiting it.

不出戶, 知天下	Without stepping-out the door, knows the world
不窥牖, 见天道.	Not looking out the window, sees Heaven's way (ch.47)

However, to deny citizens of enlightenment for ease of control, is not a defensible paradox.
By our enlightened 21st century standard, it is a violation of basic human rights.

古之善为道者	Ancient person good at practicing Dao
非以明民	Not by enlightening the people
将以愚之	But keeps them ignorant
民之难治	People are difficult to manage
以其智多	Because they have much cleverness (ch.65)

It is counter-intuitive to refer to the use of emptiness, to the weak overcoming the strong and such.
However, Laozi does acknowledge his unconventionality when he says positive sayings seem negative.

无之以为用	Empty it, to be of use (ch.11)
知其雄, 守其雌	Knowing the male (role), hold the female (role) (ch.28)
弱之胜强	The weak triumph over the strong (ch.78)
正言若反	Positive sayings seems negative (ch.78)

In fact Laozi anticipates misunderstanding, expecting lesser scholars to laugh at his sayings!

上士闻道, 勤而行之	The high scholar learn of Dao, diligently practice it
中士闻道, 若存若亡	The average scholar learn of Dao, like existing like not existing
下士闻道, 大笑之	The lesser scholar learn of Dao, loudly laugh at it
不笑不足以为道	Without laughing, not (silly) enough to be Dao (ch.41)

Laozi has postulated invisible Dao, the primal entity, to account for the visible universe.
Dao appears empty like the bellows which 'produces' energy that is inexhaustible for the fire.
Dao is perceived to have created the universe gently and silently, taking no credit, no ownership.
The seemingly negative attributes of Dao make Laozi appreciates the negative aspects of all things.
He is convinced that, like water, the weak and gentle will triumph over the strong and hard.
Hence, he favors yielding, not-contesting, and assuming the supportive role of the female.
Not attacking in war but rather retreating in defense to ensure minimal loss of life and destruction.
Believes and actions that are contrary to the accepted norms of positive, go-for-it types of mentality.
The paradoxes of Daoism often make sense and are more conducive to world peace and harmony.
But not all paradoxes are defensible and denying people of an education is certainly not one of them.

Paradoxically, the counter-intuitive Laozi reminds us, the positive aspects of negativity.

Laozi's thoughts

On Problems and difficulties

In life, it is often said that 90% of times, we suffer problems and difficulties, and we are not happy.
So what does the *DDJ* say that can help us reverse such unhealthy circumstances?

合抱之木, 生于毫末	Trees of large girth, grow from micro seed
九层之台, 起于累土	Tower of 9-stories, rise from accumulated earth
千里之行, 始于足下	Journey of thousand miles, starts beneath the feet (ch.64)

The forest giant grows from an acorn, and the journey of a thousand miles is accomplished step by step.

图难于其易; 为大于其细	Plan the difficult when it is easy; do the big when it is small
天下难事, 必作于易	The world's difficult affairs, should be done when it is easy
天下大事, 必作于细	The big affairs in the world, should be done by starting small
圣人终不为大, 故能成其大	The Sage till the end does not do it big, hence can achieve it big (ch.63)

Hence, the Sage never attempts Big, but makes easy and small efforts, that accumulate into something Big!

夫, 轻诺, 必寡信	Indeed, lightly promise, certainly lack trust
多易, 必多难	More easiness (early), certainly more difficulties (later) (ch.63)

Do not make easy promises, then we don't have the extra problems of honoring them later.

其安易持; 其未兆易谋	Things stable, easy to manage; no sign (of problem), easy to prevent (ch.64)

It is easy to take pre-emptive measures when things are stable and before there is any sign of problem.

其脆易破; 其微易散	Brittle is easy to break; micro is easy to scatter
为之于未有; 治之于未乱	Action before it (problem) exists; manage it before turmoil (starts) (ch.64)

The brittle breaks and the micro-size disperses, so be mindful of potential problems and take precautions.

民之从事	The people working on a project
恒于几成, 而败之	Often near finishing, then fail it
慎终如始	Careful at finish as at beginning
则无败事	Then no fail project (ch.64)

Often the cause of failure in daily tasks is that people take care at the start but are careless towards the end.

圣人犹难之, 故终无难已	The Sage expects it's difficult, hence ultimately no difficulty indeed (ch.63)

As the Sage does not take it easy on any task and put in extra efforts, the Sage has no difficulties.

The *DDJ* offers great insights as to where many of our problems and difficulties come from.
Forest giants grow from acorns, 1000-miles journeys from first step, are images of the Big, achieved stepwise.
Hence the Sage avoids big difficult tasks, but through small easy efforts, makes big achievement.
The *DDJ* warns us not to make promises easily, giving ourselves extra problems in fulfilling them later.
It warns us to recognise potential problems, like glass will break, hence, we are to take precautions.
It also warns that failure in our daily life is often due to carelessness towards the end of our tasks.
Hence, learn from the Sage who treats all tasks as difficult, put in extra effort, and hence has no difficulties.

Plan small, no easy promises, be vigilant, are ways to reduce our oft self-inflicted problems and difficulties.

Laozi's thoughts

On Purpose of Life

Especially when we are unhappy, we invariably ask, "What is the purpose of life?"
Is there any enlightenment from the *Dao De Jing*?

Laozi says, in the beginning of Heaven and Earth, there is nothing.
无, 名天地之始　　　　　　Wu (Have-not), to name the beginning of Heaven & Earth (ch.1)

He postulates Dao, that exists before Heaven and Earth.
有物浑成, 先天地生　　　　Have matters (Dao) mixed and formed, exists before Heaven & Earth (ch.25)

He also perceives that Dao creates and nurtures all things, but Dao is master of none
衣, 养万物, 而不为主　　　　Clothes, nourishes all things, but (Dao) not be master (ch.34)

And that Dao takes all actions for no selfish motives.
道恒, 无为, 而无不为　　　　Dao primal, with no motive, then nothing will not do (ch.37)

Laozi suggests that we should emulate Dao, and not cling to personal wealth and glory.
金玉满堂, 莫之能守　　　　Gold and jade filling the hall, none who can guard (ch.9)
功遂身退, 天之道　　　　　Success achieves, self retires, way of Heaven (ch.9)

He concludes that the way to go is by acting to benefit, not to harm and not to contest.
天之道, 利而不害　　　　　Way of Heaven, benefit and not harming (ch.81)
圣人之道, 为而不争　　　　Way of the Sage, action but not contesting (ch.81)

Laozi says we are all free people as Dao never claim to be master and demand no worship.
Our purpose in life is not to accumulate wealth or to win glory.
Laozi is wise to say we need no unnecessary stress; we need not pitch against each other to excel.
Rather, we should act to benefit, not to harm and not in contest.
Emulating Dao, we should be unselfish in all actions.

Science tells us, the universe is 93 billion light-years across. (Wolframalpha.com)
The age of the universe is computed to be 13.7 billion years, time lapsed since the last Big Bang.
By October 2011, the latest estimate puts us passed 7 billions, all riding on the surface of the Earth.
Spinning in the darkness of space, on a journey to nowhere (see book cover).
So, what is the purpose of it all?
Till this day, the truth is, nobody knows.
We do not know the beginning, neither will we know the end, at any time soon.
And hard science does reveal, that we are just bags of genes (DNA) that know of our own existence.
Each of us is here by accident, when a random sperm cell unite with an egg cell.
So while here on earth, let us make ourselves comfortable by our own labor, and not at the expense of others.
This is our humble purpose of life; for really, we are not borned to be burdened with this or that mission.

Hence, we should work together for the benefit of all.
In complementary harmony for we have different talents.
Not in contest, for contest will lead to winners and losers, strife and rivalry, misery and sadness.
And this is how we can achieve our humble purpose of life, as Laozi says:
无为, 而无不为　　　　　　Not selfish, in all our actions (ch.48)

Life is an accident really, so let's live by our own labor, share and enjoy life in harmony with others.

Laozi's thoughts

On Retribution

Living in the feudal system of his time, Laozi must has observed much injustice in society.
The oppression of the people by the ruling class.
The strong and the powerful taking advantage of the weak.
So what thoughts does Laozi have on matters of justice and injustice?

Laozi admits not knowing Heaven's like or dislike, for to act or not to act, the result is unpredictable.
But he believes that Heaven's justice net never leaks and retribution will be meted out in due course.

勇于敢, 则杀	Brave to dare, then get kill
勇于不敢, 则活	Brave to not dare, then survive
天之所恶	What Heaven dislike
孰知其故？	Who knows the reasons ?
天网恢恢	Heaven's net far and wide
疏而不失	Widely-meshed but do not leak (ch.73)

Oppressed people fear no death; hence, cannot be governed by the threat of death.
Well-governed and well-off people fear death; hence, can be governed by threat of the death punishment.

民不畏死	The citizens do not fear death
奈何以死惧之？	Then why use death to threaten them ?
若使民恒畏死	If can cause citizens to constantly fear death
而为奇者	And whoever commits strangeness (crime)
吾得执而杀之, 孰敢？	I will catch and execute, then who dares ? (ch.74)

As Heaven will have it agents and ways to punish the wrong-doers.
Laozi advises us not to take justice into our own hands, else our action may back-fire on us.

恒有司杀者杀。	Dao have executioner to execute
夫代司杀者杀,	Whoever substitutes for the executioner in execution
是谓代大匠斫。	This is called substituting for master-carpenter to chop
夫代大匠斫者,	Whoever substitutes for master-carpenter to chop
希有不伤其手已。	Rarely has not injured own hand indeed (ch.74)

Rather, we may emulate the unselfish and accommodating conduct of the Daoist.
We can respond to injustice with virtue in order to break the vicious cycle of revenge and retaliation.

为无为	Act not for self-purpose
事无事	Serve not for self-affair
大小多少	Big or small, more or less (injustice)
报怨以德	Repay injustice with virtue (kindness) (ch.63)

Often we do not know the full reasons for our actions and the results are often unpredictable.
Hence, Laozi warns that taking justice into our hands can back-fire on us with justice miscarriage.
And rather, that we respond to injustice with virtue which may break the vicious cycle of violence.
We should trust that Heaven will punish the evil-doers in due course, for evil begets evil.
Ultimately, it is good governance that produces well-off people who need not deviate for survival.
No crime, no punishment.

Universal practice of pacific Daoism will make retribution obsolete.

On Salvation

Individuals are vulnerable, needing support for recovery especially after natural disasters or human errors. Does the *Dao De Jing* offers hope and salvation for people in dire circumstances?

Dao, the conceived originator of all things is also conceived to be the refuge for all things.
Laozi suggests that rulers should do likewise, offering salvation to all who request.

道者, 万物之奥	Dao, the refuge of all things
故立天子	Hence crowning the emperor
置三公	Appointing the 3 senior ministers
虽有拱璧以先驷马	Though have Jade Seal preceding the 4-horse chariot
不如坐进此道	Not comparable to sitting-in (installing) this Dao
古之所以贵此道者何？	What is the ancient's reason for valuing this Dao ?
不曰: 求以得	(Is it) not saying: appeal and be given
有罪以免邪？	Have guilt will be forgiven ? (ch.62)

Laozi sees salvation everywhere provided we be flexible.
Be able to bend and yield initially to survive, to suffer grievance initially and be straightened later.

曲则全	Bend and be whole (preserved)
枉则直	Incriminated and be straightened (vindicated) (ch.22)

All citizens to receive salvation regardless of being trustworthy or untrustworthy.

不善者吾亦善之, 德善	With a no-good person I am also good, virtuous goodness
不信者吾亦信之, 德信	With a trust-unworthy person I will also trust, virtuous trust (ch.49)

The Sage ruler with primal virtue will offer salvation to all people and abandon nobody

圣人恒善救人	The Sage with absolute Goodness saves people
故无弃人	Hence there are no abandoned people (ch.27)

Hence the Sage ruler is always on hand to help with loans, not to pressure with taxes

圣人执左契, 而不责于人	The Sage holds the left contract, and not demand of others (ch.79)

And to all grievances, big and small, the respond should always be forgiveness and reconciliation.

大小多少	Big or small, more or less (injustice)
报怨以德	Repay injustice with virtue (kindness) (ch.63)

Heaven may not has favoritism in showing salvation.
Nevertheless, the good people receive double salvation through their own virtuous conduct.

天道无亲	The Heaven's way has no favoritism
恒与善人	Always help the good people (ch.79)

The *DDJ* speaks of universal salvation with the hypothetical Dao being the refuge for all things.
The Sage ruler will do likewise, offering salvation and forgiveness to all who request.
Individuals are urged to sow no grievances and to respond to injustice with kindness.
Heaven shows no favoritism, but Laozi believes virtuous individuals ensure their own salvation.
Laozi speaks not of supernatural power of salvation from the hypothetical Dao.

Laozi speaks of universal salvation in the practice of pacific Daoism.

Laozi's thoughts

On Self

Laozi rightly observes that often we know our enemies better than we know ourselves. That we are our own worst enemy but at the same time we are also our best friend.

Through simple meditation, we can help ourselves with the right thinking.
Concentrate the mind on One (Dao), breath like a baby, discard all fantasy thoughts.
Cultivate love for people and country, take the female support role, and use knowledge not just for self gain.

载营魄抱一	Carry and nourish the body-spirit to embrace One (Dao)
能无离乎？	Possible not to stray away (from Dao) ?
专气至柔	Focus on the breath till gentleness (achieve)
能如婴儿乎？	Possible to be like the baby ?
涤除玄览	Wash and remove mysterious visions (supernatural thoughts)
能无疵乎？	Possible without blemishes ?
爱民治国	Love the citizen and manage the state
能无为乎？	Possible without self-agenda ?
天门开阖	Heaven's door open and close (affairs of the world)
能为雌乎？	Possible to assume the female (mother role) ?
明白四达	Clear understanding in 4 reaches (all knowledgeable)
能无知乎？	Possible not aware (of knowledge's power for self gain) ? (ch.10)

Laozi points out that self-promotion behaviors show us up to be superfluous.
Self-promotions do not work and should be discarded like left-over food.

企者, 不立	Whoever is on tip-toe, cannot stand (firm)
跨者, 不行	Whoever is standing astride, cannot forward (fast)
自见者, 不明	Whoever is self-centered, not enlightened
自是者, 不彰	Whoever is self-righteous, not illustrious
自伐者, 无功	Whoever is self-praising, no credit
自矜者, 不长	Whoever is self-important, no authority (ch.24)

It is easier to know others; hence, knowing self is enlightenment.

知人者智	Whoever knows people is knowledgeable
自知者明	Whoever knows self is enlightened (ch.33)

And all cultivation of virtues starts with the Self, then extends to family and then to the world.

修之于身, 其德乃真	Cultivate it in self, the virtue is real
修之于家, 其德乃余	Cultivate it in family, the virtue is more
修之于天下, 其德乃普	Cultivate it in world, the virtue is universal (ch.54)

Defeating the enemies is indeed easier than defeating self.
We can see the faults of our enemy but self-denial prevent us from seeing our own faults.
Self-denial may seem to 'protect' us for the moment but at the end it will destroy us.
Laozi has shown us the problem and also the way out, through practicing pacific Daoism.
He suggests meditation for cultivating pacific Daoism, starting with Self.

Laozi prescribes, that ultimately we are the only ones who can help ourselves.

Laozi's thoughts

On Success and Failure in Life

Has Laozi set any level of achievement to qualify for success and failure in life?

Laozi observes that Dao creates and nurtures all things, yet has not claim credit for the success.
万物恃之而生而不辞	All things depend on Dao to exist but Dao will not speaks of it
功成不名有	Success achieve but (Dao) is not named (or credited) (ch.34)

Emulating Dao, the Sage do likewise, acts and claims no credit for success.
圣人为而不恃	The Sage contributes but not presumptuous
功成而不居	Success achieved and not claim (credit)
其不欲见贤	As not wishing be seen virtuous (ch.77)

Laozi has observes that self-promotion invariably will backfire and cause failure.
企者, 不立	Whoever is on tip-toe, cannot stand (firm)
跨者, 不行	Whoever is standing astride, cannot forward (fast)
自见者, 不明	Whoever is self-centered, not enlightened
自是者, 不彰	Whoever is self-righteous, not illustrious
自伐者, 无功	Whoever is self-praising, no credit
自矜者, 不长	Whoever is self-important, no authority (ch.24)

Hence, he suggests that it is best to follow Heaven's way, to retire after success is achieved
功遂, 身退	Success achieves, bodily retires
天之道	Way of heaven (ch.9)

To assure success, Laozi has suggested tackling problems early and starting big project from a small base.
图难于其易, 为大于其细	Plan for difficulty when it is easy, do the big by starting it small
天下难事, 必作于易	The world's difficult affairs, should be done when it is easy
天下大事, 必作于细	The big affairs in the world, should be done starting small (ch.63)

To avoid failure, Laozi suggests that people should take similar care of their projects, from start to finish.
民之从事	The people working on projects
恒于几成, 而败之	Always near finishing, then fail it
慎终如始	Careful at finish as at beginning
则无败事	Then no fail project (ch.64)

In the last chapter, Laozi concludes that we should benefit and do harm, take action but not in contest. Implying that individuals who can achieve these, are successes in life.
天之道	Way of Heaven
利, 而不害	Benefiting, and not harming
圣人之道	Way of the Sage
为, 而不争	Acting, but not contesting (ch.81)

Laozi advises starting big project small and taking care from beginning till end to ensure success.
But he has set no standards to judge whether an individual has succeeded or failed in life.
Dao has created all things and yet has not been credited; hence, worldly fame and wealth is no gauge either.

In pacific Daoism, success in life is that one benefits and does no harm.
A fair proposition, as success at this level is within the control and capability of all of us.

Laozi's thoughts

On Triumph of the Weak

In the feudal world of his time, Laozi must have seen plenty of suffering of the weak.
Taking courage in the weakness of Dao, the compassionate Laozi offers much hope for the weak and gentle.

Laozi firmly believes that the weak and gentle will triumphs over the the strong and powerful.
This seems paradoxical and counter to conventional sense.

弱之胜强	The weak triumph over the strong
柔之胜刚	The gentle triumph over the hard
天下莫不知	In the world, none do not know
莫能行	None can implement (ch78)

But has it not been conventional wisdom that force and violence does not pay?

强梁者不得其死	The ruthless person may not die a good death (ancient maxim) (ch.42)

Having hypothesized the existence of Dao, Laozi is impressed by its perceived weak attributes.
Existing in the emptiness of the bellows, Dao is weak as the air in it which is not depleted in use for creation.

天地之间	Heaven and earth, the space in-between
其犹橐籥乎?	Is it not like the bellows (barrel and plunger) ?
虚而不屈	Empty but not conforming
动而愈出	Move (plunger), yet more come out (air feeding the fire) (ch5)

Laozi also takes inspiration by observing the behavior of water.
Soft and yielding by nature, water can corrode hard rocks and shape mountains.

天下莫柔弱于水	In the world, none gentler and weaker than water
而攻坚强者莫之能胜	But attacking the hard and strong, none can surpass (ch78)

Laozi is further convinced from what he observes in real-life.
The soft and suppleness of the living contrasting with the hard and rigidity of the dead.

人之生也柔弱	People when living is gentle and weak
其死也坚强	When dead is hard and stiff (ch76)

However Laozi also realizes the disadvantages of the weak and gentle in strength and power.
Hence he encourages resourcefulness for the weak and gentle to resist and to triumph over the strong.
There are ways and means to bait and soften up the strong and powerful.

将欲歙之, 必固张之	Wishing to shrink it, must first expand it
将欲弱之, 必固强之	Wishing to weaken it, must first strengthen it
将欲废之, 必固举之	Wishing to topple it, must first promote it
将欲取之, 必固与之	Wishing to take it, must first give it
是谓微明	Is said to be subtle enlightenment
柔弱胜刚强	Gentle and weak triumph over strong and powerful (ch36)

In advising resourceful tactics and strategies for the weak, Laozi has been accused of being devious.
Well, a knife can cut both ways, depending whether you use it for defense or aggression.
Likewise, civic hackers are employed to protect computer systems against criminal hackers.

Defying expectation, the gentle and the weak do triumph by deployment of strategies and tactics.

Laozi's thoughts

On Trust

Laozi rightly says, " In good relationship, there is trust".
言善, 信　　　　　　　　　　Communication good, has trust (ch.8)

Of course, when there is not enough of trust, there will be no trust in respond.
信不足焉　　　　　　　　　　Trust when not enough
有不信焉　　　　　　　　　　There is no trust then (ch.17)

Laozi observes, having rituals to regulate behavior, indicate the lack of trust, and the beginning of disorder.
夫礼者　　　　　　　　　　　This Etiquette entity,
忠信之薄, 而乱之首　　　　　Thin in loyalty and trust, it is the beginning of disorder (ch.38)

Optimistically, Laozi advises trusting the trust-unworthy, to gain trust and effect changes in the latter. Presumably, in doing so, one takes precautions at the same time to avoid any possible contingencies.
信者, 吾信之　　　　　　　　With a trust-worthy person, I will trust
不信者, 吾亦信之, 德信　　　 With a trust-unworthy person, I will also trust, virtuous trust (ch.49)

Laozi observes that promises easily given, are usually not trustworthy, as there are too many to be fulfilled.
夫, 轻诺, 必寡信　　　　　　Indeed, lightly promise, certainly lack trust (ch.63)

Finally, Laozi warns, trustworthy words are not sweet; and sweet words are often not trustworthy.
信言, 不美　　　　　　　　　Trustworthy words, are not beautiful
美言, 不信　　　　　　　　　Beautiful words, are not trustworthy (ch.81)

Laozi recognizes deficiencies in Etiquette, saying it is sign of lack of trust and the beginning of disorder. He highlights signs of trust-unworthiness such as, promises lightly given and disarmingly sweet words. In good relationship, there is trust, and trust begets trust.

Counter-intuitively, Laozi bravely advises trusting the trust-unworthy to gain trust!

Laozi's thoughts

On Uncertainties of Life

In life, uncertainties abound; one moment one wins a lottery and the next moment, one gets murdered for it.
Or one suddenly becomes ill and misses the plane that crashes shortly after took off.
People are confused, and for protection turn to ancestral worship, consulting oracles, and religions.
So, is there advice from *DDJ* for handling the uncertainties of life?

To rulers, Laozi says the world is sacred; it is not possible to take for private ownership.
Reasons are the uncertainties of matters and events of the world; it may blow hot, it may blow cold.
So the best response is to cultivate good conduct, discard excesses, extravagance, self-aggrandizement.

将欲取天下而为之	Wishing to take the world and govern it
吾见其不得已	I see that cannot be done
物或行或随, 或歔或吹	Matter may progress, may follow, may blow-hot, may blow-cold
或强或羸, 或载或隳	May be strong, may be weak, may carry, may destroy
是以圣人去甚	Hence the Sage discards excesses
去奢, 去泰	Discards extravagance, discards grandiosity (29)

Laozi observes that good-fortune and misfortune are intimately intertwined.
Hence, the Sage ruler helps with good governance, no oppression, no pomposity, and abandons nobody.

祸兮, 福之所倚	Misfortune indeed, where good fortune depends
福兮, 祸之所伏	Good fortune indeed, where misfortune lurks
孰知其极?	Who knows the limit ?
其无正	There is no normals
正复为奇, 善复为妖	Normals back to be abnormals, good back to be evil
是以, 圣人方而不割	Therefore, the Sage gathers together and not cut-away (abandon)
廉而不劌	Incorruptible and sharp but not injuring
直而不肆	Straight and direct but not unruly
光而不耀	Bright but not dazzle (ch.58)

Life's uncertainties, we may be killed or survive, who knows what Heaven wants?
Nevertheless, retribution from Heaven will come sooner or later.

勇于敢, 则杀	Brave to dare, then get kill
勇于不敢, 则活	Brave to not dare, then survive
此两者	This two entities
或利或害	May be beneficial may be harmful
天之所恶	What Heaven dislike
孰知其故?	Who knows the reasons ?
天网恢恢	Heaven's net far and wide
疏而不失	Widely-meshed but do not leak (ch.73)

Laozi's advice applies to rulers and all individuals as each of us is a leader of sorts at our own level.
Laozi knows not Heaven's likes and dislikes, and believes retribution from Heaven will come without fail.
To face uncertainties of life, Laozi advises cultivating compassion, no aggression, no excesses.
Laozi has been wise not to suggest that there is any supernatural power of Dao that can help us.

Pacific Daoism is a good response to the uncertainties of life.

On Wars

For obvious reasons, nobody wants wars, but sometime war is inevitable.
So when is war justified, and what is Laozi's position on this very serious matter?

The Daoist does not advise war to leader, as war begets war and years of hardship follow wars.
After victory in an unavoidable war of defense, do not boast, massacre, be arrogant or dominate.

以道佐人主者	Whoever uses Dao to assist master of people
不以兵强天下	Do not use army to dominate the world
其事好还	Such affairs lead to retaliation
师之所居	After the army had occupied
荆棘生焉	Thistles and thorns grow indeed
大军之后	Big army (employment) afterward
必有凶年	Certain to have bad years
善有果而已	Good to have fruits (victories) only
不敢以取强	Not daring to take dominance (ch.30)

An instrument of misfortune, the army is to be used minimally if its use is unavoidable.

兵者,不祥之器	This Army entity, instrument of misfortune
非君子之器	Not instrument of the Gentleman
不得已而用之,恬淡为上	Unavoidable then use it, best done peacefully, minimally (ch.31)

In war, people are killed in such great numbers that we should be sad and be filled with grief.
Even in victory, we should not celebrate but rather hold funeral rites for the dead.

杀人之众,以悲哀泣之	Killed people in large number, with sorrow to grief it
战胜以丧礼处之	Fight and victorious, with funeral rites administer it (ch.31)

Livelihoods are destroyed when wars are started by discontented, greedy kings, bend on expansionism.

天下有道,却走马以粪	The world has Dao, walk horses with manure (to fertilize the fields)
天下无道,戎马生于郊	The world has no Dao, war horses give birth in the country-side
祸,莫大于不知足	Disaster, none greater than not knowing contentment
咎,莫大于欲得	Crime, none greater than desire to possess (ch.46)

Hence the good strategist prefers to retreat in defense, so as to minimize destructions and killings.

用兵有言:	Warfare strategist has a saying:
"吾不敢为主	" I not dare be the master (aggressor)
而为客	But be the guest (defender)
不敢进寸	Not dare advance an inch (attack)
而退尺"	But retreat a foot (in defense)" (ch.69)

Certainly Laozi is against wars, calling the army an instrument of misfortune.
He abhors wars for their destruction, the years of hardships and the large numbers of people killed.
He chides discontented lords and greedy kings, for embarking on expansionism wars.
He agrees that fighting is unavoidable only in defense and should never be for aggression.
And victory, even in defense, is not to be celebrated but rather funeral rites should be held for the dead.

In pacific Daoism, truly there is no place for war.

Laozi's thoughts

On WuWei (无为)

Wu (无) means "no" or "nothing" and Wei (为) means "action" or "motive".
WuWei therefore may mean "no action" or "no motive".

The actions of a ruler should be without selfish motive but for the good of the people.
In this way, no people are ungovernable.

为无为	Act for no motive (unselfish)
则无不治	Then none not governable (ch.3)

Can a ruler love his people and manage the state with no selfish motive or self-agenda?
Yes, by not building grand palaces, and by not pursuing personal greatness through expansionism warfare.

爱民治国	Love the citizen and manage the state
能无为乎？	Possible with no motive? (ch.10)

Laozi observes that Dao has no motive in all of its action, creating all things of the universe.
He suggests that rulers do likewise, have no selfish motive and all things will be alright.

道恒, 无为, 而无不为	Dao primal, with no motive, then nothing will not do
侯王若能守之	Lords and King if can uphold Dao
万物将自化	All things will self-develop (ch.37)

Laozi suggests that we embrace the virtues of Dao and cultivate our minds to lose all unnecessary desires.
That is, with no selfish motive, we perform all of our actions.

为学, 日益	Take-up learning, daily gain (of knowledge, desires)
为道, 日损	Practice Dao, daily reduction (of desires)
损之又损	Reducing it yet reducing
以至于无为	To reach till no motive (unselfish)
无为, 而无不为	No motive, then none not actionable (ch.48)

Laozi reiterates that if rulers emulate Dao's no-motive attribute, then people will self-regulate.
It is natural that when rulers lead with good examples, people will follow the good examples.

我无为, 而民自化	I have no motive, and citizens will self-develop
我好静, 而民自正	I love quietude, and citizens will self-regulate
我无事, 而民自富	I have no agenda, and citizens will self-prosper
我无欲, 而民自朴	I have no desires, and citizens will self-humble (ch.57)

Laozi highlights the benefit of having no personal motive, hence no personal failure.
Like ruler who rules the people for the people, has not personalized power; hence, never feel lost of power.

是以, 圣人无为, 故, 无败	Therefore, the Sage has no motive, hence, no failure
无执故无失	No holds-on hence no loss (ch.64)

In the *Dao De Jing*, WuWei (无为) occur 11 times.
As shown in the chapters above, translating with "no motive" makes sense, and the message is consistent.
Try substituting with "no action", and we shall see that the message is not so sensible!

"No motive" or better, "no selfish motive" is a powerful message from the Dao De Jing.

On WuWei, WuBuWei (无为,无不为)

The preceding page has shown that WuWei means "no motive", or "not selfish", but certainly not "no action ".
Directly expressed, WuBuWei means "none not actionable"; positively expressed, it means "for all actions".
Simply stated, WuWei, WuBuWei means "not selfish, for all actions".
It has been said that this statement may summarize the whole of Laozi's philosophy of Pacific Daoism.

Dao creates and nurtures all things, but never claim to be their master.
万物恃之而生而不辞	All things depend on Dao to exist but Dao will not speaks of it
衣养万物而不为主	Clothes and nourishes all things but Dao will not be their master (ch.34)
万物归焉而不为主	All things subjected to Dao but Dao will not be their master (ch.34)

Dao has been "unselfish in all its actions", and Laozi suggests that we do likewise, especially the rulers.
恒道, 无为, 而无不为	Dao primal, without self-interest, then nothing will not do
侯王若能守之	Lords and King if can uphold Dao
万物将自化	All things will self-develop (in accordance with Dao) (ch.37)

When a ruler has "no motive, no agenda, and no desires", the citizens remain undisturbed, and will prosper.
故圣人云：	Hence the Sage said:
我无为, 而民自化	I have no motive, and citizens will self-develop
我好静, 而民自正	I love quietude, and citizens will self-regulate
我无事, 而民自富	I have no agenda, and citizens will self-prosper
我无欲, 而民自朴	I have no desires, and citizens will self-humble (ch.57)

The benefits from WuWei, is that rulers will find all people governable, and will never experience failure.
为无为	Act for no self-interest (not selfish)
则无不治	Then none not governable (ch.3)
圣人无为, 故无败	The Sage has no self-agenda, hence no failure
无执, 故无失	No holds-on, hence no loss (ch.64)

And "Not selfish, for all actions" is to be the ultimate goal in the daily practice of Daoism.
为道, 日损	Practice Dao, daily reduction (of desires)
损之又损	Reducing it yet reducing
以至于无为	To reach till no motive (unselfish)
无为, 而无不为	Not selfish, then no task not actionable (ch.48)

Firstly, "no motive" or "not selfish", removes stresses from all pre-conceived duties to perform.
Dumping all the baggages and pre-conditions, liberates the mind and relaxes the body.
Then "all actions" conceive afterwards in this enlightened state, can only be good for the self and for others.

WuWei, WuBuWei (无为,无不为): "Not selfish, for all actions"; pacific Daoism in a nutshell.

SUMMARY

Summary

The *Dao De Jing* (*DDJ*), widely translated like the *Bible* but is hardly read outside the academies. The reason is, scholars have evolved the *DDJ* into the realm of religion, spiritualism or mysticism. Commentaries and translations are often incomprehensible, and hence, are unable to attract new readers. Therefore this monograph re-examines text of the *DDJ* directly, and try not to be prejudiced by others.

Laozi, the legendary philosopher is first quoted extensively by Zhuangzi (c.369-286 BC). According to Sima Qian (145-87BCE), he serves as an archivist in the court of the Zhou Dynasty. Laozi is credited with authorship of the *DDJ* of about 5,000 Chinese characters. The *DDJ* is written in terse verses like the Yi Jing (Book of Change c.1,066 BCE). On the balance of available evidence, the *DDJ* may be dated in the time of Confucius (551-479). Ideas and concepts are not presented sequentially in the *DDJ*, but are scattered among the chapters. They are therefore grouped and summarized here under 16 broad headings for a clearer perspective.

1. Quest for the Ultimate Reality
Laozi's primary quest is to understand creation of the universe (ch.1).
Admits not knowing the absolute Dao, his vague terminology suggests exploration not mysticism (ch.1).
He recognizes that a name is not absolute, and hence, to him naming is a hypothetical process (ch.1).
Naming the beginning of Heaven and Earth as Wu (Have-not or Nothing), he sees a godless universe. (ch.1).
Correlatives are naturally occurring, hence, he advises respect for all, the beauty and the non-beauty. (ch.2).
Laozi is a thinker, a philosopher scientist on the quest for the Ultimate Reality.

2. Dao
Seems formless as Laozi sees nothing in the bellows, yet Dao is inexhaustible in use. (ch.4,5)
He postulates Dao, a primal entity, that exists before Heaven and Earth, mother of all things (ch.25)
In the female/male procreation process, it seems semen is the substance of Dao (ch.6,21).
Nevertheless elsewhere, however he looks, he cannot detect Dao with any senses (ch.14,35)
Dao, cyclical in action and gentle in use, is perceived in the seasonal changes yearly. (ch.40)
But he can observe that Dao the formless can 'enter the hardest', like fire melting the bronze. (ch.43)
Laozi has not found 'Dao', but neither have we proven the 'Big Bang' theory today.

3. Heaven and Earth
Heaven and Earth's perceived selflessness, is a model for ever-lasting sustainability (ch.7)
Heaven and Earth's power is limited, like storm, lasting not a day; hence, how can dynasties last? (ch.23)
Heaven's way, reduces the have-excess and supplement the not-enough. (ch.77)
Heaven's way, benefits and not harming. (ch.81)
Laozi wishes we learn from these perceived virtues of Heaven and Earth (or Dao).

Summary

4. Freedom
Freedom for all as Dao creates and nurtures all things but claims no ownership. (ch.34)
Freedom for all reiterated as Dao creates and not possess, leads and not control. (ch.51)
Laozi sees absolute freedom for all things under his hypothetical Dao which is master of none.

5. Daoism
Is anonymity, is non-violent, is unselfishness, is harmony, is refuge for all (ch.39,42,48,55,62)
"Enlightened Dao like dim, etc", seems paradoxical and laughable to the uninitiated (ch.41)
Makes governing easy as cooking small fish, as people with daoism are self-governing. (ch.60)
The 3 treasures of Daoism: Love, Thrift and Not-dare-be-world's-first. (ch.67)
Daoism is quietly benefiting, not harming, not contesting, conducive to peaceful co-existence.

6. Daoists
Are individuals who are not intrusive in behavior and not confrontational in conduct. (ch.15,20)
Are strong, self-assured individuals who cannot be influenced for good or bad. (ch.56)
Are individuals who have humility and take responsibilities in government (ch.28,57)
Daoists are simple, honest, gentle, peace-loving people who can co-exist in any community.

7. Individual-Self
"Breath gentle as a child, cleanse of all fantasies", simple meditation techniques for self cultivation. (ch.10)
"Whoever stands on tip-toe, not stable", self-promotion is counter productive. (ch.24)
"Knowing people is knowledge, knowing self is enlightenment", it is self-denial at work. (ch.33)
"Cultivating virtues in self, family, village, nation, then the world", rightly starts with self. (ch.54)
Self-knowledge is highly valuable, for it is not easy to find fault with oneself.

8. Conventional Virtues
Benevolence, righteousness and such, are traditional helps extended after loss of civility. (ch.18)
Virtues done without selfish motive or claim to be virtuous, are true virtues. (ch.38)
True virtues wish anonymity and done without motives; virtues on display are not virtuous.

Summary

9. Primal Virtues
Individuals are advised, be not-contesting like water. (ch.8)
Be not a hoarder, for halls of gold and jade cannot be guarded. (ch.9)
Be selfless, then will have no fears or worries for body and life. (ch.13)
Humility, honesty, unselfishness and such are primal civility in individual-self.(ch.19)
Be unselfish in all action, especially with individuals in leadership positions. (ch.37)
Be contented for there is no greater crime than the desire to possess. (ch.46)
Be respectful of all talents, recognize and employ them for their strength. (ch.68)
Primal virtues are: humility, unselfishness, contentment, not-contesting, and respect for all.

10. Human Failings
Beware, indulging the senses, self-promotion, frivolity and temptation. (ch.12,24,26,53)
Beware, not knowing and act knowing is sick (ch.71)
Beware, best to sow no grievances (ch.79)
Laozi identifies common failings that are the causes of much difficulties and misery in life.

11. Life-Death Cycle
The certainty of death mellows people, makes them more accommodating and fair. (ch.16)
Loss of life versus gaining fame and wealth, it is our choice. (ch.44)
A third of deaths are premature, that survivors avoid by not getting into harms way. (ch.50)
The certainty of death humbles, makes us live better lives, helps us avoid premature death.

12. Salvation
"Bend and be whole", that is first to yield to survive, then return to fight another day. (ch.22)
"The Sage with absolute goodness saves all people, all things", salvation is universal. (ch.27)
"Trust the trust-unworthy, gain trust", trust to inspire trust where there is none. (ch.49)
"Open to desires, life-long no salvation", so self-discipline is needed for own salvation. (ch.52)
Salvation needs strategic yielding to survive, trust to gain trust, self-discipline against desires.

13. Retribution
"Heaven's net widely-meshed, do not leak", warns of unfailing justice for evil doers. (ch.73)
"Justice from society risks self-injury", warns of miscarriage of societal justice (ch.74)
Laozi promises retribution from Heaven, and warns against justice from society.

Summary

14. Rulers

Rulers are advised not to glorify themselves, not to hoard wealth, and to be unselfish in government. (ch.3)
Rulers ranking: best, not disturbing, not heard; next, feared; next, despised. (ch.17)
Nobody is likely to succeed in conquering the world as it is highly unpredictable. (ch.29)
Rulers to embrace Daoism for government, be contented, no grand palaces, no expansionism wars. (ch.32)
Rulers are told that there is nothing better than Thrift for nation building. (ch. 59)
Rulers are urged to practice humility in diplomacy, so as to promote harmony among nations. (ch.61)
Rulers are advised, to rule is to serve, to rule with Daoism, not with cleverness. (ch.66,65,60)
Rulers are told, high taxes and oppression cause hunger and rebellion. (ch.75,72)
Laozi is clearly very much a philosopher of the people rather than of the rulers.

15. Wars

They cause mass destruction, mass killings, and years of hardship for citizens in the aftermath. (ch. 30,31)
Wars are started through the discontentment and greed of Kings, bend on expansionism. (ch. 46)
When unavoidable, wars may be considered for defense, and to be fought with compassion (ch. 69).
Wars are instruments of misfortune.

16. What Paradoxes ?

"Emptiness, utility of the Hub", reality of negatives like no answer is also an answer. (ch.11)
"To take it, must first give it", it is true that to catch a fish, you must first give it a bait. (ch.36)
"Greatness not apparent", as the talented can make achievement so easy and simple. (ch.45)
"Travel more, know less", testifying to the power of the written archives (ch.47)
"Cycles of good-fortune and misfortune", like the springs and winters taking turns. (ch.58)
"Repay grievance with kindness", such depth of wisdom, breaking cycle of injustice. (ch.63)
"Journey of a thousand miles start beneath the feet", greatness be achieved stepwise. (ch.64)
"Laozi's sayings easy to know, not easy to implement", like honesty, easy to know, not easy to keep. (ch.70)
"Gentleness, path to life; rigidity, path to death", observation that inspires a gentle philosophy. (ch.76)
"Triumph of the weak and gentle", giving hope to those who need it. (ch.78)
"Small nation, few citizens", not a ridiculous idea given the over population today. (ch,80)
Laozi's thoughts seems paradoxical because he looks from the oft neglected negative aspect of things.

Summary

With 5,000-odd Chinese characters, Laozi presents a wealth of unconventional wisdom.
Seeking to explain existence of the universe, he postulates the primal entity, Dao.
In the bellows and in the procreation process, he cannot substantiates the formless Dao.
Nevertheless from his perception of the silent attributes of Dao, Laozi spawns pacific Daoism.
He has pragmatic advice for conducting our lives as individuals, as rulers, in wars and in peace.
He reveals our failings, warns of dangers and retribution, teaches survival and freedom.
But most important, Laozi has inspired us with the spirit of seeking for the Ultimate Reality.
Moving forward, when all individuals seek, the Ultimate Reality will unite us all in harmony and peace.

For there is only one Ultimate Reality.

157   CONCLUSION

158   Laozi's legacy 1: Quest for the Ultimate Reality (Dao)

160   Laozi's legacy 2: Pacific Daoism (dos and don't s) (De)

166   Benefits from reading the *Dao De Jing* (de-stressing, liberating)

169   Going forward

Legacy 1 (Dao)

Quest for the Ultimate Reality (Dao)

This is one legacy of Laozi that I admire, the spirit of inquiry to learn the Ultimate Truth.
The why and how of our existence and that of the universe has been a puzzle since the dawn of time. Some 2500 years ago Laozi thought hard and deep on this question.

Laozi postulates existence of the primal matter, born before Heaven and Earth
有物浑成	There are matters that mixed and formed
先天地生	Created before Heaven and Earth (ch.25)

Laozi terms it Dao, the inexhaustible creator of the universe and all things.
道冲, 而用之或不盈	Dao charges out (bellows), yet use it, cannot be depleted
渊兮, 似万物之宗	Deep indeed, seems to be the originator of all things (ch.4)

Dao exists and pervades in the huge bellows of space between Heaven and Earth.
天地之间	Heaven and Earth, the space in-between
其犹橐龠乎？	Is it not like the bellows (barrel and plunger)？
虚而不屈	Empty but not yielding
动而愈出	Move (plunger), yet more come out (air, feeding the fire) (ch.5)

Dao seems to exist as the Valley spirit in the female role in procreation.
谷神不死	Valley spirit (of fertility) never dies
是谓玄牝	Is said to be the primal female (ch.6)

Dao as substance in the semen in the male role in procreation, is describes in vague and obscure terms.
道之为物, 惟恍惟惚	Dao itself as substance, all vague all elusive
惚兮恍兮, 其中有象	Elusive indeed vague indeed, within there is image
恍兮惚兮, 其中有物	Vague indeed elusive indeed, within there is substance
窈兮冥兮, 其中有精	Faraway indeed dim indeed, within there is essence (semen)
其精甚真, 其中有信	The essence is very real, within there is trust (ch.21)

Dao seems invisible, inaudible and cannot be held.
Look from high and low, front and back, and Dao seems formless, the image of nothingness.
视之不见, 名曰夷	Look at it (Dao) and see not, name it Unseen
听之不闻, 名曰希	Listen to it and hear not, name it Rarefy
搏之不得, 名曰微	Grasp it and hold not, name it Micro
其上不皦, 其下不昧	It's top not bright, it's bottom not dark
绳绳不可名	Connect to something yet cannot be named
复归于无物	Again return to no-matter
是谓无状之状	This is called the formless form
无物之象	The image of nothing
迎之不见其首	Go up to it, and not see it's head
随之不见其后	Follow it, and not see it's back (ch.14)

Collected at bellows-exit, Dao has no smell, is invisible, inaudible, and not enough for a meal, being all air!

道之出口	Dao's emerging exit (manifestations)
淡乎, 其无味	Dilute indeed, it has no smell
视之, 不足见	Look at it, not enough to see
听之, 不足闻	Listen to it, not enough to hear
用之, 不足既	Use it, not enough for a small-meal (very little substance) (ch.35)

Hence, Laozi famously admits in the first line of the *Dao De Jing*, the primal Dao cannot be fully described.

道可道, 非恒道	Dao that can be described, is not the primal Dao (ch.1)

Laozi looks high and low, in all nooks and crannies for Dao in substance.
Reading the *Dao De Jing* today, we can still feel how hard Laozi has tried to prove the existence of Dao.
However, with the advance sciences of today, we can see that the existence of Dao may not be proven.

Nevertheless, in quest for the Ultimate Reality, our best scientists have not fared better than Laozi.
To explain the beginning of the universe, the 'Big Bang' theory is equally untenable to be the final answer.
For it is equally legitimate for us to ask what existed before the 'Big Bang'?
The latest attempt at this quest is published in *'The Grand Design'* (Hawking and Mlodinow, 2010).
Instead of explaining the universe, they propose the existence of multiple universes (multiverse).
This is rather unhelpful, as only theoretical physicists can understand the M-theory and such.
This also destroys the original concept of the universe, for it includes all things, including the multiverses!
So the quest goes on; and the whole problem of existence may be put into a nutshell (below).

Quest for the Ultimate Reality in a Nutshell
When was the Beginning, the "Dao" or the "Big Bang"?
Where is the End on a journey to nowhere?
In pacific Daoism, we contribute by our own labor, we share fairly and we enjoy in harmony.
In quest for the Ultimate Reality, we continue to bear Laozi's torch in search to the end of the universe.

Pacific Daoism (De)   Legacy 2 (De)

What may constitute pacific Daoism, or De (Virtue)?
The following are the dos and don't s of pacific Daoism (PD).
They are so abundant that they can be taken directly from most of the 81 chapters of the *Dao De Jing*.

二章	**Chapter 2**
圣人处无为之事	The Sage manages all tasks unselfishly
行不言之教	Practice non-verbal teaching (by setting good examples)
万物作而不辞	Observes all things in action but makes no comment (never criticize)

PD is, to work unselfishly in all tasks, teach by setting good examples and never be critical of others.

三章	**Chapter 3**
不尚贤	Not coveting to be virtuous-talented
不贵难得之货	Not valuing hard to obtain commodities

PD is, to lead by not coveting honor and wealth so that citizens will not contest for honor, and rob for wealth.

八章	**Chapter 8**
水善, 利万物, 而不争	Water good, benefits all things, yet not contending
居众人之所恶	Resides where all people will hate (bottom)
居善地	Residence good, has place (humble)
心善渊	Heart (feeling)good, has depth
与善仁	Relation good, has kindness
言善信	Communication good, has trust
政善治	Government good, has management
事善能	Service good, has capability
动善时	Action good, has timing

PD is, emulate water, not contesting, be humble, relate with goodwill, kindness, trust, capability & efficiency .

九章	**Chapter 9**
金玉满堂, 莫之能守	Gold and jade filling the hall, none who can guard
富贵而骄, 自遗其咎	Rich and noble but arrogant, self bequeath own destruction
功遂身退, 天之道	Success achieves, self retires, Way of heaven

PD is, not hoarding excessive wealth, not arrogant in power and retires to safety after success is achieved.

十章	**Chapter 10**
载营魄抱一, 能无离乎？	Composes body & spirit to embrace One (Dao), possible not to stray ?
专气至柔, 能如婴儿乎？	Focus on breath till gentleness, possible to be like baby ?
涤除玄览, 能无疵乎？	Cleans to remove mystery visions, possible without blemishes ?
爱民治国, 能无为乎？	Loves citizen, manages state, possible without self-agenda?
天门开阖, 能为雌乎？	In affairs of the world, possible to assume the female (Mother role) ?
明白四达, 能无知乎？	In use of all knowledge, possible not be aware of its power for self gain ?
生, 而不有	Create, and not possessing
为, 而不恃	Contribute, and not presumptuous
长, 而不宰	Senior, but not controlling (life and death)

PD is, to meditate for the primal virtues of harmony, unselfishness, support, not possessing, not dominating.

Legacy 2 (De)

十二章	**Chapter 12**
五色, 令人目盲	Five colors, cause people's eyes blindness
五音, 令人耳聋	Five tones, cause people's ears deafness
五味, 令人口爽	Five flavors, cause people's mouths tasteless

PD is, knowing the dangers of over-indulgence of the senses.

十三章	**Chapter 13**
及吾无身, 吾有何患?	When I have no body (prepared to die), what trouble do I have?

PD is, being prepared to make the ultimate sacrifice to release stress and fear, and be relaxed to enjoy life.

十五章	**Chapter 15**
保此道者, 不欲盈	Whoever keeps this Dao, does not wish being full

PD is, not to be overly possessive and trying to grab it all, but to leave others their shares.

十六章	**Chapter 16**
知常曰明	Knowing Death-inevitable is called Enlightenment
知常容	Knowing Death-inevitable, will be accommodating
容乃公	Being accommodating, will be fair
公乃全	Being fair, will be all-embracing

PD is, to know the inevitable life-death cycle, be mellowed, be fair, be accommodating and be all embracing.

十九章	**Chapter 19**
见素, 抱朴	Show plainness, embrace original-self
少私, 寡欲	Lessen selfishness, reduce desires

PD is, being your humble self, reducing selfishness, wants and desires.

二十章	**Chapter 20**
人之所畏, 不可不畏	What people are afraid of, cannot be not afraid

PD is, be warned by what others fear and take the same good care and precautions as others do.

二十二章	**Chapter 22**
曲则全	Bend and be whole (preserved)
枉则直	Incriminated and be straightened (vindicated)

PD is, prepared to bear injustice, or grievance to survive a crisis, so that matters can be resolved later.

二十四章	**Chapter 24**
企者, 不立,	Whoever is on tip-toe, cannot stand (firm)
跨者, 不行	Whoever is standing astride, cannot forward (move)
自见者, 不明	Whoever is self-centered, not enlightened
自是者, 不彰	Whoever is self-righteous, not illustrious
自伐者, 无功	Whoever is self-praising, no credit
自矜者, 不长	Whoever is self-important, no authority

PD is, to recognize that self-promoting behaviors are self-defeating efforts.

Legacy 2 (De)

二十六章
轻则失根
躁则失君

Chapter 26
Frivolity causes loss of roots (base support)
Impatience causes loss of kingship

PD is, to know the bad consequences of frivolity and impatience.

二十七章
圣人恒善救人, 故无弃人
恒善救物, 故无弃物

Chapter 27
Sage's absolute Goodness saves people, hence no abandoned people
With absolute Goodness saves things, hence no abandoned things

PD is, not abandoning anybody or anything, that is leaving no-one and nothing behind.

二十八章
知其雄, 守其雌
知其荣, 守其辱

Chapter 28
Knowing the male (role), hold the female (role)
Knowing the honor, hold the disgrace

PD is, taking the supportive role of the female (Mother), and taking responsibility for all consequences.

二十九章
圣人去甚, 去奢, 去泰

Chapter 29
The Sage discards excesses, extravagance and grandiosity

PD is, to discard excessess, extravagance and grandiosity.

三十章
不以兵强天下
果, 而不得已
果, 而勿强

Chapter 30
Do not use army to dominate the world
Victories, that cannot be avoided (in defense)
Victorious, but do not dominate

PD is, not to dominate with military might; to fight only in defense, and in victory, not to oppress.

三十三章
知人者, 智
自知者, 明
不失其所者, 久
死而不亡者, 寿

Chapter 33
Whoever knows people, is knowledgeable
Whoever knows self, is enlightened
Whoever has not lost life-direction, will last long
Whoever is dead but not forgotten, is long-lived

PD is, to have no self-denials, know our own strength and weakness, and not lose our own direction.

三十八
上德, 不德, 是以有德
居其实, 不居其华

Chapter 38
High Virtue, not claiming virtue, hence has virtue
Dwell in the solid (trust), not dwell in the flowery (Etiquette)

PD is, not wearing virtue like a badge, being solidly trustworthy and not be pretentious and superficial.

三十九章
不欲琭琭, 如玉
珞珞, 如石

Chapter 39
Not wanting be cut and polish, like jade ,
But be uncut and rough, like stone.

PD is, wanting to be useful, and humble like the rock; rather than be the decorative, polished jade.

Legacy 2 (De)

四十四章 — Chapter 44
知足, 不辱　　Know contentment, not be disgraced
知止, 不殆　　Know the limit, not be endangered

PD is, to know contentment and not be dishonored, to know the limit and not be endangered

四十六章 — Chapter 46
祸莫大于不知足　　Disaster never greater than not knowing contentment
咎莫大于欲得　　Crime never greater than desire to possess

PD is, knowing the disastrous consequence of discontentment and the desire for possession

四十八章 — Chapter 48
为道日损　　Practice Dao, daily reduction (of desire)
无为, 而无不为　　Not selfish, then none not actionable

PD is, to practice pacific Daoism daily so as to achieve the ideal state of being unselfish in all our actions.

四十九章 — Chapter 49
不善者吾亦善之, 得善　　With a no-good person I am also good, virtuous goodness

PD is, to accept and be good to those who are no-good so that they may be converted to being good.

五十二章 — Chapter 52
塞其兑, 闭其门, 终身不勤　　Block the portals, close the doors (to desires), life-long no regret
开其兑, 济其事, 终身不救　　Open portals, promote affairs (desires), life-long, no salvation

PD is, to block off unhealthy desires else we may live to suffer the consequences for life.

五十五章 — Chapter 55
知和曰常, 知常曰明　　Knows harmony is Nature, knows Nature is enlightened
益生曰祥, 心使气曰强　　Beneficial living is good fortune, heart controlling breath is strong
物壮则老　　Matters prime will age

PD is, harmony, healthy living, not allowing emotion that lead to forceful action and early bodily decline.

五十八章 — Chapter 58
祸兮, 福之所倚　　Misfortune indeed, where good fortune depends
福兮, 祸之所伏　　Good fortune indeed, where misfortune lurks
圣人方, 而不割　　The Sage holds together, and not cut-away (abandon)
廉, 而不刿　　Incorruptible sharp, but not injuring
直, 而不肆　　Straight and direct, but not unruly
光, 而不耀　　Bright, but not dazzle

PD is, to be hopeful in misfortune and be cautionary in good-fortune
PD is, to emulate the Sage, all embracing, not harming, not unruly, and not dazzling in conduct.

六十二章 — Chapter 62
人之不善, 何弃之有？　　People being no-good, how can they be abandoned ?

PD is, to help everybody and give up on nobody, not even the bad and the ugly.

Legacy 2 (De)

六十三章	Chapter 63
报怨以德	Repay injustice with virtue (kindness)
图难于其易; 为大于其细	Plan for difficulties when it is easy; do the big when it is small
夫, 轻诺, 必寡信	Indeed, lightly promise, certainly lacks trust
多易, 必多难	More easiness (early), certainly more difficulties (later)

PD is, never seek revenge, tackle problems when they are still small and easy, and never over promise.

六十四章	Chapter 64
其安, 易持; 其未兆, 易谋	Things stable, easy to maintain; no sign (of problem), easy to prevent
合抱之木, 生于毫末	Trees of large girth, grow from micro seed
九层之台, 起于累土	Tower 9-storeys high, rise from accumulated earth
千里之行, 始于足下	Journey of thousand miles, starts beneath the feet
慎终如始, 则无败事	Careful at finish as at beginning, then no fail project

PD is, to start small, build from the first level, take the first step, and be careful all the way to success.

六十七章	Chapter 67
我有三宝, 一曰慈, 二曰俭	I have got 3 Treasures, first is Love, second is Thrift
三曰不敢为天下先	Third is Not-dare-be-world's-first

PD is, to have Love, practice Thrift and not dare to take the lead (unless selected and recommended).

六十八章	Chapter 68
善为士者, 不武	Whoever good at being a scholar, not violent
善战者, 不怒	Whoever good at fighting-wars, never angry
善胜敌者, 不与	Whoever good at overcoming the enemy, never engage
善用人者, 为之下	Whoever good employing people, be humble

PD is, non-violence, not be angry, not be threatening, and always be humble like the talented above.

六十九章	Chapter 69
祸, 莫大于轻敌	Disaster, none bigger than to underestimate the enemy

PD is, to know there is no greater disaster than underestimating one's enemy.

七十章	Chapter 70
吾言, 甚易知, 甚易行	My words, very easy to know, very easy to implement
天下, 莫能知, 莫能行	The world, none able to know, none able to implement

PD is, easy to know and easy to implement, yet is easier said than done.

七十一章	Chapter 71
不知, 知, 病	Not knowing, yet acts knowing, sick

PD is, to know what one does not know.

Legacy 2 (De)

七十二章   **Chapter 72**
圣人自知, 不自见   The Sage is self-aware, but not self-important
自爱, 不自贵   Self-loving, but not self-aggrandizing
PD is, to emulate the Sage in not indulging in self-importance, and self-grandiosity.

七十三章   **Chapter 73**
天之所恶, 孰知其故？   What Heaven dislike, who knows the reasons ?
天网恢恢, 疏而不失   Heaven's net far and wide, widely-meshed but does not leak
PD is, to know there is retribution, for evil deeds beget evil consequences.

七十五章   **Chapter 75**
民之饥, 以其上, 食税之多   The people's hunger, because their rulers, tax too much
PD is, to know that hunger and poverty below, is due to the authority above taking too much.

七十六章   **Chapter 76**
坚强者, 死之徒   The hard and strong, path to death
柔弱者, 生之徒   The gentle and weak, path to life
PD is, to appreciate that gentleness is the way to life whereas aggression is the way to death.

七十七章   **Chapter 77**
损有余, 而补不足   Reduce have-excess, to supplement not-enough
PD is, to take from those with excess, to supplement, and help those who are insufficient.

七十八章   **Chapter 78**
弱, 之胜强   The weak, triumph over the strong
柔, 之胜刚   The gentle, triumph over the hard
正言若反   Positive sayings seems negative
PD is, to know that though it may sound paradoxical, the gentle and weak can triumph over hard and strong .

七十九章   **Chapter 79**
有德司契   Has virtues, administers contracts
无德司彻   Without virtues, administers taxes
PD is, to administer contracts, not taxes.

八十一章   **Chapter 81**
圣人, 不积   The Sage, does not accumulate (for self)
利, 而不害   Benefiting, and not harming
为, 而不争   Acting, but not contesting
PD is, to emulate the Sage in not hoarding, benefit and not harming, and not contesting in all actions.

Benefits from reading the *Dao De Jing (DDJ)*

When feeling stressed, ideas in the *DDJ* can liberate the mind, relax the body, and suggest courses for action. Pacific Daoism seems to have advice for every departments of human activities.

Face with rebellion at home, and unappreciative behavior at large, be liberated with:
生, 而不有　　　　　　　　Creates, but not possesses (ch.2)

Trouble with getting recognition for work done in the office, be patient, for credit will not be lost:
功成, 而不居　　　　　　　Success achieved, but not dwell (take credit).
夫惟不居, 是以不去　　　　Only when not taken, then (credit) does not go away (ch.2)

Fear of disaster, imagined or otherwise, de-stress with readiness to sacrifice self.
If one is prepared for the worst, what else does one fear?
吾所以有大患者, 为吾有身　Reason I have big trouble, is I have a body (self)
及吾无身, 吾有何患?　　　When I have no body (prepared to die), what trouble do I have ? (ch.13)

When suffering a disastrous experience, think positive, as something good may come out of it:
祸兮, 福之所倚　　　　　　Misfortune indeed, where good-fortune depends (ch.58)

Ostracize by others, then be prepared to self-criticize for it is more difficult to find fault with oneself
知人者智, 自知者明　　　　Knows people is clever, knows self is enlightened (ch.33)

After suffering a grievance, respond with reconciliation, to break the vicious cycle of revenge and retaliation.
报怨以德　　　　　　　　　Repay injustice with virtue (kindness) (ch.63)

Be prepared for difficulties, then, you will have no difficulties.
图难于其易, 为大于其细　　Plan for difficult when it is easy, do the big when it is small (ch.63)

Be encouraged, start big task small, like taking the first step of a long journey.
千里之行, 始于足下　　　　Journey of thousand miles, starts beneath the feet (ch.64)

Be prepared to bend initially for survival, then be able to resolve the crisis later and be whole again.
曲则全　　　　　　　　　　Bend and be whole (preserved) (ch.22)

Reading benefits

Be warned, indulgences are harmful.
五色, 令人目盲	Five colors, cause people's eyes blindness
五音, 令人耳聋	Five tones, cause people's ears deafness
五味, 令人爽	Five flavors, cause people's mouths tasteless
驰骋田猎,	Galloping fast on the flats hunting,
令人心发狂	Cause people's heart develop madness (ch.12)

Be warned of the futility of self-promotion.
企者, 不立	Whoever is on tip-toe, cannot stand (firm)
跨者, 不行	Whoever is standing astride, cannot forward (fast)
自见者, 不明	Whoever is self-centered, not enlightened
自是者, 不彰	Whoever is self-righteous, not illustrious
自伐者, 无功	Whoever is self-praising, no credit
自矜者, 不长	Whoever is self-important, no authority (ch.24)

Be warned of the futility of greed.
金玉满堂	Gold and jade filling the halls
莫之能守	None who can guard (ch.9)

Be warned not to sow evil, for Heaven's retribution never fails as one harvests what one sow.
天网, 恢恢	Heaven's net, far and wide
疏, 而不失	Widely-meshed, but do not leak (ch.73)

Treasure of 3 attributes recommended, Love, Thrift and Dare-not-be-world's-first.
慈, 故能勇.	Love, hence can be brave
俭, 故能广	Thrift, hence can be far-reaching
不敢为天下先	Not daring to be the world's first
故能成器长	Hence can become the world's leader (ch.67)

Attributes not recommended, the sickness of pretending to know when one does not know.
It is disastrous not knowing contentment and desiring for more and more possessions.
不知, 知, 病	Not knowing, yet (acts) knowing, sick (ch.71)
祸, 莫大于不知足	Disaster, never greater than not knowing contentment
咎, 莫大于欲得	Crime, never greater than desire to possess (ch.46)

167

Emulate virtuous water, benefit and not contesting, less rivalry, a gentle path for survival in life.
水善, 利万物, 而不争　　　　Water good, benefits all things, yet not contending (ch.8)

Emulate Dao, do not take advantage of others to benefit self, then any action can be taken.
道恒, 无为, 而无不为　　　　Dao primal, without self-interest, then nothing will not do (ch.37)

Simple meditation: breathing gently like the child, banishing all evil and supernatural thoughts.
载营魄抱一　　　　Carry and nourish the body-spirit to embrace One (Dao)
能无离乎?　　　　Possible not to stray away (from Dao) ?
専气至柔　　　　Focus on the breath till gentleness (achieve)
能如婴儿乎?　　　　Possible to be like the baby ?
涤除玄览　　　　Wash and remove mysterious visions (supernatural thoughts)
能无疵乎?　　　　Possible without blemishes ? (ch.10)

In short, the *Dao De Jing* offers pacific Daoism, all actions of benefiting, not contesting, and not harming.
天之道, 利而不害　　　　Way of Heaven, benefit and not harming
圣人之道, 为而不争　　　　Way of the Sage, action but not contesting (ch.81)

The versatility of the *Dao De Jing* is quite unique in answering life questions.
Lost in life's direction, one often asks simply, "How?"; without even knowing, "about what?"
It has been said that all teachings in the *Dao De Jing* can be summarized in:
无为, 而无不为　　　　With no motive, then no action cannot be taken (ch.48)
This is a very simple, but powerful direction for further action in answer to the question, "How?".
Firstly, "no motive": we free ourselves of all motives, for good or for bad.
Because, with any motive, there is always the pressure to perform, and the duty to fulfill it.
Hence, some of us are over stressed, and are lost.
Without any motive or pressure, we are liberated in body and mind to perform well in further actions.
But of course, all actions must not infringe on the rights of others.
Putting down all our baggages is certainly the first step to finding our lost-selves back.

The *Dao De Jing* offers guidance in all areas of human activities.
It is the one book that comes to mind when I need some advice.
The book is small with only 5000 odd Chinese characters in 81 chapters.
Almost every other line in the *Dao De Jing* offers an insight that all humanity can benefit.

It is astonishing that so many can be taught so much with so few words.

Going Forward (The Vision Thing)

Daoism has been expanded into the realm of mysticism and religion by individuals who came after Laozi.
But Dao as the Ultimate Entity is just a theory and clearly cannot be substantiated today.
Dao the primal entity may not exist, but the perceived attributes of Dao are clearly useful as pacific Daoism.

Pacific Daoism is humility, is benefiting and not harming, is not self-serving, in all actions.
It is contributing, but not taking more, not claiming success, not wishing to have control over others.
The pacific Daoist has no grand desires, is at ease with the self and makes no demand of others.
The cultivation of pacific Daoism is therefore good for each individual, good for all humankind.

Going forward, we only need to raise awareness of pacific Daoism and what it means.
We need only to teach it in school together with other philosophies and religions
Let each individual decide whether to cultivate pacific Daoism or not.
Hence, going forward does not demand big planning, big organization, or big expenses.
Pacific Daoism should not be institutionalized, so that it may not be hijack by strong, but selfish individuals.

Pacific Daoism in our hearts, unseen, unheard, and only show in our unselfish actions.

170 BIBLIOGRAPHY

171   Publications in English

172   Publications in Chinese

BIBLIOGRAPHY

Publications in English

Chan, Alan (2007). *Laozi*. In. Stanford Encyclopedia of Philosophy. Http://plato.standford.edu/entries/laozi.

Clearly, Thomas (1998). *The Essential Tao*. New Jersey, USA, Castle Books. ISBN 0-7858-0905-8.

Gao, Huaping (2010). *Laozi*. Nanjing, Nanjing University Press. ISBN 978-7-305-06607-8.

Gu, Zhengkun (1995). *Lao Tzu: The Book of Tao and Teh*. Beijing, Peking University Press. ISBN 7-301-02815-6/B.144.

Harrington, Spencer P.M. (1998). *Laozi Debate*. Archaeology, newsbriefs, Vol.51, No. 6.

Hawking, SW, Mlodinow L (2010). *The Grand Design*. Bantam Books, US. ISBN 9780553819229.

Henricks, Robert G. (1991). *Lao-Tzu Te-Tao Ching*. London, Rider. ISBN 0-7126-4645-0.

Lau, D.C. (1994). *Lao-Tzu Tao Te Ching*. Alfred A. Knopf, New York, Everyman's Library. ISBN 0-679-43316-3.

Littlejohn, Ronnie (2005)..*Laozi (Lao-tzu)*. The Internet Encyclopedia of Philosophy, Http://www.iep.utm.edu/laozi/.

Maurer, Herrymon (1985). *Lao Tzu / Tao Teh Ching*. New York, Schocken Books. ISBN 0-8052-3985-5.

Merkin, Maury (2008). *Daoism in Brief*. Http://www.his.com/~merkin/DaoBrief.html.

New Encyclopedia Britannica (1988). *Taoism*. Vol. 28, 5th ed. Encyclopedia Britannica Inc.Chicago, USA.

Star, Jonathan (2001). *TaoTe Ching*. New York, Penguin. ISBN 1-58542-099-9.

Seymour-Smith, Martin (1998). *The 100 most influenctial books ever written: the history of thought from ancient times to today*. Secaucus, N.J.: Carol Publ.Group. ISBN 978-0806520001.

Stein, Jess (1984). Chief editor, *Random House College Dictionary*. Revised edition, Random House, USA. ISBN 0-394-43600-8.

Wolfram Mathematics (2011). Http://www.wolframalpha.com.

Publications in Chinese

Chen, Qinghui (2002). *Laozi direct interpretation.* In (classical Chinese culture, the true interpretation), edited by Cui Fuzhang, Hangzhou: Zhejiang Culture and Art Publishing House. (陈庆惠 (2002). 《老子直解》. 见《中国文化經典真解》, 崔富章主編, 杭州:浙江文艺出版社).

Liu, Hao (2001). Edit. *Dao De Jing, (Spring and Autumn Period, Lao Dan).* Yanbian University Press. (劉浩 (2001). 主编, 《道德經》, (春秋, 老聃). 延边大学出版社). ISBN 7-5634-1491-6 /G.265.

Liu, Mian Yi (1991). Edit. *Ancient Text Pictograms for the Arts.* Changsa Shi, Hunan Arts Publisher. (刘勉怡 (1991). 编. 《艺用古文字图案》. 长沙市, 湖南美术出版社). ISBN 7-5356-0393-9 /J.

Liu, Xiaogan (2006). *Laozi ancient and modern: Five Text Versions for Analysis, Evaluation and Discussion.* Beijing, China Social Sciences Press. (劉笑敢 (2006). 《老子古今: 五種對勘輿析評引論》. 北京, 中国社會科学出版社). ISBN 7-5004-5605-0.

Lou, Fei (2006). Edit. *Laozi (Spring and Autumn Period). Zhuangzi (Warring States).* Beijing, Beijing Publishing House. (楼霏 (2006). 编. 《老子》(春秋). 莊子(战国). 北京, 北京出版社). ISBN 7-200-06509-9.

Mao, Peiqi, Li Zefeng (1989). Edit. *Of History, Mountains and Rivers: Chinese History in Pictures.* Shanghai Ancient Books Publishing House. (毛佩琦, 李泽奉 (1989). 主编. 《崴月山河: 图说中国历史》. 上海, 古籍出版社). ISBN 7-5325-0591-X /K.54.

Peng, Hao (2000). Edit. *Guodian Chu Bamboo-slip Laozi Proof-read.* Hubei People's Publishing House, Wuhan. (彭浩 (2000). 校编. 《郭店楚简老子校读》. 湖北人民出版社, 武汉). ISBN 7-216-02741-8 /B.147.

Sha, Shaohai, Xu Zihong (2004). Annotate. *Laozi.* Taipei, Taiwan Ancient Texts published. (沙少海, 徐子宏 (2004). 譯注. 《老子》. 台北市, 台灣古籍出版). ISBN 978-986-7743-831.

Scholars (Song, 960-1279CE; Yuan, 1271-1368CE). Annotated. *The 4 Books and 5 Classics.* Tianjin, the Ancient Shop printed, 1988. (宋元人 (960-1279CE; 1271-1368CE). 注. 《四書五經》. 天津市, 古店影印, 1988).

Wang, Jun (2007). Compiled. *Shi Ji (Sima Qian, Han).* Beijing, Zhonghua Book Company. (王军 (2007). 编. 《史記 (司馬迁, 漢)》. 北京, 中华書局). ISBN 978-7-101-05146-9.

Xu, Shen (Han, 206BCE-220CE). *Words Explain.* Tianjin Antiquarian Bookshop printed, 1994. (许慎 (漢). 《说文解字》. 天津市古籍書店影印, 1994.)

Zhang, Xiuping, Wang Nai Zhuang (1993). Edit. *100 cultures which has affected China.* Nanning, Guangxi People's Publishing House. (张秀平, 王乃庄 (1993). 主编. 《影向中国的100文化》. 南宁市, 广西人民出版社). ISBN 7-219-02307-3 /G.

Zhang, Xiuping, Wang Xiaoming (1993). Ed. *100 books which has affected China.* Nanning, Guangxi People's Publishing House. (张秀平, 王晓明 (1993). 主编. 《影向中国的100本書》. 南宁市, 广西人民出版社). ISBN 7-219-02339-1 /K.

Zhou, Bingjun (2001). Annotate. *Book of History.* Hunan Changsha City, Yuelu Bookstore. (周秉鈞 (2001). 譯注. 《尚書》. 湖南长沙市, 岳麓書社). ISBN 7-80665-093-8.

173	**APPENDICES**
174	Acknowledgments
175	After thoughts
176	List of important dates
177	Glossary
178	The Chinese Language
180	*Illustration 12 Evolution of Chinese Characters*
181	Concordance Analysis
183	Copyright & Disclaimer
184	Alphabetical index

Appendices

Acknowledgments

The author is greatly indebted to all authors listed in the bibliography and many others that are not listed. Most of the publications listed here have not been cited directly in the text of this study. But all of them have been read and much consulted, for my understanding of the *Dao De Jing*. And most importantly, I am indebted to the legendary Laozi himself for writing the *Dao De Jing*.

The great editorial help of Lisa Cole from HyperLife Editing Services, is much appreciated. Many thanks for suggesting that use of words with close meanings may give a broader perspective. I have left them in place in the different sections and not try to achieve consistency with one word. I am most thankful for the very positive assessment of Leigh Blackmore, The Manuscript Appraisal Agency. The suggestion that illustrations be put in to enliven the pages, will certainly enhance readers' enjoyment.

I sincerely thank the National Library Singapore for issuing the complimentary ISBN and CIP. Applications for a Deposit Web account, an ISBN and CIP are all completed within 2 weeks. It has been a breeze working with the Legal Deposit Office, Singapore.

Last but not least, I salute Lightning Source (Ingram) for providing on-demand printing (POD). Also, world-wide distribution services, which is particularly helpful to self-publishers like myself.

Due diligence has been exercised to be honest and acccurate with facts and figures used inthis book. Nevertheless, all the errors and omissions that still remain in this book are entirely mine.

Appendices

After Thoughts

I have asked myself, "Do I have the qualifications to study Laozi's *Dao De Jing*?"
"Do I have the talents to write a monograph on my findings?"
Indeed, I am no philosopher and do not know how to develop a topic philosophically.
Indeed, I am no scholar of the Chinese language and of ancient Chinese texts.
However from a very young age, I am given to wonder, "How does the universe come to exist?"

A Westerner once wrote, the Chinese should do more to introduce their own culture.
Living and breathing the culture, a Chinese is more facilitated than a Westerner looking in from the outside.
I am encouraged to, and with great humility, carry this study to completion.
This monograph is my first, written after retirement.
I have tried to address all comments and criticisms received, before publication.
It is presented at the Google site: https://sites.google.com/site/laoziappreciation/ and is free for viewing.

It seems that my study may have done Laozi a disservice, calling his primal entity Dao, non-existing.
But I offer no apology for treating the 'Dao' of Laozi as, just his theory for explaining the universe.
In fact, the theory of 'Dao' compares well with the 'Big Bang' theory of our time.
Both are unsubstantiated and both remain, theories only.
In spite of our great advancement in science today, we have not done better than Laozi in c.500 BCE!

Laozi has left us with 2 great legacies:
In 'Dao', his spirit of quest for the Ultimate Reality.
In 'De', his philosophic prescription for peace and harmony on earth.

Appendices

List of Important Dates	In chronological order
Old stone age (石器时代)	600,000 – 9,000 BCE
New stone age (新石器时代)	8,000 – 4,000 BCE
Bronze age (铜器时代)	2,100 - 771 BCE
Emperor Yao (尧)	c.24th - 23rd century BCE (Legendary ruler of ancient China)
Emperor Shun (舜)	c.23rd - 22nd century BCE (Legendary ruler of ancient China)
Emperor Yu (禹)	c.22nd - 21st century BCE (Legendary ruler of ancient China)
Xia Dynasty (夏朝)	2,100 – 1,600 BCE (China's 1st dynasty, with no written language)
Shang Dynasty (商朝)	1,600-1,066 BCE (China's 2nd dynasty, writing on shells, bones)
Zhou Dynasty (Western) (西周)	1,066 – 771 BCE (China's third dynasty, with written history)
Zhou Dynasty (Eastern) (东周)	770 – 221 BCE (China's third dynasty, with Capital moved east)
Spring Autumn period (春秋)	770 – 476 BCE (numerous vassal states coalesced into 7 majors)
Warring States period (战国)	475 – 221 BCE (7 major vassal states fighting for supremacy)
Qin Dynasty (秦朝)	221 – 206 BCE (China's 4th dynasty with a unified language)
Han Dynasty (汉朝)	206BCE–220CE (China's 5th dynasty with unification consolidated)
Jin Dynasty (Eastern) (东晋)	317-420 CE (a troubled period with invasions by 5 northern tribes)
Song Dynasty (宋朝)	960-1279CE (China stabilized after a long period of turmoils)
Yuan Dynasty (元朝)	1271-1368CE (China under the rule of Mongolian Emperors)
Yi Jing (*Book of Change*, 易经)	c. 1,066 BCE (largely by Wen, founder-king of Zhou Dynasty)
Shang Shu (*Book of History*, 尚书)	c. 500 BCE (records of Xia, Shang, Zhou dynasties)
Shi Jing (*Book of Poems*, 诗经)	c. 500 BCE (records of poems from the vassal states of Zhou)
Shi Ji (*Historical Records*, 史記)	c.100BCE (author, Sima Qian, Han Dynasty)
Laozi (老子)	c. 580 BCE (Zhou, Spring Autumn period, philosopher)
Kongzi (Confucius, 孔子)	551 – 479 BCE (Zhou, Spring Autumn period, philosopher)
Mengzi (Mencius, 孟子)	c. 372 – 288 BCE (Zhou, Warring States period, philosopher)
Zhuangzi (庄子)	c. 369 - 286 BCE (Zhou, Warring States period, philosopher)
Hanfeizi (韩飞子)	c. 280 - 233 BCE (Zhou, Warring States period, philosopher)
Heshanggong (河上公)	c. 179 BCE (Han, author of a commentary on Laozi)
Sima Qian (司马迁)	c. 145-87BCE (Han, author of Historical Records, 史記)
Wang Bi (王弼)	226 – 249CE (author of a commentary on Laozi)
Xu Shen (许慎)	c. 58 – 147CE (Han, author of Words Explain, 说文解字)
Laozi, text on bamboo-slips	c. 350 BCE (Chu tomb at Guodian, Jingmen, Hubei)
Laozi, text on silk	c. 200 BCE (Han tomb at Mawangdui, Changsha, Hunan)

Glossary

Dao (道):	"Path"; to name Laozi's hypothetical Primal Entity that creates the universe.
De (德):	"Virtue"; to name Laozi's hypothetical derivative of Dao, it nurtures all things.
Dao De Jing (道德经):	*The Primal and Virtue Classic*; Laozi's book of 5000 Chinese Characters.
Fuxi (伏羲):	c. 2900 BCE; mythological sovereign of ancient China, traditionally credited with inventing the trigrams of the *Yi Jing* (*易经, Book of Change*).
Guodian (郭店):	An archaeology excavation site, where the *Dao De Jing* on bamboo-slips were recovered from a Chu tomb (c.350 BCE), in Jingmen, Hubei, in 1993.
Han Dynasty (汉朝):	206 BCE–220CE; Emperor Han consolidated unified China.
Hanfeizi (韩飞子):	c. 280 - 233 BCE; philosopher, Warring States period, Eastern Zhou Dynasty.
Heshanggong (河上公):	c. 179 BCE; author of a commentary on *Laozi*, Han Dynasty.
Jin Dynasty, Eastern (东晋):	317- 420 CE; latter half of Jin Dynasty, much troubled by 5 northern tribes.
Kongzi (Confucius, 孔子):	551 – 479 BCE; philosopher, Spring Autumn period, Eastern Zhou Dynasty.
Laozi (老子):	c.580 BCE; philosopher, Spring Autumn period, Eastern Zhou Dynasty.
Li (礼):	Etiquette, rites, traditional form of virtue expression.
Mawangdui (马王堆):	An archaeology excavation site, where 2 copies of *Dao De Jing* on silks were recovered from a Han tomb (c.200 BCE), near Changsha, Hunan, in 1973.
Mengzi (Mencius, 孟子):	c. 372 – 288 BCE; philosopher, Warring States period, Eastern Zhou Dynasty.
Qin Dynasty (秦朝):	221 – 206 BCE; Emperor Qin defeated 6 eastern states, and unified China.
Ren (仁):	Benevolence, compassion, traditional form of virtue expression.
Shang Dynasty (商朝):	1,600 – 1,066 BCE; first to have written language on oracle bones and shells.
Shang Shu (尚书):	c. 500 BCE; *Book of History*, archives of the Xia, Shang, Zhou Dynasties.
Shi Jing (诗经):	c.500 BCE; *Book of Poems*, archives of poems, feudal states, Zhou Dynasty.
Shun (舜):	23rd - 22nd century BCE; Legendary ruler of ancient China.
Sima Qian (司马迁):	c. 145-87 BCE; author of *Historical Records (史記)*, Han Dynasty.
The Chinese Bellows:	Big box with a plunger which is used to push air out to fire the furnace.
Wang Bi (王弼):	226 – 249 CE; author, a commentary on *Laozi*, Cao Wei, the Three Kingdoms.
Wu (无,):	"Have-not"; Laozi uses to name the beginning of Heaven and Earth (ch.1).
WuWei (无为):	Laozi's philosophy of "no motive", or "not selfish"; but not "no action".
WuWeiWuBuWei: (无为无不为)	Laozi's philosophy of unselfish-living, with "no motive" that removes all pressure to perform, that clears the mind and body "for further actions".
Xia Dynasty (夏朝):	2,100-1,600 BCE; China's first established dynasty with no written language.
Xu Shen (许慎):	c. 58 – 147CE; author of *Words Explain (说文解字)*, Han Dynasty.
Yang (阳):	Denotes all things bright and positive, like the Sun, Heaven, male, hot, etc.
Yao (尧):	24th - 23rd century BCE; Legendary ruler of ancient China.
Yi Jing (易经):	c.1,066 BCE; *Book of Change*, largely by King Wen, founder, Zhou Dynasty.
Yi (义):	Righteousness, Justice, traditional form of virtue expression.
Yin (阴):	Denotes all things dark and negative, like the moon, Earth, female, cold, etc.
You (有):	"Have"; Laozi uses to name the 'Mother of all things' (ch.1).
Yu (禹):	22nd - 21st century BCE; Legendary ruler of ancient China.
Zhou Dynasty, Eastern (东周):	770 – 221 BCE; China's third dynasty, the late period, capital in the East.
Zhou Dynasty, Western (西周):	1,066 – 771 BCE; China's third dynasty, the initial period, capital in the West.
Zhuangzi (庄子):	c. 369-286 BCE; philosopher, Warring States period, Zhou Dynasty, Eastern.

Appendice

The Chinese Language

Words are square pictograph characters, that can be placed vertically or horizontally to form sentences.
A pictogram can be used as noun, verb, adjective, as name, and with minimal of grammatical requirements.
By its radicals, a pictogram informs if an object is a tree, a bird, made from stone, water-related, etc.
A written script sound different in dialects, but all readers are united in the comprehension of its content.
Uniquely, the written Chinese Language is a unifying language for all individuals who write it and read it.
Though hard to speak and listen, it is easy to read and understand, and exciting to write in calligraphic style.

Evolution of the Chinese Scripts
For about 3000 years, the Oracle Bone script evolved in continum to the present day Standard script.
At any one time several scripts are in used, as new script needs time to evolve and does not appear suddenly.
Primitive pictographic forms giving way to strucutred stroke formats, and simplification with less strokes.

Shell-bone script (甲骨文, jia gu wen) - Inscribed directly with a sharp instrument on turtle shells and oxen bones. Well developed during Shang Dynasty (c.1400 - 1200 BC) mainly for recording of oracles.

Bronze script (金文, jin wen) - Cast on bronze vessels, weapons and coins. Well developed during the ZhouDynasty (c.1100 - 256 BC) for religious celebrations and recording of important events.

Large Seal script (大篆, da zhuan) - Curved in stones and brushed on bamboo slips. Well developed during the Zhou Dynasty (c.1100 - 256 BC), this script is highly varied among the 6 warring states in the East.

Small Seal script (小篆, xiao zhuan) - This is the script of the State of Qin in the West. When Emperor Qin Shi Huang stablished the Qin Dynasty (c. 221 -207 BC), this script was imposed over all unified China.

Clerical script (隶书, li shu) - For need of simplification, this script was developed by lowly officials during the Qin Dynasty. It was well developed and established during the Han Dynasty (207 BC – 220 CE).

Standard script (楷书, kai shu) - Evolving from the Clerical script, it gained popularity after the Han Dynasty. It was well established by the the Eastern Jin Dynasty (317- 420 CE) and use to the present day.

Running script (行书, xing shu) - Evolving in tandem, it is the popular form of writing the Standard script. With the artistic deletion and combination of strokes, the continuity between words flow like a stream.

Draft script (草书, cao shu) - Also evolving in tandem, this is equivalent to the short-hand writing of the Standard script. Often illegible to others, it is of no practical use, but for the expression of freedom by some caligraphers.

Simplified script (简体字, jian ti zi) - More simplification by reduction and combination of strokes. Used since 1949 in the People's Republic of China (PRC). Also used in Singapore.

Romanization of the Chinese Language.(汉语拼音, hanyu pinyin) - Has been used in the People's Republic of China (PRC) since 1958. This stabilizes the phonetics, but causes loss of the beautifully written pictograhic characters, and the loss of instant recognition and appreciation of meanings by their radical compositions.

Chinese Phonetics (注音符号, zhuyin fuhao) - This was developed in China in 1913, and is still used in Taiwan. This is not popular as it is difficult to learn a new set of phonetics which is unfamilial.

Appendice

Creation of Chinese Characters

Xu Shen (c.100AD) in his *Words Explain,* first clarified, that Chinese characters are formed by 6 techniques.
1. Ideograms (指事字, zhishizi), example, top (上) and bottom (下). (radicals formation)
2. Pictograms (象形字, xiangxingzi), example, sun (日) and moon (月). (radicals formation)
3. Phono-semantic compounds (形声字, xing sheng zi), example, broad river (江) and river (河).
4. Ideogrammic compounds (会意字, huiyizi), example, martial (武) and trust (信).
5. Transformation variants (转注字, zhuanzhuzi), example, old (考) and old (老).
   (The character for longevity (寿), is known to have great than 100 forms, but no new word creation).
6. Loan words (假借字, jiajiezi), example, decree (令) and elder (长).
   (Common today, borrowing characters with same sound for translating foreign words; like clone, 克隆).

Controversy in Punctuation Placement
There is a paucity of punctuation in ancient Chinese texts.
And depending where we choose to break a sentence with a comma, the meaning can be quite different.
As illustrated below, the 2 Concepts of Wu (Have-not) and You (Have) have become Nameless and Named.

无, 名天地之始	Wu (Have-not), to name the beginning of Heaven and Earth
有, 名万物之母	You (Have), to name the mother of all things

(this study, 2012)

无名, 天地之始	As <u>Nameless</u>, it is the origin of all things
有名, 万物之母	As <u>Named</u>, it is the mother of all things

(Star, 2001)

Difficulty in Comprehending Grammatical Usage
In the English language, words as nouns or verbs have different spellings to differentiate their usage.
In the Chinese language, the same characters are written, whether in use as nouns or verbs.
This difficulty can be seen in the first 2 lines of the first verse of the Dao De Jing.

道可道, 非恒道	If <u>Dao</u> can <u>be described</u>, it is not the primal Dao
名可名, 非恒名	If <u>Name</u> can <u>be named</u>, it is not the primal name (ch.1)

Problem with Direct and Implied Meanings
The actions of a ruler should be without selfish motive and for the common good, hence people are governable.
It seems inaction to govern and regulate is not a good idea after we saw the melt-down of Wall Street, 2008.

为无为	Act for <u>no motive</u> (unselfish)
则无不治	Then none not governable (ch.3)

(this study, 2012)

为无为	Act in accordance with this principle of <u>inaction</u>
则无不治	And the world will be kept in order everywhere (ch.3)

(Gu, 1995)

The earliest known version, Guodian *Laozi was* written in the Large Seal script of the State of Chu.
Mistakes of omissions, additions and mis-transcription of the *Laozi* in the different scripts could have occur.
In spite of diffficulties in interpretaion and transcription error, the *Dao De Jing* has remained cohesive.
Today in the 21st century, it still consistently reflects the spirit and thoughts of Laozi.

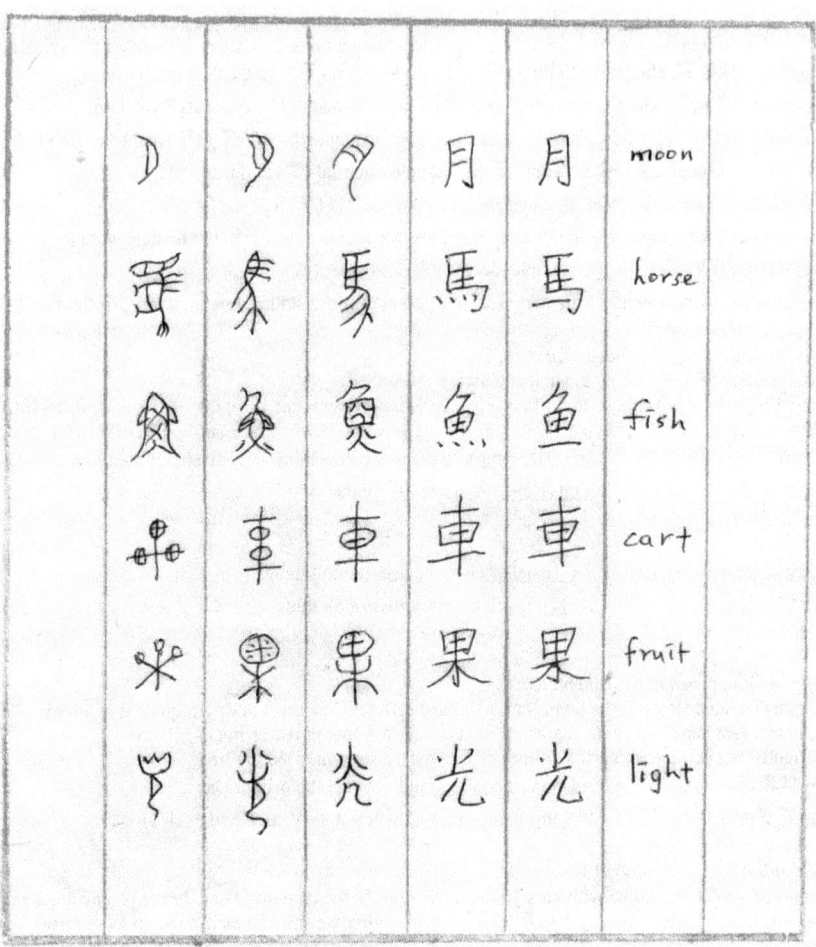

Evolution of Chinese Characters

From left to right:
Shell-bone script - Shang Dynasty (c.1400 - 1200 BC)
Bronze script   - Zhou Dynasty (c.1100 - 256 BC)
Small seal script - Qin Dynasty (221-206BC)
Standard script - Eastern Jin Dynasty (c.317 – 420 BC) to day, 21st century
Simplified script - Used since 1949 in the People's Republic of China.
           Also used in Singapore.

Appendices

Concordance Analysis

The version of the *Dao De Jing* here adopted has a total count of 5282 characters. There are 800 unique characters, of which 323 characters occur once only in the text. The rest have usages ranging from 2 times to the maximum of 251 times.

The 12 characters with most frequent usages are:

之 zhi	- its, itself, their (251x)		不 bu	- no, not (239x)	
以 yi	- by-which (163x)		其 qi	- its, itself, their (143x)	
而 er	- but, and (122x)		为 wei	- motive, action, as, be (114x)	
无 wu	- Have-not, nothing (102x)		天 tian	- Heaven (93x)	
者 zhe	- person, zhe (91x)		人 ren	- people (87x)	
下 xia	- below (83x)		有 you	- Have, has (83x)	

Chinese Language need characters like 之(its, 251x), 其 (their,143x) for grammatic assignment of ownership.

行不言, 之教　　　　　Does non-verbal, <u>its</u> teaching (by setting good examples) (ch.2)
虚其心, 实其腹　　　　Humble <u>their</u> heart, fill <u>their</u> stomach (ch.3)

Paradoxically, negative words like, 不 (not, 239x), 无 (no, 102x) are often used in positive context.

生, 而<u>不</u>有; 为, 而<u>不</u>恃　　Creates, but <u>not</u> possessive; contributes, but <u>not</u> presumptuous (ch.2)
爱民治国, 能<u>无</u>为乎？　　Love the citizen and manage the state, possible <u>no</u> self-agenda? (ch.10)

Words like, "以 (by-which 163x)" and "而 (but, 122x)" are also needed to connect the abundance of ideas.

恒无, 欲<u>以</u>观其妙　　　　Primal Wu (Have-not), if wishes <u>by-which</u> to observe Dao's wonders (ch.1)
万物作焉, <u>而</u>不辞　　　　All things in action, <u>but</u> makes no criticism (ch.2)

High usage of 为 (wei, 114x), with multiple meanings like, "motive (27x)", "action (27x)" and "as, be (60x)".

是以: 圣人处无<u>为</u>之事　　Therefore: the Sage manages no <u>motive</u> (unselfish) tasks (ch.2)
生, 而不有; <u>为</u>, 而不恃　　Creates, but does not possesses; <u>action</u>, but not presumptuous (ch.2)
天下皆知美之<u>为</u>美, 斯恶已　All the world know beauty <u>as</u> beautiful, then non-beauty is known (ch.2)

Most often, 无 (wu, 102x) means "not, none" and 有 (you, 83x) means "has". But they have also been used to name the Dao derivatives, 无 (Wu or Have-not, 5x) and 有 (You or Have, 6x)

为无为, 则<u>无</u>不治　　　Act <u>not</u> in self-interest (not selfish), then <u>none</u> not governable (ch.3)
生, 而不<u>有</u>　　　　　　Creates, but does not <u>has</u> (ch.2)
<u>无</u>, 名天地之始　　　　Wu (Have-not), to name the beginning of Heaven and Earth (ch.1)
<u>有</u>, 名万物之母　　　　You (Have), to name the mother of all things (ch.1)

When 天 (Heaven , 93x) does not mean Heaven, it is used in the phrase, 天下(the world, 61x).

<u>天下</u>, 莫柔弱于水　　　In the <u>world</u>, none gentler and weaker than water (ch.78)
<u>天</u>之道, 利而不害　　　Way of <u>Heaven</u>, benefiting, and not harming (ch.81)

Appendices

Concordance Analysis

Other usage of 者 (zhe, 91x) like, interjection (13x) with no meaning, besides person (54x), and entity (24x).

天地, 所以能长且久者	Heaven and Earth, the reason for being long and lasting, <u>zhe</u> (ch.7)
古之, 善为道者	In ancient time, <u>persons</u> good at practicing Dao (ch.15)
此两者, 同出而异名	These 2 <u>entities</u>, are from the same source but differently named (ch.1)

Of all the 人 (people, 87x) mentioned, it refers to the 圣人 (Sage), 31x.

既以为人, 己愈有	With working for <u>people</u>, self will have more (ch.81)
圣人不积	The <u>Sage</u> does not accumulate (for self)

Almost 3 quarters of 下 (below, 83x) are tied up in 天下(the world, 61x), not depicting lowliness, humility.

不以兵强天下	Do not use army to dominate the <u>world</u> (ch.30)
善用人者, 为之下	Whoever good at employing people, be <u>humble</u> (ch.68)

道 (Dao, 76x) and 德 (De, 43x) in the *Dao De Jing*, almost exclusively name the primal entity and its virtue.

有物浑成, 先天地生	There are matters that mixed and formed, created before Heaven and Earth
吾不知其名, 字之曰道	I do not know its name, in word call it <u>Dao</u> (ch.25)
失道, 而后德; 失德, 而后仁	Lost <u>Dao</u>, then comes <u>Virtue</u>; lost <u>Virtue</u>, then comes Benevolence (ch.38)
万物, 莫不尊道而贵德	All things, none do not respect <u>Dao</u> and value <u>Virtue</u> (ch.51)

The traditional virtues 仁 (Ren, 8x), 义 (Yi, 5x), and 礼 (Li, 5x) are beneath 道 (Dao, 76x) and 德 (De, 43x).

失道, 而后德; 失德, 而后仁	Lost <u>Dao</u>, then comes <u>De</u>; lost <u>De</u>, then comes <u>Ren</u> (ch.38)
失仁, 而后义, 失义, 而后礼	Lost <u>Ren</u>, has <u>Yi</u>; lost <u>Yi</u>, has <u>Li</u> (ch.38)

The characters, 阴(Yin) and 阳(Yang) occur once only, and so certainly are not expounded as concepts here.

万物负阴, 而抱阳	All things carry <u>Yin</u> (female energy), embrace <u>Yang</u> (male energy) (ch.42)

From the character counts, the concordance is revealing on the contents of the book.
It is about 人 (people, 87x), the 圣人 (Sage, 31x), who embrace the 道 (Dao, 76x) and 德 (De, 43x).
Traditional 仁 (Ren, 8x), 义 (Yi, 5x), 礼 (Li, 5x) count much less, certainly not 阴(Yin, 1x) and 阳(Yang, 1x).

The paradoxical style of Laozi is reflected in plenty of, 不 (not, 239x), 无 (no, 102x), and 下 (below, 83x). These negative words are used in positive context, especially with positive characters like 为 (action, 114x).

Chinese characters are essentially agrammatic with no indications of belonging, gender, time, etc.
Sentences need plenty of 之(its, 251x), 其 (their,143x) to assign ownership.
And characters like, 以 (by-which, 163x) and 而 (but, 122x) are needed to connect events and thoughts.
Also 天 (Heaven , 93x) may not be Heaven when used in combination, like 天下(the world, 61x).
One must be mindful as to when characters are names, like 无 (Wu, Have-not 5x) and 有 (You, Have, 6x).
Other usage of characters like, 者 (*zhe*, 91x) as interjection (13x) with no meaning, just adding verbal emotion.

The Concordance is enlightening on the contents, style of the author, and colors of the Chinese language.

Copyright © 2011
This work is registered with the UK Copyright Service.
All rights reserved.
Copying is allowed for individual private use.
Copying is not allowed for commercial trade.

Disclaimer:
Every precaution has been taken in the preparation of this book. The publisher and author apologize for any errors and omissions that may remain. The publisher and author assume no liability, whatsoever, for damages resulting from the use of this book.

Laozi: Quest for the Ultimate Reality

This monograph may be used as a handbook for understanding the *Dao De Jing* and Laozi's thoughts. The Chinese text / English translations may also facilitate students who are learning a second language. Hence for this guide on the *Dao De Jing*, indexing is made comprehensive with the following 3 approaches. The concordance of the English translation section yields 1594 unique words, and all are included. Stimulating phrases from the comment sections and punch-lines, are liberally referenced by cross-entries Lastly, the Contents pages are also indexed for convenient access from back of the book.

Alphabetical Index

1
1 hub..............................31
10, 3 of which prematured deaths..............................75
100 most influential books..............................6
100-fold..............................39
2
2 entities..............................19
3
3 entities..............................34, 39
3 of 10, long-lived..............75
3 senior ministers..............87
3 Treasures..............................93
4
4-horse chariot..................87
6
6 family-relationships....38
9
9-stories Tower..................90
A
a..............................26, 33, 40
A fair proposition..........144
A mystic, Laozi ?..........112
a quest..............................47
a religion? not Daoism...57
A scientist, Laozi!........115
a step backward..............91
A word of caution..........16
Abandon..............39, 83, 93
abandoned................49, 87
abandoning virtues!........39
abandons nobody............87
able..............34, 40, 73, 96
abnormal..........................83
about..............................67
above..............41, 62, 92

absolute..................50, 74
absolute compassion......49
absolute freedom..........153
abundance, is contentment
..............................56
abundant........................79
accepted norms........65, 138
accommodating..............36
accomplished..................72
accomplishing................99
accomplishment............37
accord..................41, 78
accordance............36, 44
accords..............................44
accumulate..................107
accumulated..................90
accumulating................84
achieve..............26, 54, 88
achieve big, small efforts
..............................88
achieved..........29, 37, 103
Achieves..............20, 57, 76
Acknowledgments........174
act..................21, 35, 72, 90
Act for no motive..........149
acting..............................36
action....28, 36, 62, 90, 101
action directed, meditation
..............................136
actionable........................73
actions without motives. 67
acts..................20, 103
acts knowing, sick..........97
Additional........................39
addressing Dao..............47
adjusting, bow..............103
administer........................54

administers taxes..........105
administration................21
Admitting ignorance......22
advance..........................95
advanced........................60
advancing........................65
advantages over others. 131
advices, facing fears.....127
Affairs..................52, 88, 96
afraid..........................40, 98
after..................47, 52, 91
After Thoughts..............175
aftermath of wars..........155
afterward 52
again..................36, 50, 77
against desires..............154
age..............................52, 80
age of universe................13
agenda..................26, 73, 82
aggressor........................95
ahead..............................92
aids..................................49
air..............................24, 69
alert..................................83
alive..................................63
alive, supple and soft....102
all............20, 37, 40, 74, 93
All Matters..........55, 63, 66
all things..................57, 90
all things created by.......64
all things, refuge of........87
All things' creation..........66
All-things........................20
allegiance 86
alliance............................86
alone..........................40, 47
already..........................55

184

also......................58, 74, 85
Always................70, 86, 91
am..............................40, 74
ambition..............21, 54, 56
ambitions......................101
an..............................73, 95
an anthology? No..........110
analogy of a bow..........103
analyzes rebellion...........98
analyzing survival..........75
ancestor 22
anchor.............................40
anchors...........................48
Ancient.........35, 41, 43, 91
ancient maxim.................66
ancient's.........................87
ancients...........................94
and........51, 66, 81, 93, 100
angry................................94
anonymity, Daoism........63
another............................56
anti-dotes, discuss.........133
anything..........................34
apart.................................40
appalled by.....................52
appeal.............................87
appear..............................38
APPENDICES..............173
    Acknowledgments..174
    After Thoughts.......175
    Chinese Characters. 179
    Chinese Language. .178
    Concordance Analy 181
    Copyright © 2011 ..183
    Disclaimer...............183
    Glossary..................177
    Important Dates 176
application 84
Appointing......................87
appropriate.....................86
archive of knowledge.....72
archives...........................72
are..........64, 76, 92, 96, 102
argue..............................107
arise..........................61, 82
arm............................62, 95
armies..............................95
Army....52, 54, 75, 82, 102

army, misfortune, discuss
....148
arrogant....................29, 52
as............20, 35, 39, 57, 63
ascending........................40
assist................................52
assume.............................30
astray...............................78
astride..............................45
at....................49, 58, 65, 75
attack...............................95
attacking.......................104
attain................................63
attaining..........................63
attempts...........................90
attributes of Dao............65
authority...................43, 45
Authorship, DDJ..........110
average............................65
avoid................................75
avoid premature death..154
avoided............................52
aware 30
away..........................30, 41
awed by Dao, no............76
B
baby..............30, 40, 50, 80
back..............20, 34, 77, 83
back to basics 106
back-role........................26
back-to-tribal society....106
bad....................................52
bad years follow wars. .148
baggage...........................48
balanced..........................69
banner-signs...................78
barrel...............................24
base..........................48, 63
based...............................63
basic human rights.......138
basis of pacific Daoism 120
battle................................54
be...............50, 55, 57, 60, 81
Be contented 70
be contented, be safe......68
be prepared,difficulties...88
Be unselfish.............26, 61
be vigilant...............90, 139

be whole (preserved)......43
bears nation's dirt.........104
beasts..............................80
beautiful........................106
Beautiful words...........107
Beauty......................20, 40
Because......43, 57, 91, 101
become............................93
been.................................83
before........................47, 90
began..............................77
beginning............19, 34, 90
behavior, Daoist............35
behind.............................92
being..................36, 50, 92
being-full........................35
BELLOWS..............58, 69
    Dao charges out........22
    Dao's emerging exit..58
    fascinates Laozi......118
    Illustration................23
    space,Heaven,Earth. .24
Bend for salvation..........43
beneath...........................90
beneficial..................80, 99
benefit......................31, 39
benefit, do no harm......144
benefit, not harming.....107
benefited...................66, 81
benefits....................28, 67
benefits all things...........27
Benefits reading Laozi. 166
Benefits, does no harm...50
benefits,Daoist harmony 80
Benevolence.............38, 62
Benevolence, discuss...124
benevolent......................24
bent.................................69
bequeath.........................29
best...........................37, 54
best medicine................61
best friend, Self...........143
bestowed.........................87
better.........................24, 29
BIBLIOGRAPHY........170
    Chinese...................172
    English...................171
Big................33, 52, 68, 86

185

Big Bang..................3, 13	broken.........................83	charity of others............124
Big Bang creation...........66	bronze..........................67	charity works.................124
Big Bang theory.............47	Bronze Tripod..................4	Charity, relieving
Big Bang/Dao, Ultimate	building...................65, 79	symptoms......................61
Reality.......................159	built in small steps..........90	chasing glory, wealth...125
Big nation.....................86	burdened.......................92	Chastising Lords, Kings..78
Big or small..................88	bury..............................75	chickens.......................106
bigger..........................95	but.........................96, 99	chiefs............................78
billion years..................13	By............75, 78, 82, 86	child.....................22, 50
billion years since..........3	by-paths........................78	children 74
birds.............................80	C	Chinese Bellows.....23, 118
birth.....................70, 75	call.........................45, 47	Chinese Bronze Tripod ...4
black............................50	called.....................34, 36	Chinese Characters,
blade............................75	called One.....................34	creation.......................179
Blank............................40	calmly.........................103	Chinese Language.........178
blemishes.....................30	can.....................43, 55, 104	Chinese Scripts, evolution
Blend............................22	cannot..........40, 44, 51, 81	178
blend-in................74, 81	capability......................28	ChineseText DaoDeJing 16
blind pursuit of fame ...126	capability of all individuals	choose..........................32
blindness......................32	144	chop............................100
Block............................77	carefree life.................135	chop-down....................52
Blocks..........................81	Careful..........................90	citizens. 37, 39, 55, 82, 101
blow-cold.....................51	cares.......................32, 76	citizens are free.............82
blow-hot.......................51	carpenter, master..........100	Civilization took off.......72
blue planet.....................3	Carry..................30, 51, 78	claim...........................103
Blunt............................22	cart..............................31	claiming........................62
Blunts...........................81	catch...........................100	claw..............................80
boast.............................52	cattle.............................40	claws............................75
boats...........................106	cause.....................32, 100	clay...............................31
bodily...........................29	causes....................21, 48	clear.................30, 36, 63
body...................33, 68, 92	causes of difficulties.....154	Clear-minded...........40, 69
body-spirit....................30	causes of hunger..........101	cleared..........................35
Bones...................21, 80	causes of wars.............125	cleverness.....................91
book structure, style.......16	celebration....................40	close.................30, 81
border...........................65	center............................24	close doors to desires.....77
boring...................40, 83	Certain 52	Cloth.............................78
bosom-held...................96	certainly................68, 88	Clothes..........................57
both.....................19, 85	champion of the weak....60	clothes, superfluous........45
bottom............28, 34, 37	chances of survival.........75	clothing 106
bountiful.....................107	change...........................47	clumsy..........................69
bow analogy...............103	change others.................56	co-exist, community.....153
Brave....................93, 99	changed.........................50	coarse-jacket.................96
break....................90, 102	character................35, 56	coldness........................69
breath............................30	Charge...........................66	collapsing.....................63
breath, control by heart. .80	charges 22	colors............................32
Bright...................34, 83	charging 69	come..............................24
Brittle...........................90	chariot...........................87	comes............................62
broad............................65	chariots.........................48	comfort.........................58

comfortable....................48
commanded....................55
comment.........................20
Comments......................16
commits.........................100
commodities..............21, 32
common..................40, 48
common benefit of all....73
common failings............154
common good..............130
common people........37, 69
common sickness...........97
common social ills..........68
Common virtues' faults. .38
Commoners....................63
Communication..............28
comparable..............80, 87
compare.........................67
compassion....................83
compassionate................95
complete..................57, 65
completes.......................76
completing.....................65
comply...........................62
computed to be..................3
CONCEPTS.......................
    Chinese Bellows.....118
    Correlatives.............123
    Dao, primal entity...119
    De, primal virtues...120
    Naming......................122
    Wu, You..................121
CONCLUSIONS.................
    Going Forward.......169
    Legacy 1, Spirit......158
    Legacy 2, Daoism...160
    Quest in a Nutshell. 159
    Reading benefits.....166
Concordance Analysis..181
condition.........................41
conduct....................44, 87
conduct, Daoist..............40
conflicts..........................22
confronting....................95
Confucianism...............124
confuse..........................49
confused..............21, 43, 82
confusion.......................83

consequences of wars...125
considerate of others....131
Constant...................36, 80
constantly...............21, 100
construct the universe...121
Constructive words........65
Contained......................80
container 31
contemporary, elder.....109
contending................28, 43
contented.......................70
contention......................43
contentment...........68, 154
Contentment is wealth..125
contentment, disastrous not
knowing..........................70
Contentment, discuss...125
contentment, has
abundance......................56
contentment, knows limits
....68
CONTENTS.....................7
Contents 41
contest............................92
contesting..................94, 99
continuously..................25
contracts.......................105
contrasting.....................91
Contribute......................30
contribute to harmony....64
contribute, not contest..107
control............................76
controlling...............30, 80
conventional virtues.......39
Conventional virtues,
summary......................153
conventional wisdom...145
cooking a small fish.......85
Copyright © 2011 183
core values of ancient...124
correlatives....................20
Correlatives, concept....123
counter-intuitive.............31
counter-intuitive Laozi. 138
Counter-intuitively.........29
counter-productive.........45
counting.........................49
country-side 70

cover artwork...................2
Create.............................30
created..............47, 64, 66
created all things,
You(Have)?....................64
created before Heaven....47
created from Nothing!....64
creates.....................20, 76
creation..........................41
Creation of all things!....66
Creation, Chinese
Characters....................179
creation, summary........152
creation, the universe.....66
creations........................20
credit.......................20, 43
credited..........................57
creek..............................50
crime......................70, 100
crime, none greater.......125
crises handling, discuss 127
crisis resolved, meditation
......................................136
critical of others, no.......20
Crop..............................78
crossing 35
Crowning.......................87
Cultivate........................79
cultivate our minds.......149
cultivate pacific Daoism
......................................143
cultivate primal virtues...30
Cultivate selflessness.....33
cultivating virtues...........79
curing society's ills.........61
cut..................................63
cut-away........................83
cutting...........................50
cycle of Life-death.........36
cycles......................36, 64
Cycles of fortune...........83
cyclical in action, Dao....64
D
daily...............................73
danger..................26, 55, 77
danger, fame/wealth.......68
DAO.................................
    more attributes..........65

DAO ....
  a concept, discuss...119
  action and use...........64
  as substance........41, 58
  at exit of bellows.......58
  birth of......................47
  enter no space...........67
  give rise, all things....66
  has no form...............22
  has no motive..........149
  hypothetical nature...19
  in bellows between
  HeavenEarth..............24
  legacy 1 of Laozi....158
  naming..34, 47, 57, 122
  Not Dao, early demise
 52
  not detectable............34
  prevails the world......85
  procreation, female...25
  procreation, male......41
  refuge for all..............87
  small-meal.................58
  summary..................152
  When lost..................38
Dao and Daoism, introd. 15
Dao created One...........66
Dao creates....................76
DAO DE JING..................
  Act not selfish (63)...88
  ancient Daoist (15)...35
  Army killings (31)....54
  attain One(Dao)(39). 63
  Authorship..............110
  Bend be whole (22). .43
  Big grievance (79)..105
  big nation (61)..........86
  Brave to dare (73).....99
  building virtue (54)...79
  Carry-nourish (10)....30
  Contain-virtues (55). 80
  Dao charges (4)........22
  Dao create One (42). 66
  Dao creates (51)........76
  Dao described (1).....19
  Dao is Great (67)......93
  Dao over-flows (34). 57
  Dao substance (21)...41

Dao to assist (30)......52
Dao unselfish (37)....61
Dao, no name (32)....55
Dao, refuge (62).......87
Dating.....................109
Emerge in birth (50). 75
End Sage-hood (19)..39
fame vs life (44)........68
Favors, Insults (13)...33
Five colors (12)........32
good like water (8)...28
Govern. nation (60). .85
Great Dao lost (18)...38
Great ruler (17).........37
Great success (45)....69
Have matters (25).....47
Heaven lasting (7)....26
Heaven-Earth (5)......24
Heaven's way (77)..103
Heavy is root (26).....48
high scholar (41).......65
High Virtue (38).......62
Holds and fills (9).....29
honest governm.(57).82
hunger, taxes (75)...101
In cycles, Dao (40)...64
Know the male (28)..50
Knows not, act (71). .97
knows people (33)....56
knows,not speak(56).81
learn,daily gain(48). .73
Less talk nature (23). 44
living, gentle (76)...102
Look, see not (14).....34
Manage people (59)..84
move, no trails (27). .49
My words (70)..........96
natural limits (53).....78
Not exalting (3)........21
not fear death (74). .100
not fear power (72)...98
on tip-toe (24)...........45
practicing Dao (65)...91
Respect for Talents
(68)............................94
Rivers and seas (66). 92
rulers, boring (58).....83
Sage no wishes (49)..74

Small nation (80)....106
stable is easy (64).....90
stepping-out (47) 72
take the world (29)...51
Thirty spokes (11)....31
till emptiness (16)....36
to shrink it (36).........60
Trustworthy (81).....107
Uphold image (35) ...58
Valley-spirit (6)........25
Warfare strategy (69)95
world beauty (2).......20
world began (52)......77
world has Dao (46)...70
world, gentler (78)..104
world's gentle (43) ...67
"Wei", "Ah" (20)......40
Dao De Jing, Chinese text
.....................................16
Dao De Jing, English
Translation...................16
Dao in creation.............66
Dao in procreation....25, 41
Dao is Great !................93
Dao models after Nature 47
Dao, concept discuss....119
Dao, enter no space........67
Dao, master of none.......57
Dao, not detectable...34, 58
Dao, not found 152
Dao, Primal Entity........119
Dao, summary..............152
Dao's Greatness............130
DAO's Name......................
  Faraway.....................47
  Going-forth...............47
  Great..................47, 57
  Micro........................34
  One.....................30, 43
  Rarefy.......................34
  Returning..................47
  Small...................57, 77
  Uncarved-wood........55
  Unseen......................34
DAOISM............................
  Daoism is, humility. .66
  for easy governing....85
  for government.........87

188

harmony is present....80
is anonymity.............63
is laughable!.............65
is unselfishness 73
Legacy 2 of Laozi...160
like water, triumphant
.................................104
three treasures:..........93
Daoism and Dao, introd. 15
Daoism for rulers...........55
Daoism in a nutshell.......73
Daoism is anonymity.....63
Daoism is non-violence..66
Daoism, by example.......67
Daoism, discuss.............160
Daoism, easy to know....96
Daoism, in a nutshell......61
Daoism, not a religion....57
Daoism, refuge for all
things...............................87
Daoism, summary........153
Daoist denounces wars...52
Daoist leadership.............50
Daoist mysticism............80
Daoist's happiness........131
DAOISTS...........................
behavior....................35
can co-exist.............153
conduct.....................40
in government...........82
incorruptible.............81
leadership................50
not self-serving........82
Daoists, discuss...............131
Daoists, summary..........153
dare....................21, 90, 99
dares..................................100
daring..........................52, 93
dark...................................34
Dates, important list.....176
dating, Dao De Jing......109
day.........................44, 48, 80
days.....................................83
dazzle..........................22, 83
De, concept discuss......120
dead............................56, 102
dead, hard and stiff.......102
deafness............................32

dearer................................68
death......36, 66, 68, 75, 93, 100
death, life, summary.....154
death, prematured...........75
Death, Survival, discuss
.................................135
debased............................81
debater.............................69
decreed by Dao...............76
DEDICATION...................3
deem.................................57
deep....................22, 84, 91
defeating self, discuss. .143
defects..............................45
defender...........................95
defense................52, 93, 95
deficient...........................69
Defying expectation.....145
demand big planning, no
.................................169
demand of De, self-
discipline....................120
demands of others........124
demise..............................52
denounces wars..............52
depend..............................57
depends............................83
depleted....................22, 25
deployment.............52, 54
deploys............................82
depreciated.....................66
depth........................28, 35
Deputy............................54
derivatives of Dao........121
describe...........................35
described........................19
desirables........................21
desire......21, 39, 61, 70, 73
desire to possess...........125
desires............57, 61, 81, 90
Desires, failings, discuss
.................................133
desires, salvation..........154
desiring...........................61
despair not, the weak......43
Destiny............................36
destroy..............................51

destroy by indulgence....32
destruction.....................29
detest...............................45
detriment, health,life....125
develops.........................76
device.............................31
dew..................................55
diameter of universe.......13
die.......................25, 33, 66
differences....................28
different.........................40
differently.....................19
difficult............88, 91, 101
difficulties.....................88
difficulties, discuss.......139
difficulty...........20, 88, 101
Dignify...........................35
diligently........................65
Dilute.............................58
dim...........................41, 65
diplomacy with humility 86
direct..............................83
dirt..................................104
Disaster...............70, 77, 95
disaster, none greater....125
discard....................32, 98
discard excesses.............51
Discards.........................51
discards extremes, discuss
.................................133
discerning..............40, 83
Disclaimer...................183
discontentment, discuss 133
DISCUSSION...............108
Authorship DDJ 110
Benevolence, etc.....124
Chinese Bellows.....118
Concept of Dao 119
Concept of De 120
Concept, Naming....122
Correlatives............123
Dating the DDJ........109
Desires, Failings.....133
Happiness, Daoist...131
Laozi a mystic?.......112
Laozi religious?......113
Laozi, a pessimist?. 116
Laozi, for rulers?....111

Laozi, laughable?....117
Laozi, philosopher? 114
Laozi, scientist?......115
Life Death Survival 135
On Contentment.....125
On Fame, Wealth....126
On Fears, Crises.....127
On Femininity.........128
On Freedom............129
On Greatness..........130
On Humility............134
On Meditation.........136
On Not-Contesting. 137
On Paradoxes..........138
On Problems...........139
On Purpose of Life. 140
On Retribution........141
On Salvation...........142
On Self...................143
On Success Failure 144
On Triumph Weak..145
On Trust..................146
On Wars..................148
On WuWei 149
Uncertainties, Life..147
WuWei, WuBuWei 150
disgrace....................50
disgraced..................68
dislike................66, 99
disorder....................62
disperse 50
display...................106
disputes....................81
Disregards................26
distanced..................81
do......41, 44, 82, 88, 95, 99
do not go harm's way.....75
does...............72, 76, 88, 92
does not leak...................99
dogs....................24, 106
dominance..................52
dominate....................52
dominate the world.......148
don't......................22, 80
done.......................54, 88
done without motives...153
door...................30, 72, 81
door-ways....................19

doors..........................77
doorway.....................25
down.........................103
down-to-earth talents......94
down-to-earth treasures..93
downfall.....................63
drought......................63
dry...........................102
due............................63
dull............................83
Dumping all baggages..150
dust.....................22, 81
Dwell...............45, 54, 62
dwellings.............98, 106
E
each......................86, 95
early............52, 75, 84, 88
ears......................32, 74
earth.............26, 63, 90
ease 37
easiness.....................20
easiness, then difficultiies
.................................88
easy....................88, 90
easy government............85
easy promises, no.........139
easy to know, to do........96
edges....................22, 81
educate the citizens........91
education, basic human
rights.........................138
effective....................63
elder contemporary......109
elusive......................41
embrace........30, 39, 66, 98
embraces....................43
embracing.................79
Emerge 75
emerging...................58
emperor...............22, 87
employing.................94
emptiness............31, 36
emptiness and utility......31
emptiness, bellows, Dao.24
empty.............24, 31, 78
emulate Dao, discuss....149
enables......................69
encourage hope............43

end.......................39, 88
end of the universe......159
end-of-life.....................77
endangered..............36, 68
ends...........................80
enemy.....................94, 95
enemy, Self................143
energies......................66
energy........................66
engage...................43, 94
English Translation........16
enjoy in harmony.........159
enjoying....................40
Enjoyment................106
enlightened...43, 56, 65, 77
enlightened state...........150
enlightening.................91
enlightenment.....36, 49, 77
enlivened 35
enough....37, 39, 50, 58, 65
enter....................67, 86
entities....19, 34, 39, 62, 99
entity.........................54
entrusted....................33
epitome,pacific Daoism. 63
equipments................106
era.............................40
eradicating poverty.........61
erect...........................80
especially..................96
essence...................41, 80
establishes.................91
ethics.........................40
Etiquette...................62
Etiquette, discuss..........124
euthanasia.................56
even....................44, 72
Ever..........................75
evergreen..................36
everybody's world.........51
evidence of Dao............58
evidence, solid...........109
evil...........................83
evil doers..................99
evil schemer.............60
Evolution, Chinese text 180
exalting......................21
example..............43, 50

190

examples............20, 67
excess...............78, 103
excess food................45
excess to offer world....103
excesses................51, 75
execute.......................100
executioner................100
executioners..............100
Exercise........................69
exhaustible..................69
exist.................37, 39, 57
existence......................84
existing............22, 25, 65
exists...........................90
exit, Dao emerging.........58
exotic...........................82
expand.........................60
expansionism........101, 125
expansionism wars.......155
expense of others, no....140
expenses.......................68
exposes faults of virtues.38
extend 86
extinction.....................63
extolled......................124
extravagance................51
extravagance of rulers. .101
extravagances, discuss. 133
extremes......................51
eyes..................32, 74
F
facing fears, crises........127
fail...................51, 79, 90
failed in life, discuss.....144
Failings, discuss...........133
failure..........................90
faint 65
fair..............................36
falsehood.....................38
fame............................68
Fame, wealth, discuss...126
families.......................79
family..................38, 79
fantasy, not Daoism........24
far-away...............41, 106
far-reaching..........91, 93
Faraway......................47
farther.........................72

fascinated by bellows...118
fast.................32, 45
Faults of virtues, discuss
...................................124
favoritism 105
favors...............33, 54
fear..................37, 63, 100
feared..........................78
fearful.........................35
Fears, Crises, discuss...127
feast............................40
feeding........................24
Feeds..........................76
feeling.........................28
feelings.......................21
feet 90
fellow travelers...............3
female....25, 30, 50, 66, 80, 86
Female in procreation.....25
femininity, discuss.......128
fertility.........................25
fertilize........................70
festivity........................40
few citizens.................106
fields....................70, 78
fierce...........................80
Fight only in defense......95
fighting-wars...............94
filial love......................39
filial piety....................38
filled..................43, 63
filling..........................29
fills.............................29
find fault with oneself. .153
find faults in others........56
finds..................26, 75
finery..........................78
finest 63
finish..........................90
finishing.....................90
finite or infinite..........3, 13
fire.............................24
firm............................45
firm 84
First..................60, 93
fish...................60, 85
Five............................32

flat..............................78
flats............................32
flavors........................32
flawed.........................69
flexible, path to life......102
Floating.....................40
Flow-together..............35
flowery-facets of Dao.....62
flowing........................86
focus..................30, 74
follow.................34, 51
follower......................45
Follower of Dao............44
following....................93
food...........58, 78, 106
food, excess.................45
fool............................40
foot............................95
for..................29, 100
Force..........................47
forces.........................56
forgiven 87
form..................34, 65
formed.......................47
formless..........22, 34, 47
forms..............20, 22, 76
fortune..........54, 83, 91
found.........................58
foundation..................25
founded..............28, 63
fragile 102
free-thinker................57
FREEDOM......................
    Dao, not master........57
    for all things...........153
    inherent right........129
    respect, not decree....76
    world for everyone...51
freedom for all..............76
Freedom, discuss........129
Freedom, summary......153
friend, Self................143
frighten......................33
frightened..................33
frightening................33
Frivolity 48
frivolity, discuss.........133
from...37, 40, 45, 48, 60, 64

191

front.................................20
front-role.........................26
frown upon society.......100
fruits..................................52
Fulfilled...........................36
fulfilling..........................36
full......................................35
fullness.............................69
funeral..............................54
G
gain.....................30, 68, 73
gain trust.......................146
gained..............................43
gains.........................39, 86
Galloping........................32
gathers.............................83
generals..........................54
gentle......................35, 102
gentle in use, Dao...........64
gentle path of life..........102
gentle, peaceful people...35
Gentle, triumph............104
Gentleman......................54
gentleness................30, 77
gentleness, philosophy. 128
genuine virtue.................62
get.................75, 86, 90, 99
ghosts..............................85
girth..................................90
give............................60, 70
given........................39, 87
gives.................................65
giving, self is bountiful 107
glorifies...........................54
glorify..............................54
glory and wealth............125
Glory/wealth endanger. 135
Glossary.......................177
Go.....................................58
go-away....................20, 50
go-for-it mentality........138
goat..................................40
godless universe...........152
goes..................................72
Going Forward.............169
Going-forth....................47
Gold................................29
gone.................................41

good........20, 35, 52, 83, 87
Good-fortune............80, 83
goodness...................20, 28
goods.........................78, 90
goodwill begets goodwill
.....................................105
got.....................................93
govern...............51, 91, 101
govern a nation...............91
governable, all citizens...21
Governing, makes easy. .85
government................28, 83
government, Daoism......87
government, Daoist........82
governs............................82
Grainless, self-salutation 63
granary............................78
grand..........................48, 78
grand palaces...............149
grandiose........................63
Grasp................................34
Grass..................36, 78, 102
Great.......38, 58, 69, 91, 93
great principle, Respect 123
Great successes..............90
greater..............................70
greatest enemy, self........56
greatly..............................49
Greatness..................57, 93
greatness by quietude.....69
greatness paradoxically. .69
Greatness, discuss........130
Greats of Dao.................65
Greats of the Universe....47
greed for fame/wealth....68
greed for power,wealth. .70
greedy kings.................148
grievance......................105
grievances......................88
grieve..............................54
grip..................................80
ground.............................75
grow..........................52, 90
Grows..............................76
Gu, 1995..............117, 179
guard...............................29
guest........................35, 95
guests 55

guilt.................................87
H
had...........................81, 96
hailed............................104
Halls full of gold............29
hand...............................100
handle..............................54
handling crises.............127
happily.............................40
happy..........44, 54, 92, 106
happy daoist, discuss....131
happy person.................125
hard..................32, 90, 102
hard-to-obtain.................21
hardest.............................67
hardship...........................77
harm's way......................75
harmed.................58, 81, 92
harmful............................99
harming...........................50
harmonize................22, 66
Harmonizes....................81
Harmony.............20, 38, 80
harmony among nations. 86
Harmony is Dao.............80
harmony with others.....140
Harrington, 1998............13
harvest what we sow......99
has.............................31, 56
has no motive, Dao........149
hate...........................28, 54
have.............19, 34, 52, 77
Have (You), concept....121
Have (You), created all
things.............................64
Have-excess.................103
Have-not....................19, 20
Have-not (Wu), concept
.....................................121
Have-not created Have...64
Have, Have-not, no space
....67
Having...............40, 62, 84
Hawking and Mlodinow,
2010.............................159
head.................................34
heads of robbers.............78
hear..........................34, 58

192

heard............................106
heart.............28, 32, 40, 74
heart controlling breath. .80
heart of the Sage..............74
Heaven....................26, 63, 99
HEAVEN & EARTH.........
   Benefit, not harm ...107
   not exist for selves....26
   perceived virtues.....152
   power limited............44
   supplement not-enough
  103
Heaven's..........................94
Heaven's retribution......99, 154
Heaven's way........103, 107
HeavenEarth, summary 152
Heavenly-attuned............36
Heavyness........................48
help....................................90
help others, discuss......124
help ourselves, discuss. 143
Hence.....44, 51, 54, 57, 84
here....................................98
Hesitant...........................35
high.....20, 28, 92, 102, 103
high taxes, hunger.........101
High Virtue.....................62
highest.............................63
highly 33
highway 78
hijack by strong
individuals....................169
hills..................................75
history.............................34
hit target, bow analogy. 103
hoarding.........................68
hoardings, discuss........133
hoarse..............................80
Hold........24, 34, 50, 93, 95
holds......................29, 51, 90
holds-on..........................90
honest thinker..........22, 34
honesty............................82
honesty above all..........132
Honesty, discuss...........132
honesty, low-profile.......83
honey...............................55

honor........................50, 63
Honorable.......................87
honored...........................81
hope for the weak...........43
horn..................................75
horrified, mass killing....54
horse................................87
horses..............................70
hot....................................51
hotness.............................69
How....................79, 82, 87
however........................103
howling...........................80
hub...................................31
Human....................44, 47
HUMAN FAILINGS.........
   causes difficulties...154
   frivolity......................48
   Indulgence, senses....32
   Not knowing, knows.97
   problems, discuss....133
   self-centered..............45
   sowing grievances. .105
   Temptation.................78
Human Failings, summary
....154
human nature..................56
humankind......................41
humankind's...................41
humble..........21, 28, 83, 94
humiliation.....................65
humility......50, 66, 86, 154
Humility for diplomacy..86
Humility, discuss..........134
hundred...........................92
hunger...........................101
Hunger, high taxes.......101
hunting...........................32
hurt..................................75
hurting......................81, 85
hypothetical Dao....19, 153
hypothetical naming.....122
I
I..............33, 36, 40, 51, 95
I do not know.................46
ice.....................................35
ideal world....................106
ideas flow, meditation. .136

If.................19, 55, 61, 93
ignorance, discuss........133
ignorance, Laozi's........132
ignorant...........................91
illnesses of society.......124
ILLUSTRATIONS.............
   Bend and be whole...42
   Chinese Bronze...........4
   Chinese Characters. 180
   good like water........27
   Journey, 1000 miles..89
   Killed, large number 53
   Laozi, text on silk 11
   Matters mixed...........46
   Not stepping-out.......71
   Wishing to take it.....59
   Wu (Have-not)..........18
   You (Have)...............18
illustrious..................43, 45
image....................34, 41, 58
Image great, no form......65
impartiality.....................24
Impatience......................48
implement....................104
important............45, 49, 68
in........20, 28, 36, 44, 48, 54
in our hearts..................169
in our unselfish actions 169
in-between......................24
in-depth...........................35
inactive............................35
inactivity........................69
inarticulate.....................69
incessant pursuit...........125
inch..................................95
inclination.......................20
incompatible..................52
inconspicuous................22
Incorruptible..................83
incorruptible Daoist........81
increase............................82
Incriminated..................43
incriminating.................49
indeed...35, 74, 86, 95, 100
indistinct........................34
individual glory............130
Individual-Self, summary
....153

individuals................75
Indulgence of senses......32
indulgence, discuss.......133
inexplicable................48
infinite........................3, 13
infinite success, Dao......65
infinity........................50
influenced, not Daoist....81
ingenuity................39, 82
inherent, Freedom........129
initiate....................62, 86
initiated concept Dao...118
injured........................100
injuring........................83
injustice........................88
inner peace.................131
innocence..........40, 50, 65
insects..........................80
inspiring legacy..............56
installing......................87
institutionalized, not to be
................................169
instructions...................39
instrument................51, 54
instruments...................50
instruments of misfortune, wars..........................155
insult............................37
Insults..........................33
intelligence............38, 39
interact.........................85
intimated......................81
into..............................98
INTRODUCTION..........12
    Dao and Daoism.......15
    Dao De Jing, quotes..14
    Laozi........................13
    writing style..............16
intrusion.......................98
invention, written words 72
investigated 34
invisible........................65
is......................26, 50, 61
it........22, 37, 47, 51, 55, 58
it's...............................35
Its..................22, 36, 47, 69
itself......................41, 57
J

jacket..........................96
jade..............29, 63, 87, 96
Journey........................90
journey to nowhere..........3
journey to nowhere!.....159
Journey, thousand miles.90
judgmental, no.............20
judicial punishment......100
Justice.........................62
justice from society......154
justice, injustice, discuss
................................141
justice, miscarriage.......100
K
keep......................55, 93
keeper..........................33
keeping........................91
keeps.....................22, 35
kill........................54, 99
Killed..........................54
killed, great numbers....148
Kindness................28, 62
king.............................36
kingdoms......................55
kings.......55, 61, 66, 78, 92
Kings'..........................63
kingship........................48
knotting.......................49
know21, 34, 41, 50, 55, 81, 91
know ourselves............143
knowing............36, 55, 96
knowing the world.........79
knowledge............38, 73, 78
knowledgeable..........35, 56
knowledgeable, unknown
................................107
known..........................35
knows.................72, 81, 84
Knows not knowing.......97
knows one's limits..........68
L
labor............................77
lack..............................88
lacking..............24, 63, 83
Lacking, self-salutation..66
language......................92
language, civilization.....72

LAOZI..............................
    a mystic?................112
    a pessimist?............116
    a philosopher?.........114
    a scientist?..............115
    Introduction.............13
    laughable?..............117
    Legacy 1 (Dao).......159
    Legacy 2 (De).........160
    religious?................113
    Ultimate Reality.......13
    writing for rulers?...111
Laozi advises................83
Laozi advocates Daoism 55
Laozi declares ignorance
................................132
Laozi, not mystical.........84
Laozi, text on silk...........11
Laozi's ideal world.......106
Laozi's pragmatism........93
Laozi's primary quest...152
Laozi's sayings..............96
Laozi's teachings...........66
Laozi's thinking.............16
Laozi's torch in search..159
Laozi's wisdom...............56
large......................54, 90
last.......................44, 56
last long.......................56
lasting..............26, 68, 84
late..............................65
later.............................88
laugh...........................65
laughable, Laozi ?........117
laughing matters? No...117
laughing scholar.............65
lavishly......................101
Laws............................82
lead.............................52
leader...............50, 93, 101
leaders.........................63
leadership-care..............86
leadership, Daoist..........50
Leading........................92
leak 99
Learn............................90
learning..................39, 73
learning, daily gain..........73

194

learns...65	limit...36, 68, 83	make...31
leaves...49	limitation of power...44	makes...20
left...54, 57	limits...29, 55, 78	male...41, 50, 66, 80, 86
left contracts...105	List: Important Dates..176	manage...20, 30, 51, 91
Legacy 1, Spirit of Dao 159	Listen...34, 58	management...28
Legacy 2, Daoism...161	little...58	manifest...90
legacy of problems...77	live...75, 101	manifestations...19, 20
legendary author...109	live better lives...154	manipulate...21
legendary Laozi...63	live by our own labor...140	manure...70
less...43, 72, 88	livelihood...98	many...83
less selfishness, desires 124	living...80, 102	marching...95
Lessen...39	living, gentle, weak...102	market...87
lesser scholar loudly laughs...65	loan contracts...105	mass destruction...52
let...29	lock...49	mass killings...54
let-go...79	lock-up...49	master...48, 52, 57, 95
Level...65	Lonely...63	master of none...57
Li, Etiquette...124	Lonely, self-salutation...66	master of none, Dao...153
liberate ourselves...57	long...20, 26, 68, 84	master-carpenter...100
liberates the mind...150	long-lasting...36	masters...96
life..30, 36, 44, 68, 75, 101	long-lived...56	matching...94
Life -survival...68	Longevity, remembrance 56	material...49
Life is an accident...140	Look...34, 58	materials...82
life uncertainties...83	Looking...40	Matter...51
LIFE-DEATH CYCLE......	Lords...55, 61, 66, 78	Matters...52, 80
death humbles...154	Lords'...63	matters...47, 54
Life versus wealth...68	lose...51, 90	maxim, non-violence...66
life-death discuss...135	Losing...33	may...22, 51, 66, 99
mellowing impact...36	loss...44, 68, 90	me...96
premature death...75	loss of civility...153	meal, small...58
life-direction...56	lost...38, 56, 95	medicine, best...61
Life-essence...80	loud...40	meditation...30, 36
Life-long...77	loudly...65	Meditation, discuss...136
Life, Death, discuss...135	Love. 33, 37, 68, 78, 82, 93	meet...75, 86
life, Death, Summary...154	loving...49	mellowing impact...36
life's purpose, discuss...140	low...20, 74, 103	melting...35, 67
Life's success, discuss..144	Low Virtue...62	mentality, go-for-it...138
Life's uncertainties, discuss ...147	Low-lying...43	mention...57
light...77, 81	low-profile...22, 81, 83	Merkin, 2008...117
light-years across...3, 13	lowest position...104	message is not mysticism ...112
lightly...88, 101	lowly...33, 40	method...79
lightly promises, discuss ...133	loyal...38	micro...34, 90
lightness...48	Loyalty...62	miles...90
lights...22	lurks...83	mind...36
like...35, 40, 84	lying, a sickness...132	minimally...54
likely...33, 45, 54	M	ministers...38, 87
	M-theory...159	minority liberated...57
	madly...32	miscarriage of justice...100
	maintain...29, 36, 90	

misery in life.................154
misfortune.............54, 83
mistakes...................49, 90
Mix................................31
mixed.....................34, 47
models..........................91
models, all after nature...47
models, government.......91
modern science today.....66
Momentum....................76
more.......43, 68, 79, 82, 88
more by expansionism. 125
morning.........................44
most.......................40, 67
mother................19, 47, 77
mother of all things........18
motive...................62, 67, 82
mouths..........................32
move................24, 48, 75
movement.....................49
Moving..........................47
much.................68, 91, 101
muddle..........................38
muddy..........................35
multiplied 79
multiverse....................159
Music............................58
Must....................60, 92
mutually.......................55
my.....................78, 93, 95
My words......................96
myriad..........................36
mysterious..............19, 30
Mystery........................19
mystical powers............33
mystical, Laozi !.............94
mysticism, discuss........112
mysticism, not Daoist.....80
mystified interpretation..75
N
naked 80
name............19, 34, 41, 47
named..................19, 34
nameless......................61
names...................55, 72
Naming, concept..........122
nation......38, 79, 82, 85, 91
nation building, Thrift....84

nation's thief..................91
nations..........................79
nations, ideally small....106
natural..........37, 44, 78, 99
naturally.................55, 76
nature......................79, 90
nature, ultimate model...47
near..............................90
nearly.....................78, 95
needs......................49, 65
negative aspect, summary
....................................155
negative sayings, positive
....................................104
negativity, positivity.....138
neglect..........................63
Neighboring nations.....106
neighbors.....................35
net of retribution............99
never....................25, 76
never leaks....................99
next..............................37
Nice..............................87
No....................88, 95, 98
no desires.....................82
no desires, Daoist...........81
no laughing matters......117
no nation ungovernable..21
no place for war............148
no selfish motive..........149
no space.......................67
no-good..............20, 49, 87
No-grain, self-salutation.66
no-march......................95
no-matter.....................34
Nobility........................63
noble............................29
non-beauty..............20, 40
non-verbal....................20
non-violence..........66, 128
none..21, 29, 39, 43, 55, 70
none able to know, to do 96
none not governable.....149
Normal..........................83
norms of society............65
not................83, 85, 88, 92
not a bad idea..............106
not a mystic...................93

not a religion.................76
not attacking.................95
not be influenced, Daoist
......................................81
not be seen virtuous......103
not contending..............27
not contesting...94, 99, 153
Not dare................21, 95
Not daring....................93
not easy to fulfill, Daoism
......................................96
not happy, discuss........139
not harming................153
not just for self gain.......73
Not knowing, knows !....97
not self-serving.............82
not selfish....................21
Not selfish, for all actions
....................................150
not to educate citizens!...91
not-contesting........28, 154
Not-Contesting, discuss
....................................137
not-dare.......................99
Not-dare-be-world's-first93
not-desire....................90
Not-enough.................103
not-existing.............25, 65
Nothing.................34, 84
nourish.........................30
nourishes......................57
nourishing-mother.........40
now..............................41
nowhere.............3, 40, 75
number.........................24
numbers................49, 82
nurtures........................76
nutshell, Daoism..........150
Nutshell, Quest............159
O
observations.................41
observe..................19, 79
observed.......................36
obsoleted, retribution...141
obssessions, discuss.....133
obtain.....................21, 32
occupation....................40
occupied......................52

occupies...........................47
of..................22, 25, 29, 31
offer..............................103
official............................50
oft neglected..................155
Often.........................82, 90
ominous..........................36
omnipotence, Dao...........67
omnipresent, Dao...........67
on............32, 35, 40, 87, 90
on display, virtues........153
one.............................19, 47
One (Dao).....30, 34, 43, 63
One created Two............66
one Ultimate Reality....156
oneself............................35
Only...........52, 78, 84, 103
only for defense, wars....95
Open.................30, 40, 77
Open-minded..................35
opened............................49
opened to bias, abuse...124
opening...........................81
opposing.........................95
oppressing......................98
oppression......................98
optimist, Laozi.............116
or....................................88
order........................50, 91
original-self...................39
origins............................96
other.........................79, 95
others.............40, 60, 105
out..................22, 24, 72, 75
over.................56, 60, 86
over-flows......................57
Over-indulge..................78
over-indulgence.............32
Overcome................84, 95
overcomes......................69
overcoming....................94
overgrown......................78
oversees.........................41
own..................29, 74, 100
own labor.............140, 159
P
Pacific Daoism.........26, 66
Pacific Daoism,discuss.160

Pacific Daoism,nutshell. 73
pacific philosophy..........76
pacific principles............64
pacifist............................35
Palace.............................78
PARADOXES...................
  Gentle path to life...102
  injustice, kindness....88
  Journey, 1000 miles..90
  Misfortune, fortune...83
  negative aspects......155
  not stepping-out 72
  of greatness..............69
  positive, negative....104
  Small nation, few....106
  Triumph, the weak....60
Paradoxes, discuss........138
Paradoxes, Summary....155
passers-by......................58
past.................................63
path................65, 78, 102
path to death 102
path to life 102
paw.................................80
Peace..............................58
peace on Earth...............86
peace with society..........81
peace-loving..................81
peace-loving people.....153
peaceful...................22, 63
peaceful co-existence...153
peacefully.......................54
people.....32, 40, 52, 66, 83
people's....................94, 98
people's heart................74
people's philosopher......98, 111
People's way.................103
perceived attributes........67
perceived virtues, Dao....65
perceived, Heaven........152
perfect world of Dao....124
perforce 35
performed......................37
person.................48, 66, 81
personal....................26, 77
personalized power......149
persons............................35

pervasive........................57
pessimist, not Laozi......116
phallus............................80
philosopher of people...155
philosopher of rulers!...111
philosopher scientist..6, 47, 152
philosopher, Laozi?......114
philosopher, people's......37
philosophy, gentleness. 128
physical evidence, Dao. .58
physical form of Dao.....41
piety...............................38
pig..................................40
pillar of Daoism, not-contesting....................137
pillar principle..........50, 70
pillar principles..............28
place..................28, 48, 86
plagiarized...................115
plainness........................39
Plan................................88
Plan small....................139
plunger..........................24
point...............................45
Poisonous.......................80
polished.........................63
poorer............................82
portals............................77
position..........................24
positive negativity........138
Positive sayings, seems negative........................104
possess...............20, 70, 76
possessing......................30
possession......................78
Possible.........................30
Possibly.........................33
poverty eradicating.........61
power......................30, 98
power for self-gain.........30
power limited................44
power over others.........131
Power, the archives 72
powered.........................85
powerful........................60
powerful message.........149
powers............................85

197

powers, not mystical......33
Practice....................65, 73
practicing............35, 77, 91
pragmatic advices.........127
pragmatic Laozi, Thrift. .84
pragmatism, Laozi..........88
praise...............................37
pre-conceived duties....150
pre-empt crises.............127
preceding................22, 87
precious..........................96
predates Confucius.......124
PREFACE........................6
Prefers............................48
prehistoric......................40
premature death......75, 154
Prepared.........................35
present.....................34, 80
preserved........................43
preserving......................75
press.............................103
presumptuous...20, 30, 103
prevailing.......................85
prevent...........................90
prevention......................32
primal................55, 61, 76
primal entity..................58
Primal Entity, Dao........119
Primal union, Dao..........22
primal union, Daoist.......81
Primal Virtue, De.........120
Primal Virtues..........30, 76
primal virtues of Dao...124
Primal virtues, summary
......................................154
prime.......................52, 80
principle..................66, 84
principles................77, 91
private-agenda...............26
problem..........................90
problems, discuss.........139
Proclaiming....................55
procreation, female........25
procreation, male...........41
profile............................74
Progeny.........................79
progress..........................51
progressively 35

prohibitions....................82
project............................90
Project great, infinite......65
proliferate......................82
promise..........................88
promises lightly given..146
promises lightly, lack trust
....88
promote...................60, 77
prosperity.......................58
protect............................93
Protector........................87
Protects..........................76
psyche............................36
PUBLICATION DATA...2
pull.................................62
Purpose of Life, discuss
......................................140
pursue own dreams.........82
pursuit, fame/wealth.....126
pushing..........................29
put-in.............................75
putting oneself last.........92
Q
quality............................65
QUEST..............................
    already revealed........19
    for book title.............16
    for Dao......................47
    in a nutshell............159
    Ultimate Reality,
    discuss.....................158
Quest, summary............152
quietened.......................63
quietly benefiting.........153
quietude..40, 48, 61, 82, 86
quietude of rulers...........69
QUOTATIONS.................
    warfare strategists.....95
    'Constructive Words' 65
    "Whoever is violent..."
   66
    "Bend, be preserved"43
quotes his sources.........115
R
race 32
rain-down......................55
rain, stormy...................44

raise.........................95, 103
raise awareness of pacific
Daoism..........................169
Random House............123
rank..............................102
Ranking of Virtues.........62
rankings of rulers...........37
rare 96
rarefied...........................47
Rarefy............................34
Rarely.............37, 67, 100
rarer...............................96
reach......................36, 73
reaches...........................30
Reading Laozi, benefits166
ready..............................33
real..........................41, 79
reality.............................34
reaping what we sow......44
reason...........26, 33, 87, 92
reasons 99
reasons for wars.............70
rebellion........................98
Rebellion, oppression.....98
Receiving.......................33
recommend....................92
reconciliation................88
recording.....................106
Reduce....................39, 103
reducing........................73
reduction.......................73
redundant......................61
refuge............................87
refuge for all things,
Daoism..........................87
regarded........................33
Regulated......................61
Relation.........................28
relationship, trust..........146
relationships.................38
relationships, discuss....134
Relax in meditation......136
relaxed and care-free......40
relaxes the body...........150
relentless in his effort.....58
religion, not Daoism.......57
religious Laozi, discuss 113
remove..........................30

198

Ren, Benevolence..........124
renewed......................35, 43
Repay injustice...............88
repeatedly.......................36
repeating..........................90
replace............................104
resemblance 93
resembles.........................93
residence....................28, 54
Resides 28
residual grievances........105
Resolve............................22
resolves............................81
Resolving.......................105
resolving grievances.....105
respect..............................87
respect Dao......................76
Respect for all........20, 123
Respect for Talents..........94
respecting.........................76
responding........................99
response...............40, 44, 62
response, uncertainties. 147
responsibility...................50
restrain.............................49
retaliation........................52
retire.................................29
retreat...............................95
retreat in defense...........148
retreating.........................65
RETRIBUTION.................
　from society.............100
　net of Heaven...............99
Retribution, discuss......141
retribution, summary....154
return...........34, 36, 40, 85
Returned..........................36
Returning.........................47
returns..............................43
reverse.............................91
Rhino...............................75
Rich..................................29
ride.................................106
Rides................................67
riding................................40
riding together..................3
right..........................54, 57
Righteousness............38, 62

Righteousness, discuss. 124
rigid, path to death........102
rise 90
rites...........................54, 79
rivalry..............................28
river.................................35
Rivers........................55, 92
robbers..................21, 39, 82
robbers' chiefs................78
role......................26, 30, 50
room.................................31
root............................36, 48
roots..........................48, 84
rope...........................34, 49
ropes..............................106
rough...............................63
RULERS.......................101
　citizens ignorant!.......91
　citizens, no burden....92
　Daoism to govern.....55
　greatness by quietude
　..................................69
　humility, diplomacy..86
　Hunger, high taxes..101
　not possess world......51
　not to oppress............98
　rankings, types..........37
　self-salutations..........66
　to rule is to serve....155
　Unselfish...................21
rulers, discuss...............111
Rulers, summary..........155
run....................................40
ruthless, maxim...............66
S
sacred...............................51
sacrifice...........................33
sacrificial........................40
sacrificing.......................33
sadness............................54
safe................................106
Sage........20, 24, 32, 43, 51
Sage-hood.......................39
Sage, not accumulate....107
Sage's Greatness...........130
Sage's heart.....................74
Sage's way....................107
said...............24, 37, 49, 82

SALVATION....................
　Bend, be preserved...43
　no abandonment 49
　Pacific Daoism.........74
　self-discipline...........77
Salvation, discuss.........142
Salvation, summary......154
same................................19
Sample quotations, DDJ.14
save our planet.............106
saved...............................77
saves...............................49
saving.............................93
say.............................33, 54
saying..................43, 67, 95
sayings.....................65, 96
sayings, positive...........104
Says..........................33, 80
scatter.............................90
scholar.............................94
scholar, lesser.................65
scholars...........................54
scientist, Laozi?............115
sea.............................40, 60
Seal.................................87
seas..........................55, 92
second.............................93
secondary virtues, abuses
.....................................124
secret...............................49
see..................34, 51, 58, 72
seed 90
seeker..............................19
seeker of truth.................57
seeking the Truth............34
seem..............................104
seems.......................69, 93
seems paradoxical........155
seen........................21, 103
sees.................................72
SELF........................30, 33
　Cultivating virtues....79
　Meditation, virtues ...30
　Self-knowledge.........56
　Self-promotion..........45
　to fault oneself........153
　worst enemy...........143
self cultivation, summary

199

.................................153	separated........................60	small............50, 55, 86, 93
Self discuss...................143	separately........................86	Small (Dao)....................77
self gain.....................30, 73	sequence..........................20	small efforts, achieve big
self sufficient, Daoism. 124	serious..............................84	88
self-affair........................88	seriously.................36, 106	small fish.........................85
self-agenda..................30, 90	seriousness.....................48	Small nation..................106
self-aggrandizing............98	Serve...........................86, 88	small-meal 58
self-aware........................98	Service............................28	smell................................58
self-centered.............45, 98	setting.............................20	smile................................40
self-coming....................99	Seyour-Smith, 1998........13	so...........................75, 77, 90
self-defeating tactics......45	shall................................61	social failures................124
self-denial, discuss.......143	share................................31	societal justice...............154
Self-denial, sick..............97	share and enjoy life......140	society..................104, 106
self-designate.................63	share fairly...................159	Society's Greatness.......130
self-develop....................82	shared..............................55	soft..................................40
self-discipline...............124	sharp.....................22, 78, 82	Softly..............................25
self-discipline, salvation.77	sharpen............................29	Soldier.............................75
self-focus........................43	sharpness........................29	solicitation......................99
self-glorification, not Dao	shelters............................76	solid...........................62, 93
.................................76	short................................20	son...................................77
self-humble 82	should..............................88	soon.................................80
self-important............43, 45	Show...............................39	sorrow.............................54
self-indulgence................88	shown.............................60	Sound...............20, 65, 106
self-inflicted problems. 139	shrink..............................60	source..............................19
self-interest.....................61	shrivel............................102	sow goodwill...................99
Self-knowledge,difficult 56	shut-out all desires..........77	sow no grievances........105
Self-loving.......................98	sick............................68, 97	space.....................3, 24, 67
self-praising...............43, 45	sickness 97	space and time.................3
self-promotion................45	sides..............................106	spawning Daoism...........67
self-promotion, discuss 133	sight..............................106	speaks..............................81
self-prosper.....................82	sign.............................40, 90	Specifically.....................66
self-purpose....................88	Silent..............................47	speech.............................49
self-regulate...............61, 82	silent teaching................67	spill.................................29
self-reliance..................124	silly..................................65	Spirit...................25, 30, 63
self-righteous............43, 45	simple..............................83	spirit of 'Dao' 119
self-salutations................66	simple,honest,gentle	spirit, not-contesting.......95
self-serving.....................82	Daoists...........................153	spiritual philosopher.......93
self-stabilized.................61	simpleton........................35	splitting...........................63
self-willing.....................55	simultaneously...............36	spokes.............................31
selfish..............................21	Since..........................41, 77	spring..............................40
selfish individuals........169	Sincere............................35	Square great, no border. .65
selfishness......................39	sincere observer.............25	stabilize..........................61
Selfless like Heaven.......26	sinews.............................80	stable..............................90
selfless, in all actions.....61	sitting..............................92	stand...................45, 47, 54
selves...............................79	sitting-in.........................87	standing..........................45
semen..............................41	skill.................................69	stands..............................54
senior..............................87	skills...............................82	Star, 2001......................179
seniority...................30, 76	slight...............................48	start to finish..................90

start with self, virtue.......79	stupidity begins..............62	swallow's..........................48
starting.................55, 65, 88	subject.............................55	sweet words...................146
starting with Self.........143	subjected.........................57	swords 78
starts 90	subjects...........................55	symptomatic treatment. 124
Starts beneath the feet....89	submerged................22, 36	SYNOPSIS......................5
starts disorder.................62	subservient.....................92	systems..........................55
state..................................30	substance of Dao......41, 58	T
statement summarize Laozi 150	substitutes....................100	take............51, 60, 73, 106
	substituting...................100	Take-up..........................73
staying back for credit....29	subtle........................35, 60	takes.........................62, 82
stepping...........................72	success....20, 29, 37, 57, 69	taking......................33, 101
stepping-out the door.....71	success in life, discuss..144	talents identified............94
steps 78	such........22, 40, 52, 67, 83	talk...................................37
stepwise creation............66	SUMMARY......................	talking..............................40
stiff..................................102	Dao 152	target, bow analogy......103
still...................................93	Daoism...................153	task..................................37
Stillness....................35, 36	Daoists...................153	tasks........................20, 88
sting.................................80	Freedom.................153	Taste................................88
stomach....................21, 32	Heaven and Earth...152	tasteless.........................32
stone...............................63	Human Failings......154	tax..................................101
stop.................................58	Individual-Self........153	tax-collector..................105
stop seeking ever more.125	Life-Death Cycle....154	taxes high, hunger........101
stopped...........................40	Quest, Ultimate Reality 152	teach................................66
stopping..........................47		teach Daoism in school 169
Stormy-rain.....................44	Retribution.............154	teacher 49
Straight............................83	Rulers......................155	teaches by examples.......67
straightened...................43	Salvation 154	teaching....................20, 66
straightness....................69	Virtues, conventional 153	Teaching Thrift to rulers 84
strangeness..................100		Teloned...........................80
strategic yielding..........154	Virtues, primal........154	Temptation, beware........78
strategies and tactics.....145	Wars.........................155	ten...................................48
strategies, of the weak....60	What Paradoxes ? 155	ten thousand chariots......48
strategist........................95	superfluous clothes.........45	tender..............................80
straw 24	supernatural advices, no 127	termed......................76, 94
stray.................................30		than.............29, 70, 95, 101
strays 48	supernatural power........30	that...............51, 80, 85, 98
stream.............................50	supernatural talents!.......94	The...............35, 50, 81, 83
streams...........................55	supplement not-enough 103	The Book Structure, Style 16
strength...................56, 94	support.....................30, 48	
strengthen...............21, 60	Surely..............................43	The Chinese Bellows...118
stresses removed..........150	surface of.........................3	The Chinese Text..........16
stretch.............................62	surpass..........................104	The English Translation. 16
stretching.....................103	surplus............................40	The Grand Design........159
Strikes............................29	surprises.........................82	The Primal and Virtue Classic......................5, 14
string.............................103	survival....................26, 68	
Strong...51, 56, 77, 80, 102	Survival, Death, discuss 135	the Primal Entity, Dao..119
stubborn..........................40		the Primal Virtues, De..120
study................................72	survive.....................63, 99	The Vision Thing.........169

201

theft..............................65
Their..................63, 74, 85
them............................54, 92
then.................50, 93, 99
theory, Big Bang, Dao..119
there....................26, 38, 41
Therefore......43, 48, 51, 62
these.......19, 30, 41, 45, 65
They..................62, 75, 78
thick..................62, 75, 80
thief..............................91
thieves...................39, 82
thin...............................62
Things..........................36, 90
Third...............................93
Thirty.............................31
This...................34, 79, 94
Thistles 52
thorns.............................52
Those......................63, 75
Though..............49, 55, 87
thoughts........................30
thousand...................48, 90
threaten......................100
Three created All Matters
...................................66
three treasures................93
Thrift..............................93
Thrift, nation building....84
Thus..................63, 101
Tiger...............................75
till................41, 77, 88, 91
time......................3, 35, 41
timing...........................28
tiny minority of us..........57
tiny-grass......................35
tip-toe...........................45
tired.......................40, 92
Title availability..............2
title chosen: Quest for ...16
to..................36, 40, 44, 50
to nowhere......................3
To rule is to serve 92
together...................35, 83
Tone......................20, 65
Tone great, inaudible......65
tones..............................32
too..............................101

top.....................34, 37, 54
topple............................60
total.........................43, 49
total Freedom................76
Total freedom for all....129
Tower....................40, 90
traditional helps............153
traditional values..........124
traditional wisdom........109
traditions.......................106
trails..............................49
translated more times.....13
transport........................34
travel..............................72
travelers..........................3
Traveling........................78
treasure..................87, 95
treasured........................87
Treasures........................93
treat...............................88
treated............................24
treats..............................74
trees......................90, 102
tribal society.................106
tries................................51
triumph............60, 93, 102
Triumph, the Weak,
discuss........................145
triumphs.................86, 95
trouble............................33
trouble-free life.............77
true 82
true Greatness..............130
True virtues, anonymity
...................................153
trust........28, 44, 62, 75, 88
trust begets trust...........146
trust to gain trust..........154
trust-unworthy...............74
trust-worthy...................74
Trust, discuss..............146
truth..............................57
Truth 43
turmoil...........................90
two....................91, 99
Two created Three.........66
U
ulterior motives...........124

ULTIMATE REALITY.....
And Laozi...............13
birth of.....................47
in a Nutshell............159
in Dedication.............3
primal Dao...............19
Quest for, discuss...158
Ultimate Reality, summary
...................................152
ultimate wisdom.............94
ultimately................57, 88
unable............................63
Unavoidable............36, 54
unbridled imagination....24
uncarved-wood...50, 55, 61
uncertainties of life.........83
uncertainties, life, discuss
...................................147
uncertainty of naming. .122
uncut stone....................63
undefined......................34
underestimating.............95
understand....................96
understanding................30
understands....................72
undone..........................49
uneven...........................65
unfailing justice............154
unhappiness among us. 125
Unhurried......................99
union..............................80
unite all humankind......119
united.............................55
unites.............................81
universal........................79
Universal practice, PD. 141
universal salvation........142
universe..............3, 47, 159
universe creation............66
universe's age, size.........13
Universe's Greatness....130
unknown.......................55
unknown figure.............63
unnecessary desires......149
Unproductive, self-
salutation....................66
unruly............................83
unscrupulous.................21

202

Unscrupulously...............36
Unseen......................22, 34
unselfish....................20, 73
unselfish actions..............67
Unselfish leaders.............21
unselfishness.................154
unyielding, path to death
.....................................102
up............................34, 103
up-front..........................92
upheaval........................38
uphold..................58, 61, 77
upholding........................77
upon..............................19
Upright..........................62
uproot...........................79
use.................31, 52, 58, 69
used..............................25
uses..........................50, 52
using........................91, 106
V
vague............................41
valley...............35, 50, 63, 65
Valley-spirit...................25
valleys.......................55, 92
value.........................33, 40
value Virtue....................76
Valued...........................81
valuing............49, 76, 87, 90
varied..........................106
vast..............................99
vehicles........................106
verbal criticisms...............67
verge.............................35
versus........................40, 68
very.................41, 78, 96
victories.....................52, 54
Victorious.......................52
victorious over self.........56
Victory..........................54
view..............................45
vigilant, start to finish.....90
village...........................79
villages..........................79
vindicated.......................43
violent...........................94
virtue......41, 44, 50, 62, 79
Virtue nurtures.................76

VIRTUES (conventional)..
appear, Daoism lost..38
charity of others......120
Etiquette, etc............62
on display................153
VIRTUES (primal).............
Be contented..............70
be unselfish................61
Creates, possess not..76
CultivateSelflessness 33
has humility..............94
not be arrogant..........29
not presumptuous.....76
not-contesting...........28
respect for all..........154
senior, control not.....76
simplicity, honesty....39
Virtues, discuss............120
virtues, faults.................38
virtues, summary..........154
virtuous........................103
virtuous-talented............21
vision............................84
visions..........................30
voicing...........................99
W
wagon............................48
Walk 70
walk-paths....................78
Walking.........................75
wanting........................101
war.........................70, 93
Warfare strategist...........95
warning frivolity............48
warning of temptation....78
warns of miscarriage....154
WARS..............................
Fight, in defense.......95
instruments of
misfortune..............155
is mass destruction....52
is mass killings 54
root causes................70
Wars, discuss...............148
Wars, summary............155
Wash............................30
water......................28, 31
water weak, triumph.....104

Water, not-contesting.....28
Water, weak & gentle...104
way...........................29, 84
Way of Heaven,Sage....107
Ways...............................94
we..................................77
we know not....................3
we sow, we harvest........99
weak..........51, 60, 80, 102
weak, despair not............43
weak, gentle, triumph...104
weaken....................21, 60
weakness, triumph, discuss
.....................................145
Wealth.....................68, 78
wealth endanger...........135
wealth is contentment.....68
Wealth, discuss.............126
weapon....................75, 95
weapons.........................82
wears.............................96
well-being........................3
well-known..................107
what.........................33, 86
What Paradoxes ?
summary.......................155
Whatever.......................86
When................88, 93, 102
When, the Beginning?..159
where................28, 44, 54
Where, the End?...........159
wherever........................58
which.................66, 68, 77
whirl-wind.....................44
White.......................50, 65
who................29, 75, 100
Who can have excess?..103
Whoever.............52, 54, 56
whole........................44, 48
whose.............................22
why.................33, 48, 75, 100
Widely-meshed..............99
widespread destruction...52
Wilderness.....................40
will.................45, 48, 52, 55
win................................87
wind.........................40, 44
window....................31, 72

203

wine..............................78
winning..........................99
winter 35
wisdom, ancients'...........94
wisdom, Laozi's depth....88
wish........................35, 86
wishes......................19, 74
wishing.......51, 60, 92, 103
with....................79, 88, 92
within.............................41
without..................61, 65, 67
without stepping-out......72
without-motive 67
Wolframalpha.com.........13
wonderful.......................35
wonders.........................19
Wood.................52, 55, 102
Wood strong, will break
....102
word of caution..............16

words..........65, 87, 96, 107
working..........................90
working for people.......107
world......20, 30, 33, 55, 77
world for everyone.........51
world's.................43, 50, 93
Worn..............................43
worries...........................39
worship, not Dao............57
worst enemy, Self.........143
worthless.......................65
writing for rulers?........111
writing style, this book...16
written...........................39
written archives..............72
written archives,
civilization.....................72
wrong.............................50
Wu (Have-not).........19, 67
Wu (Have-not), concept

....121
Wu and You, no space...67
WuWei, discuss............149
WuWei, WuBuWei, discuss
....150
Y
Yang 66
yard stick........................26
years..........................26, 52
yet...........55, 66, 73, 80, 93
Yi, Righteousness.........124
yielding....................24, 64
yielding, flexible, life...102
Yin 66
You (Have).........19, 67, 77
You (Have), concept....121
You's (Have's) creation..64
"
"Ah"..............................40
"Wei"............................40

204

www.ingramcontent.com/pod-product-compliance
Lightning Source LLC
Chambersburg PA
CBHW071200160426
43196CB00011B/2145